The Philosophy of the
America ₵

11/89

The Philosophy of the American Constitution

A REINTERPRETATION OF THE
INTENTIONS OF THE FOUNDING FATHERS

Paul Eidelberg

UNIVERSITY
PRESS OF
AMERICA

LANHAM • NEW YORK • LONDON

Copyright © 1986 by

University Press of America,® Inc.

4720 Boston Way
Lanham, MD 20706

3 Henrietta Street
London WC2E 8LU England

Printed in the United States of America

ISBN (Perfect): 0-8191-5341-9

All University Press of America books are produced on acid-free
paper which exceeds the minimum standards set by the National
Historical Publications and Records Commission.

To My Father
and to the
Memory of My Mother

Foreword

BY HERBERT J. STORING

ASSOCIATE PROFESSOR

DEPARTMENT OF POLITICAL SCIENCE, UNIVERSITY OF CHICAGO

AMONG the epithets hurled by Anti-Federalists against the proposed Constitution were "mongrel," "bantling," "spurious brat," and "heterogeneous phantom." The Constitution, the opponents complained, was complex, obscure, and illegitimate. "I will not expatiate long," Mercy Warren wrote scornfully, "on a Republican *form* of government, founded on the principles of monarchy—a democratick branch with the *features* of aristocracy. . . ." She opposed the adoption of "this many-headed monster; of such motley mixture, that its enemies cannot trace a feature of Democratick or Republican extract nor have its friends the courage to denominate it a Monarchy, an Aristocracy, or an Oligarchy, and the favoured bantling must have passed through the short period of its existence without a name, had not Mr. *Wilson*, in the fertility of his genius, suggested the happy epithet of a *Federal Republic*."*

The thrust of such objections lies in the claim that the Constitution contains no principle that binds its diverse parts into one whole. According to this view, the Constitution is

---

* *Observations on the New Constitution* . . . By a Columbian Patriot (Boston: 1788), pp. 5-6. (Reprinted in Paul L. Ford, *Pamphlets on the Constitution,* where the author is incorrectly identified as Elbridge Gerry.)

essentially incomprehensible; it is merely heterogeneous. According to this view, there can be found in the day-to-day work of the Philadelphia Convention, as one recent writer has it, "no over-arching principles."* Now, if this were true, one could understand the Constitution only by resorting to some explanatory principle outside the Constitution. One might then look for hidden plots and self-serving schemes. One might look for interests that had to be compromised or constituencies that had to be pleased. One might look for some patchwork "consensus" or aggregate of opinions that the Framers sought, willy-nilly, to express. Most studies of American Founding do pursue some such external inquiry. Few give any serious attention to the primary question of whether there is in the Constitution as it presents itself a principle or set of principles that explains how its parts make a whole.

In this book, Paul Eidelberg takes up that question. He admits—indeed he insists upon—the complexity of the Constitution, but he seeks to dispel the obscurity and the aura of illegitimacy that still cloud it. He traces the different features of the Constitution; he examines what the Framers intended these features to be, how they intended their combination to work, and why they thought the result good. He argues, in brief, that the Framers intended to establish a mixed regime, new in many respects, but old in its main elements and in its purpose to promote the common good through prudent combination.

One of the few major works with an intention anything like this one is William W. Crosskey's *Politics and the Constitution*.† Both works aim to discover the true meaning of the Constitution. Both deny that the Constitution has meaning only as a product of certain historical circumstances.

* John P. Roche, "The Founding Fathers: A Reform Caucus in Action," *American Political Science Review*, LV (Dec. 1961), p. 816.
† (Chicago: University of Chicago Press, 1953)

Both deny that its essence is change. Both state their conclusions with a good deal of emphasis, at the same time
opening their evidence and reasoning to inspection. But if
Eidelberg joins Crosskey in the quest for the true meaning
of the Constitution, he differs in his conclusion as to where
the quest leads. For Crosskey, the proper study is the document itself, read in the light of the contemporary meaning
of words and ordinary rules of logic and legal interpretation.
Reliance on what the Framers *said* about what they were
doing is dangerous if not altogether illegitimate. Crosskey
eschews philosophical questions as unnecessary, pointless,
and misleading. Eidelberg, on the other hand, concerns himself very much with the deliberations leading to the Constitution and with certain other contemporary materials, as
well as with the Constitution itself. For him, the task of
seeing the Constitution as it presents itself includes looking
at what its makers intended it to be. He holds that in order
to get the full meaning out of the document, it is necessary
to explore the reasoning that went into it. This leads him
into questions of political philosophy, for he would agree
with Fisher Ames that in the United States in 1787 "legislators have at length condescended to speak the language of
philosophy."*

Two common misconceptions need to be disposed of immediately. The first is that an examination of the Framers'
political philosophy somehow implies that the Framers were
not practical politicians. Of course it implies nothing of the
sort. There is no need at all to march down the blind alley
of regarding the Framers as either metaphysicians or shrewd
ward politicians. The Framers were extraordinarily intelligent, literate, and thoughtful men engaged in a great political act. They sought to bring to bear on that act all of their

---

* Jonathan Elliot (ed.), *The Debates in the Several State Conventions on
the Adoption of the Federal Constitution* (5 vols.; Philadelphia: J. B.
Lippincott Co., 1836), II, 155.

political knowledge and skill, including the most profound understanding they could command of the ends, forms, and problems of political association. The second and closely related misconception is that an examination into the Framers' political philosophy must involve a mode of discourse radically different from that used by the Framers themselves. Eidelberg is not playing the dull game of identifying philosophical sources or getting each Framer neatly placed into the appropriate preconceived philosophical pigeon-hole. His goal is not philosophical labelling but philosophical understanding. And his book is based on the belief that such an understanding requires a reconstruction and participation in the debate, the argument, the dialectic, that produced the Constitution. Thus he begins with a singularly careful and informative examination of the rules adopted by the Convention. He pursues the debate from the introduction of the Virginia Plan through its main stages, participating in its give and take and following its movement from level to level. In this way he explores the different *reasons* that went into, for example, the construction of the Senate and the intricate and (as he shows) profoundly conceived mode of electing the President. At the same time, his method is far more sensitive to the *politics* of the framing than the usual flat, nonphilosophical studies, precisely because it exposes us to the *range* of political deliberation. It is striking, with a subject so well worn, how far the author has been able to go in clarifying and deepening our understanding of what the men at Philadelphia were doing.

This book does not deal at equal length with all aspects of the Constitutional deliberations, and the selection reflects a sound judgment about where the fundamental issues are to be found. There were two great questions. One had to do with the *powers* of the government and the reservation of individual rights. Here lay the burden of the Anti-Federalist attack, and here incidentally is Crosskey's focus. The other question had to do with the *structure* of the government. Here lay the chief problem for the Framers, and here is Eidelberg's main concern. This matter has, in turn, two parts: the relation between the state and general governments and the structure of the general government itself. It may seem curious that the author spends relatively little time with the former, which is usually presented as the central issue. His emphasis is on the structure of the general government, which has been much less discussed but which is in fact the more important matter of the two. He is concerned with the *republican* side of Wilson's *Federal Republic;* for while federalism is the husk, republicanism is the kernel of American government.

In taking up this important question, Eidelberg argues that the Framers intended to establish a mixed regime. He describes the Framers' intentions with respect to both the institutions and the way of life of that regime. He denies that it is adequate to view the Constitution as an oligarchy or (what has been more persuasively argued) as a democracy,* contending that it must be seen as a deliberate tension between democratic, aristocratic, oligarchic, and even monarchic principles. He makes a powerful case, closely reasoned and well documented, and it would be a poor man indeed who could not learn much from it. I remain doubtful about how far the Framers' intentions can be described in terms of the traditional categories. But as between the argument that the Framers intended to establish a democracy and the argument that they intended to establish a mixed regime, I am inclined to think that the latter is closer to the truth. Yet I ponder the apparently contrary view of

* Cf. Martin Diamond, "Democracy and *The Federalist:* A Reconsideration of the Framers' Intent," *American Political Science Review,* LIII (March, 1959).

* Elliot, *op. cit.,* II, 434.

James Wilson, who was in a good position to know: "In its
principle, [the government under the Constitution] is purely
democratical. But that principle is applied in different forms,
in order to obtain the advantages, and exclude the inconveniences, of the simple modes of government."* Democracy
is the beginning point, and the problem for the Framers
was to find ways to mitigate that democracy to secure its advantages and avoid its excesses. The question is whether the
democratic principle, when "applied in different forms," as
Wilson puts it, remains the democratic principle or whether
it is not thereby *transformed* into aristocratic, oligarchic, or
monarchic principles. Does the excellence of the Constitution, as the Framers intended it, depend precisely on that
transformation, which provides the elements of a mixed
regime?

Preface

VIRTUALLY every major controversy in American politics involves the Constitution. Consider the Presidency. Some commentators fear that the powers of the Presidency have grown to such an extent as to endanger the constitutional system of checks and balances, and, with it, liberty. Others maintain that this very system of checks and balances hinders the proper function of the Presidency, that the President will have to circumvent that system if he is to fulfill his paramount role as Tribune of the People. Consider the Congress. Many political scientists regard Congress as in need of radical reform. The Congress, they argue, is institutionally incapable of formulating comprehensive and coherent plans of national policy, hence of translating into law the will of the people or of popular majorities. This defect they attribute to the constitutional principle of federalism, a principle, they say, which not only renders Congress subservient to State and local interests, but which, in the Senate, unduly favors rural as opposed to urban interests. Other political scientists, however, believe that Congress, as an institution, is fundamentally sound. Its proper function, they insist, is not to represent the will of popular majorities, so much as to accommodate diverse groups on the one hand, and to protect the rights of minorities on the other. Consider, finally, the Supreme Court. Some writers praise

the Court as an instrument of democracy, extending freedom and equality through a broad interpretation of the Constitution, especially of the First and Fourteenth Amendments. Others contend that the present Court, far from interpreting the Constitution, is amending the Constitution—
fostering not freedom but licentiousness, not equality but a
leveling of all distinctions. Here, not only is the proper function of the Court in question, but so too are the very ends
or purposes of the Constitution, indeed, of American society.

Now, underlying these various controversies may be seen
a tension within the Constitution or between the Constitution and democracy. Why this tension? What is there about
the Constitution which admits of this tension? The problem
is more than academic. For the Constitution intimately involves our purpose as a nation, and today our purpose as a
nation is in doubt and in jeopardy. What, indeed, is this
Constitution? What was it intended to be by the Founding
Fathers? How may we best understand the intentions of
the Founding Fathers? To what extent are their intentions
relevant to our own times? For each of these various questions scholars have propounded different and conflicting
answers. If these answers are inadequate, then our understanding of our nation's purpose is inadequate. Whatever
the Constitution is, or whatever it was intended to be, it has
shaped the course and character of American history. Whatever the Constitution is or was intended to be, it represents
our political origin as a people. That origin is unique. It is
unique because this nation was born not by accident and
force, but from choice and reflection. Perhaps this is why
we so often go back to that origin for insight and inspiration.
And surely today, more urgently than ever before, we must
go back to that origin if we are to know where we stand,
what we stand for, and where we are going.

PAUL EIDELBERG
Raleigh, North Carolina

Contents

*The Philosophy of the
American Constitution*

1
Introduction

THIS IS an inquiry into the political philosophy of the American Constitution. It is an attempt to understand the Constitution as it was understood by the Founding Fathers. The inquiry will seek to elucidate the intended character of American society as reflected in its fundamental laws and institutions. It will try to reveal the kinds of men intended to be the leaders of this society and the great purposes they were intended to serve. The inquiry posits a central thesis, namely, that the *Republic* established by the Founding Fathers was understood by them to be a *Mixed Regime*. What

[3]

is meant by a mixed regime—what its formative principles are and how these are embodied in institutions—will unfold during the course of the inquiry.

Inasmuch as the subtitle of this work is "A *Reinterpretation* of the Intentions of the Founding Fathers," it will be necessary, in this Introduction, to consider briefly the interpretations of other commentators, as well as their methods of inquiring into the political philosophy of the Constitution. It should be understood, however, that it is not my purpose here to refute these interpretations, but rather to place in question their unexamined assumptions. This will not only justify the present inquiry; it will also enable the reader to place it within the context of philosophical and constitutional disquisition.

§

The Analogical Method of Interpreting the Constitution

The language of the Constitution, and of the debates preceding its adoption, have suggested to commentators the phrases and doctrines of almost every possible philosopher. Accordingly, these commentators derive their elucidations from a study of the history of ideas. Some scholars, whose writings provide collateral support for the thesis developed here, attempt to show the influence upon the Founding Fathers of such philosophers as Aristotle, Cicero, Locke, and Montesquieu.[1] * For some of the ideas of these (and other) philosophers may be presented as having provided the Founders with many of the organizing principles and ideals of a mixed regime. Analogies suggest influence. The difficulty with this method of explanation, as Richard McKeon has pointed out, is this: "The discovery that phi-

* Notes to this chapter appear on page 293.

losophers have used the same words, the same phrases, the same expressions of ideals as are found in a political document is not a sound basis for the argument, even when an influence is probable, that the meanings are the same."[2] In the works of the philosophers mentioned, such words as *constitution* and *mixed regime*, and such ideals as *liberty* and *justice*, occur in different contexts of principles and definitions of terms, and hence have different meanings. Consequently, it would be more than difficult to show how these philosophers could be made to father the same political institutions. Even assuming an eclectic borrowing, there would still remain the difficulty of showing how differences among these philosophers were institutionally resolved by the Founding Fathers. To complicate matters further, there is, today, a welter of different interpretations of the very doctrines which are supposed to have influenced the Founders. Which of these interpretations shall we regard as authoritative—and not for us, but for the Founders themselves—and not for the Founders collectively but individually, for each of them may have understood these doctrines in different ways! Clearly the analogical method of interpreting the Constitution may pose more problems than it solves, though this is not to say it is without relevance.

§

The Historicist Interpretation of the Constitution

Some commentators who use the analogical method may be identified with the school of *historicism* or *relativism*. It is the contention of these commentators that the thoughts of the Founding Fathers—their conceptions of man and society—were bound to the culture of their own times; that their political ideals and principles have little or no relevance today; hence, that their philosophy of government, as embodied in the original Constitution, is virtually obsolete. Now the claim of these historicists, that the thoughts of the Founders have little or no relevance for our own times, presupposes two things: first, that they understand our own times, and second, that they adequately understand the thoughts of the Founders. Whether they understand our own times need not detain us. Whether they adequately understand the thoughts of the Founders need detain us but a few moments.

In the first chapter of his book *The American Political Tradition*,[3] Richard Hofstadter presents a view of the Constitution which, in one respect, resembles my own; for he sees in that document an eighteenth-century version of what he calls the classical idea of "balanced government." By a balanced government Hofstadter means a political system in which "the aristocracy and the democracy [are] made to neutralize each other" by giving to each "its own house in the legislature," and by setting over both a "strong, impartial executive," on the one hand, and an "independent judiciary," on the other.[4] Now without actually examining these institutions, Hofstadter concludes that the Founders' philosophy of balanced government is virtually obsolete.[5] This conclusion is based on his understanding of (1) the Founders' conception of human nature; (2) their conception of property; and (3) their conception of liberty. Let us see whether his conclusion is well-grounded.

According to Hofstadter, the Founders regarded human nature as fundamentally depraved. Having "a vivid Calvinistic sense of human evil and damnation," they looked upon man as but a contentious "atom of self-interest."[6] "They accepted the mercantile image of life as an eternal battleground, and assumed the Hobbesian war of each against all; they did not propose to put an end to this war, but only to

stabilize it and make it less murderous."[7] Hence they es-
poused the constitutional system of checks and balances, a
system in which avarice was to check avarice, ambition to
check ambition—a theme familiar from *Federalist 51*. Pause,
however, and contrast the following statements of Alexander Hamilton—the first from his "Pacificus," the second
from *Federalist 76:*

> Instances of conferring benefits from kind and benevolent
> dispositions or feelings toward the person benefited, without
> any other interest on the part of the person who renders the
> service, than the pleasure of doing a good action, occur every
> day among individuals. But among nations they perhaps
> never occur.

> Th[e] supposition of universal venality in human nature is
> little less an error in political reasoning, than the supposition
> of universal rectitude. The institution of delegated power
> implies, that there is a portion of virtue and honor among
> mankind, which may be a reasonable foundation of confi-
> dence; and experience justifies the theory.[8] *

From this it appears that the Founders' conception of human
nature was not quite so dismal and simplistic as Hofstadter
would have us believe. Confidence in man enabled them to
establish a government of delegated powers; distrust in man
cautioned them to institute a system of checks and balances.
Perhaps they leaned toward, or preferred to have erred on,
the side of pessimism. But is this Hobbesian pessimism or
is it sober realism? Strangely enough, Hofstadter's first chapter is entitled "The Founding Fathers: An Age of Realism"
—which is not to say that Hofstadter regards realism and
pessimism as the same thing. It may be, however, that the
Founders' realism was based not on pessimism so much as
on *dogmatism*. Indeed, this is precisely what Hofstadter

---

* Richard Hofstadter, *The American Political Tradition*, (1948).
Reprinted by permission of the author and Alfred A. Knopf.

suggests. Again and again he points out that the Founders were convinced that human nature is permanent or unchanging.

> They were inordinately confident that they knew what man always had been and what he always would be. The eighteenth-century mind had a great faith in universals. Its method, as Carl Becker has said, was "to go up and down the field of history looking for man in general, the universal man, stripped of the accidents of time and place." (p. 7)

Contrast, however, the following passages from *Federalist 37*, the author of which was Madison:

> The faculties of the [human] mind itself have never yet been distinguished and defined, with satisfactory precision, by all the efforts of the most accute and metaphysical philosophers. . . . The most sagacious and laborious naturalists have never yet succeeded in tracing with certainty the line which separates the district of vegetable life from the neighboring region of unorganized matter, or which marks the termination of the former and the commencement of the animal kingdom. . . . When we pass from the works of nature . . . to the institutions of man . . . we must perceive the necessity of moderating still further our expectations and hopes from the efforts of human sagacity.

> Besides . . . the imperfection of the human faculties, the medium through which the conceptions of men are conveyed to each other adds fresh embarrassment. The use of words is to express ideas. . . . But no language is so copious as to supply words and phrases for every complex idea, or so correct as not to include many equivocally denoting different ideas.

Now I do not wish to suggest that Madison did not believe in a permanent human nature. But it does seem that his confidence in man's capacity to know "universals" is somewhat less than Hofstadter's confidence in man's *in*capacity to know "universals." Be this as it may, it is quite evident that Hofstadter's understanding of the Founders' conception of human nature is grossly inadequate. But this means that the first and most fundamental premise upon which he concludes that the philosophy of balanced government is obsolete is not only questionable, but untenable. I turn now to consider the second premise.

According to Hofstadter, the philosophy of balanced government presupposes a large and propertied middle class, and such a class, he contends, no longer exists: "A large portion of the modern middle class . . . is propertyless; and the urban proletariat, which the Fathers so greatly feared, is almost one half the population." Furthermore, what the Founders understood by "property" has been rendered meaningless "even for many propertied people" by "the separation of ownership and control that has come with the [modern] corporation."[9] It so happens, however, that at least some of the Founders meant by the term property *whatever is one's own;* for them the term signified not only land or real estate, as Hofstadter suggests, but also money, public securities, personal possessions, and not only material possessions, but even rights and privileges.[10] Thus, despite the changes which may have occured in the character of "property" since the time of the Founders, it cannot be concluded from this alone that the philosophy of balanced government has become antiquated. The conclusion must therefore rest on the *size* of the middle class vis-à-vis what Hofstadter calls the "urban proletariat." That "proletariat," he asserted, comprises almost half the population. From this it follows that American society is roughly divided between proletarians and non-proletarians. Does this division even suggest that the philosophy of balanced government is virtually obsolete? Or are we to believe that proletarians and non-proletarians are no longer governed by what the Founders called "self-interest"? On the other hand, is it possible that class conflict is in the process of being transcended in virtue of certain changes which have occurred either in human nature or in the character of human thought? This leads to the third premise of Hofstadter's thesis.

Throughout the course of his argument, Hofstadter more than suggests that the philosophy of balanced government was based upon a mode of thought which has undergone a radical transformation.[11] Such a philosophy of government presupposed a society which regarded "eternal conflict and rigid adherence to property rights as its integrating principles."[12] This idea of "eternal conflict," but especially the idea of "property rights," dominated the political thought of eighteenth- and nineteenth-century American society. Both ideas may be traced to the Founders' conception of human nature. "They thought man was a creature of rapacious self-interest, and yet they wanted him to be free—free, in essence, to contend, to engage in umpired strife, to use property to get property."[13] Steeped in the belief that human nature is unchanging, they thought man would ever remain a creature of "rapacious self-interest." Hence "they had no hope and they offered none for any ultimate *organic* change in the way men conduct themselves."[14] Their thoughts were culture-bound. They were merely the "intellectual heirs of seventeenth-century English republicanism."[15] Not that they were committed to what is presently understood by liberty and democracy; for "in their minds"—and consistent with the mode of thought which dominated their epoch—"liberty was linked not to democracy but to property."[16] Indeed, the Founders' regard for "civil liberties" was none "too tender."[17] Now in the light of these various remarks of Hofstadter, can we guess what transformation may have occurred in American thought so as to have rendered the philosophy of balanced government obsolete or obsolescent? Could it be a commitment to "human rights" over "property rights"? Could it be that an austere liberty, which supposedly fostered avaricious egotism, has been transformed into a "tender" liberty, a liberty suffused with compassionate altruism. Is this the "organic change" of which Hofstadter speaks, the "organic change in the way men conduct themselves," but of which the Founders had no hope and could offer no hope, steeped as they were in the belief that man is and will ever remain a creature of "rapacious self-interest"? If so, we can understand why he concludes that "any attempt . . . to tear their ideas out of the eighteenth-century context is sure to make them seem starkly reactionary."[18] Dismal and dogmatic is the Founders' conception of human nature. Antiquated is their conception of property. Reactionary is their conception of liberty, a liberty they linked to property and not to democracy. But here again there is a flaw in Hofstadter's understanding.

It may be true that the meaning of liberty has undergone a radical transformation since the time of the Founders. But it is not true that the Founders simply linked liberty to property and not to democracy. Of course, for men like Madison, who regarded liberty as a *right,* it would certainly be included under the concept of property. But Madison appears to have linked liberty also to democracy, or such may be inferred from *Federalist 37,* where he says: "The genius of republican liberty seems to demand . . . that all power should be derived from the people." Granted, the word *seems* appears suspicious, so that Madison may not have wholly identified *republican* liberty with *democratic* liberty. Nevertheless, virtually all the Founders agreed with Madison that there can be *no* liberty without *some* democracy—suggesting that the two were closely linked indeed.[19] Finally, it was this same Madison, together with many other members of the Convention, who led the First Congress of the United States to adopt the Bill of Rights, that is, to embody in the Constitution the very civil liberties of which the philosophy of balanced government, according to Hofstadter, is almost devoid![20] This philosophy may or may not be obsolete; but whether or not it is so can only be determined after we have adequately understood the thoughts of the Founders.

§

The Economic Interpretation of the Constitution

Although the economic interpretation of the Constitution came into academic vogue more than half a century ago, its influence on American thought has not greatly diminished.[21] Indeed, as the reader will have surmised, it has found a place in the historicist interpretation. But let us examine this older view on its own grounds.

Because of the prominence in the debates preceding the adoption of the Constitution of such terms as "property," "interest," and "faction," some commentators, most notably Charles A. Beard, have felt a need to investigate contemporary conditions rather than consult earlier philosophers or the history of ideas. Their elucidations of the Constitution involve analysis of economic interests and private ambitions which its words are thought to conceal, but by reference to which, they argue, it must be understood.[22] In other words, the Constitution must be understood in terms of the property interests represented by the Founding Fathers. (Stated another way, these commentators regard the language of the Constitution as concealing "oligarchic" intentions.) This method of interpretation, however, encounters the same difficulty as the *analogical* method. If consulting the history of philosophy affords little insight into the intended meaning of the Constitution, there is no possibility of explaining its statements (or those of the constitutional debates) in terms of the economic and psychological forces that led to their formulation so long as the meaning of those statements is in doubt. The sociological and psychological view of knowledge notwithstanding, it is still prudent, when examining the writings of the Founders (or of anyone for that matter), to determine what *they* thought they meant before attempting to explain their thoughts in terms of material causes and private motives. But leaving method aside, let us probe a little deeper into the meaning and consequences of the economic thesis.

In his *Economic Interpretation of the Constitution*, Beard draws the following conclusions:

> The members of the Philadelphia Convention which drafted the Constitution were, with few exceptions, immediately, directly, and personally interested in, and derived economic advantage from, the establishment of the new system. (p. 324)
>
> A large propertyless mass was, under the prevailing suffrage qualifications, excluded at the outset from participation (through representatives) in the work of framing the Constitution. (p. 324)
>
> In the ratification, it became manifest that the line of cleavage for and against the Constitution was between substantial personalty interests on the one hand and the small farming and debtor interests on the other. (p. 325)
>
> [In short:] the Constitution was essentially an economic document. . . . (p. 324)

Now the evidence with which Beard defends these conclusions—his analysis of the Founders' property holdings, his study of the economic interests which supported the Constitution, and his examination of the class-voting on ratification —all this evidence has been critically reviewed by recent writers.[23] But whether or not Beard's *evidence* has been refuted, his fundamental thesis may yet be valid; that is, it may still be argued that the *essential* purpose of the Constitution or of its authors was to protect the interests of property, or that the Constitution, as Beard maintains, "was essentially an economic document." Hence, let us assume, what Beard contends, that the supporters of the Constitution were mainly the "rich," while its opponents were mainly the "poor." By so doing, we are compelled to consider seriously the implications of the *theory of economic determinism* upon which Beard explicitly bases his interpretation.*

In the Introduction to the 1935 edition of his work, Beard disclaimed the belief that " 'all history' can or must be explained in economic terms, or any other terms." Nevertheless, it seemed to him that "economic 'forces' are primordial or fundamental, and come nearer 'explaining' events than any other 'forces.' "[24] Beard was convinced that Madison held the same views, in proof of which he cites the following passage from *Federalist 10:*

> The diversity in the faculties of men, from which the rights of property originate, is not less an insuperable obstacle to a uniformity of interests. The protection of these faculties is the first object of government. From the protection of different and unequal faculties of acquiring property, the possession of different degrees and kinds of property immediately results; and from the influence of these on the sentiments and views of the respective proprietors, ensues a division of society into different interests and parties. . . . The most common and durable source of factions has been the various and unequal distribution of property. Those who are creditors, and those who are debtors, fall under a like discrimination. A landed interest, a manufacturing interest, a mercantile interest, a moneyed interest, with many lesser interests, grow up of necessity in civilized nations and divide them into different classes, actuated by different sentiments and views. The regulation of these various and interfering interests forms the principal task of modern legislation, and involves the spirit of party and faction in the necessary and ordinary operations of the government.

After citing this passage, Beard concludes: "Here we have a masterly statement of the theory of economic determinism

---

* I might note that the division between the rich and the poor roughly corresponds to a division between the educated and the uneducated; so that the Constitution might be explained in terms of *intellectual determinism!* But of course there were many well educated men who opposed the Constitution.

in politics."[25] By economic *determinism*, Beard presumably means that economics does not merely *influence* politics—which, after all, is a matter of common knowledge—but that economics is the "primordial or fundamental" determinant of politics; or that men's political opinions can be *adequately* explained in economic terms; or that political institutions constitute, essentially, a "superstructure" based on economic grounds. Now I submit that Madison's understanding of the relation between politics and economics is closer to *common sense* than to the theory of economic determinism suggested by Beard. This may more readily be seen by considering two statements which Beard failed to cite. The first occurs immediately after Beard's elision in the above passage. Here Madison says: "The latent causes of faction are thus sown in the nature of man; and we see them everywhere brought into different degrees of activity, according to the different circumstances of civil society." In other words, the "primordial or fundamental" causes of faction, and therefore of *politics,* are latent in *human nature.* But these causes, according to Madison, are none other than the *diverse and unequal faculties of men.* Economics, it is true, influences the *activity* of these faculties; it influences men's political opinions, and how it does this depends on the different circumstances of civil society. *But men's opinions in turn influence economics.* For in the second statement which Beard failed to cite—and this occurs immediately before the passage in question—Madison says: "As long as the connection subsists between [man's] opinions and his self-love, his opinions and his passions will have a reciprocal influence on each other; and the former will be the objects to which the latter attach themselves." In other words, while man's passions will influence his opinions, so his opinions will influence his passions. Stated in terms of class interests: whereas the political opinions of the rich are biased in favor of the interests of the rich, so the political opinions of the poor are biased in favor of the interests of the poor—again, a matter of common knowledge. But Madison goes even further, much further than the economic interpretation of politics will allow.

In the passage which Beard cites, Madison has primarily in view the common run of men, be they rich or poor. But not *all* men are governed primarily by economics. For again in *Federalist 10*, Madison speaks of "enlightened statesmen," and he says that such statesmen "will not always be at the helm." This means that there will be times when *unenlightened* men will be at the helm. In other words, Madison envisions two kinds of *politicians: mediocre* politicians and *great* politicians. Mediocre politicians—and they are legion— are primarily motivated by narrow self-interest; they are very apt to identify themselves either with the rich or with the poor. Hence we can expect their political opinions to be biased in favor of the economic interests of one class or the other. In contrast, great politicians, although not free from self-interest, will not *wholly* identify themselves either with the rich or with the poor. Hence their political opinions, though not free from bias, will not simply favor the economic interests of either of these classes; their political opinions will have other kinds of interests or ends in view. Now it is precisely because great politicians are rare, and mediocre politicians legion, that Madison expects to see "the spirit of party and faction in the necessary and ordinary operations of government." This means, in part, that economic interest groups will generally influence the formulation of public policies. But the extent of their influence will depend on the caliber of the politicians who are to *regulate* the "various and interfering interests" of society. Stated another way: Just as there is a reciprocal influence between men's passions and men's opinions, so there is a reciprocal influence between economics and politics. This is as much a theory of *political* determinism as it is a theory of *economic* determinism. But again, so much depends on the caliber of the politicians.

Now the economic interpretation obscures and levels these distinctions. It posits an identity of interest between the Founders and the propertied classes. It ignores or denies the possibility that the Founders may have had *one* interest which, though perhaps consistent with the interests of the propertied classes, was nevertheless distinct from such interests: I mean their interest in politics, in *Politics as a Vocation*—to use the title of Max Weber's famous essay.[26] In other words, I am suggesting that the Founders constitute a class of their own, a class of politicians. The same may be said of intellectuals: they too constitute a class. But just as there are great and mediocre intellectuals, so there are great and mediocre politicians. Now what great and mediocre politicians have in common is trivial in comparison with their differences. Certainly all politicians are influenced by economics. But as I have said, politicians may also influence economics, and how they do this and with what ends in view will depend on their caliber as politicians. It need hardly be said that the Founders wanted to wield political power. It does need to be said that *they wanted to set their stamp on the course and character of American life.* Here they were influenced not only by economic considerations, but by political considerations, and by political ideals and principles. And it is primarily these political ideals and principles that we must try to elucidate; for these are the things that endure, that touch the question of how men should live. I do not mean to suggest by this that the Founders were primarily involved in a philosophical inquiry. But to an extent far surpassing—and *necessarily* surpassing—present-day politicians, the Founders applied philosophy to action, which is to say they were engaged in *constitutional* deliberation. Nevertheless, constitutional deliberation is political deliberation: it involves *compromise*. To understand their compromises, it will be necessary to understand the extent to which the Founders were governed by immediate considerations *and* by long-range considerations. It will be necessary to learn something about the *art* of politics, and this the economic interpretation of the Constitution obscures.*

§

The Oligarchic and the Democratic Interpretations of the Constitution

For reasons which will soon become apparent, the oligarchic and democratic interpretations of the Constitution require distinct but not separate analyses. Here I wish to point out that both interpretations frequently confuse the question of what the Constitution *is* with the question of what the Constitution *was intended to be*. Clearly, these questions are of a different order, however similar be their solutions. The first is a problem of philosophy; the second,

---

* Perhaps, I ought to mention, in a footnote, the "political realist" interpretation represented by John Roche, "The Founding Fathers: A Reform Caucus in Action," *American Political Science Review*, LV (Dec. 1961), 799-816. Following the *group interest* interpretation of politics, which denies the existence of a *public interest*, Roche argues that all the Founders tried to do was to "hammer out a pragmatic compromise which would both bolster the 'National interest' and be acceptable to the people" (p. 799). What is more, "the Constitution," he concludes, "was not . . . a triumph of architectonic genius; it was a patch-work sewn together under the pressure of both time and events"; it was guided by "no over-arching principles"; indeed, "the Constitution was neither a victory for abstract theory nor a great political success" (pp. 815-816). In other words, the Founders were merely concerned with hammering out a "consensus" or a bundle of compromises among competing interest groups. They were preoccupied with the interests of the moment, not with long-range considerations or with political ideals and principles.

I shall refute Roche's interpretation in subsequent chapters, explicitly in Chapter 9.

a problem of textual and historical exposition. The first question—for example, whether the Constitution is democratic—presupposes prior philosophic inquiry into *what is a democracy*. Such an inquiry necessitates setting forth principles and categories of explanation more concrete than the term democracy or such formulas as "political equality," "majority rule," or "popular sovereignty." Very likely, such an inquiry would have to determine what are the habits, dispositions, and beliefs of a democratic regime; what are the ends to which its activities are directed; and what are its legal and institutional structures of power. Only then would it be possible to show whether the Constitution is consistent with a democracy. But as already suggested, the results of this philosophic inquiry may be somewhat different from the results of an inquiry into what the Constitution was intended to be by the Founding Fathers. This said, I turn to consider the oligarchic and democratic interpretations, but only insofar as they profess to be explanatory of the intentions of the Founders.*

Proponents of the oligarchic interpretation generally employ as their criterion of evaluation the notion of "majority rule."[27] The material so evaluated is largely confined to the electoral laws and institutional divisions of power set forth in the first three articles of the Constitution. The manner of constituting the Senate and its ratifying power, the method of electing the executive and its veto power, and the sum and substance of the Supreme Court are declared inconsistent with the criterion of majority rule—hence, oligarchic. This, of course, is a philosophic conclusion. But it may be represented as being in accord with the views of the Founding Fathers. For it is well known that the Founders professed concern over the tendency of popular majori-

---

* In what follows concerning the oligarchic interpretation, it should be borne in mind that the latter usually incorporates the economic interpretation.

ties to encroach on minority rights, as well as to hinder the progress and good administration of government—which concern moved them to institute safeguards against such dangers and inconveniences. And it is also well known that at least some of the Founders professed "oligarchic" and "aristocratic" leanings which they are supposed to have embodied in the Senate and perhaps in other institutions as well. But these considerations do not warrant the conclusion that the Constitution *as a whole* is oligarchic in design and in intention, or even primarily so. For according to the criterion of majority rule, the method of constituting the House of Representatives, together with its powers, appears to be democratic both in design *and* in intention. And to complicate matters further, it is not entirely clear which institution of government was intended to be the most important and powerful. The criterion of majority rule, therefore, would seem to favor the thesis that the Founders intended to combine, in varying ways and degrees, oligarchic and democratic institutions (perhaps with aristocratic ones as well), and thereby to constitute some form of *mixed regime.*

However, after a somewhat more subtle examination of these same institutions, other commentators, notably Martin Diamond, conclude that they are essentially democratic, or that the Constitution is representative of a "mitigated" or "qualified" democracy.[28] One criterion of evaluation employed by Diamond is the idea of "popular sovereignty," which, be it noted, he regards as synonymous with "majority rule"—the very criterion employed by the oligarchic interpretation! To be sure, Diamond would agree with his opponents that the Founders attempted to impose institutional checks against the dangers and vices associated with the "many." Nevertheless, because the composition and power of the Senate, the executive, and the Supreme Court are ultimately derived from the people and not from *distinct orders or classes,* he regards these checks as mere "mitigations" of essentially democratic institutions.[29] This, of course, is a philosophic conclusion. But it too may be represented as being in accord with the views of the Founding Fathers. For the Founders frequently *say* they are committed to the popular form of government. And even though they admit that this form of government requires certain institutional restraints if it is to be well constituted, still they *confess* that the people are the source of sovereign power. So, whereas the oligarchic thesis discounts the Founders' professed commitment to popular government, the democratic thesis discounts the Founders' avowed leanings toward oligarchic (and aristocratic) institutions. Clearly, the terms of discourse and the intentions of the Founders appear ambiguous. But I have yet to discuss the difficulties which the democratic interpretation of the Constitution encounters.

The difficulties are many. For the moment, however, consider only those relevant to textual exposition. First, the Founders express not only a commitment to popular government, but also a concern for *liberty* and *natural justice*. Even had they spoken solely of a commitment to popular government, we should still not be justified in concluding that they *intended* to establish either a democracy or a mitigated one. In the first place, we should have to determine what they meant by popular government. In the second, even if the Founders regarded popular government and democracy as synonymous, this would not be conclusive of their *real intentions*. For one may conceal one's real intentions by deliberately confounding the terms of one's discourse. But this suggests a second difficulty. The authors of the Constitution say they favor not only the popular form of government but also the *republican* form of government. Hence the question arises: How did the Founders distinguish one form from another, and both from democracy? According to Diamond, "*popular government,*" for the Founders, "*was the genus, and democracy and republic were two species* of the genus."[30] This is controverted, however, by Hamilton in *Federalist 6*, where he says: "Sparta, Athens, Rome, and Carthage were all republics." Notice that Athens, a democracy, is here regarded as a republic. But notice too that Sparta, Rome, and Carthage are *also* regarded as republics although they were *mixed regimes* having hereditary institutions! From this it appears, contrary to Diamond's contention, that *republic is the genus,* and that democracy is but one species of that genus.[31] Nevertheless, it could still be argued that the republic established by the Founders was understood by them to be a "mitigated" democracy. But this poses a third difficulty.

Recall that the restraints imposed upon the "many" are regarded by Diamond as mere mitigations of essentially democratic institutions. Assuming that he has properly defined what constitutes a democratic institution, what, may one ask, constitutes the essential character of their supposed "mitigations"? Clearly, the character of these mitigations cannot be democratic. If they are not democratic they must be non-democratic. But we can hardly define a so-called mitigation of an institution by what it is *not*. To be sure, like the character of a virtue for Aristotle, the character of an institution may lie in a mean between extremes. For example, consider the old British House of Lords as one extreme, and the Council of Athens at the time of Aristotle as the other. Relative to the hereditary House of Lords, the original Senate appears democratic—or as Diamond says, "radically democratic." But he might have also noted that, relative to the Council of Athens, which numbered *five hundred men annually* chosen by *lot*, the original Senate appears oligarchic, if not radically oligarchic. What Diamond has done is to make an *absolute* distinction out of a *relative* one. He seems to have overlooked the possibility, well-known to Aristotle, that institutions may be democratic in some respects, and oligarchic in others. Indeed, it may be possible to so combine such institutions as to constitute a *mixed regime*. And the regime thus constituted may be so subtle as to deceive those who live in it as to its true character. Some may think it is a democracy; others may think it is an oligarchy. However this may be, again I must ask what constitutes a mitigation of essentially democratic institutions? What form would this mitigation take? Might it take the form of a unitary and indirectly elected executive exercising a suspensive veto over a more directly elected legislature? Might it take the form of a Senate sharing in the appointment power of the executive, a Senate constituted on a non-majoritarian basis and holding office three times the duration of a popularly elected assembly? Or might it take the form of a Supreme Court whose members are well insulated from the electoral process, whose members, moreover, are endowed with the power to nullify the acts of popularly elected legislatures, a power they may exercise, in effect, for life? Perhaps, from a philosophic point of view, these may yet be mere "mitigations" of essentially democratic institutions. But from the point of view of textual and historical exposition, were they regarded as such by the Founding Fathers?

That the proponents of the oligarchic and democratic interpretations of the Constitution should arrive at opposite evaluations of the same political document suggests that they started from different but not wholly unrelated philosophic assumptions. The assumption of the oligarchic interpretation is that the character of a regime must be understood primarily in *quantitative* or in non-teleological terms.[32] The measure of significance is not the *qualities* or *ends,* but the *numbers,* of those who participate in the political process or in the exercise of sovereign authority. This assumption is then used for expository purposes. But let us juxtapose this assumption with the criterion of majority rule, which, it will be recalled, was employed to determine whether institutions are democratic. Now is it not evident that the criterion of majority rule permits a drastic reduction in the number of those who participate in the political process? Indeed, that criterion, by reference to which the Constitution was deemed to have been oligarchic in intention, may permit so drastic a reduction in the number of those who participate in the political process as to make the Constitution appear rather democratic in intention! Admittedly, majority rule is a quantitative criterion and so it allows for a "more or less" determination of the extent to which a regime is or was intended to be democratic. Nevertheless, if the majority should subjugate the minority, it would seem that only the introduction of purposive, if not ethical, considerations, could extricate us from the philosophic dilemma involved.* However this may be, the criterion of majority rule does not appear to be very fruitful in gauging the intentions of the Founders.

Turning once again to the democratic interpretation: some of its proponents proceed from the philosophic assumption that the character of a regime must ultimately be understood in *qualitative* or in *teleological* terms. Accordingly, what is significant is not the *number,* so much as the *qualities* and *ends,* of those who participate in the political process or in the exercise of sovereign authority. This approach is especially evident in Diamond, who writes: "What premodern thought had seen in an aristocratic Senate—wisdom, nobility, manners, religion, etc.—the Founding Fathers converted into stability, enlightened self-interest, a 'temperate and respectable body of citizens.' "[33] Now it is true that Madison, in *Federalist 63*, describes the Senate as comprising a "temperate and respectable body of citizens." It so

---

* It could be argued, however, that the only majority which has a right to rule is that majority, in the making of which, all members of society have had an equal opportunity to participate. But this only proves that the criterion of majority rule alone is not sufficient to determine the character of political institutions. Indeed, it indicates that not only numbers but such ends or values as equality and liberty must be taken into account if the character of political institutions is to be adequately evaluated.

happens, however, that this same Madison also expected the Senate to consist of men of "wisdom and virtue."[34] And surely the early Senate of the United States eloquently confirmed his expectations. Nevertheless, let us admit that the Founders did not emphasize the aristocratic virtues to the extent, say, of Aristotle. And let us assume that the Senate was expected to consist "merely" of temperate and respectable men motivated by what Diamond calls "enlightened self-interest." But these terms are very vague. A body of men governed by *enlightened* self-interest might be very elevated indeed. Furthermore, what *we* regard as temperate and respectable men *today* might have been regarded as somewhat intemperate and undeservedly respected men by the *Founders*. It is not simply wrong, indeed it may be informative, to use the standards of excellence prescribed by philosophers such as Aristotle. But a study of Aristotle's *Politics* would reveal that much the same qualities which Diamond attributes to the Senate were regarded by the philosopher as being most characteristic, not of democracies, but of *mixed regimes!*[35]

Turning to the ends in terms of which we are to understand whether a regime is democratic, Diamond approaches the problem by asking: "What was the Founding Fathers' view of the good life? Upon what fundamental theoretical premises did that view of the good life depend?"[36] Citing Madison, he answers:

> the great principle of self-preservation . . . the transcendent law of nature and of nature's God, which declares that the safety and happiness of society are the objects at which all political institutions aim, and to which all such institutions must be sacrificed.

Unfortunately, Diamond has taken this passage out of context. For immediately preceding that passage—and it will be found in *Federalist* 43—there appears this question: "On what principle [can] the Confederation, which stands in the solemn form of a compact among States . . . be superceded without the unanimous consent of the parties?" Madison's answer, of course, is not some principle of the good life, but "the great principle of self-preservation." Now it is true that Diamond translates self-preservation into "comfortable self-preservation"—this, via the Founders' allegedly Lockean view of "happiness." He then translates "comfortable self-preservation" into the "protection of economic interests," which, he gives us to understand, is primarily what the Founders meant by "justice."[37] So here, paradoxical as it may seem, the democratic interpretation ends up with the same conclusion as the economic interpretation! Both regard the "protection of economic interests" as the ultimate purpose of the Constitution. Consider, however, the following three sentences from *Federalist 51, only the first two of which are cited by Diamond:*[38]

> Justice is the end of government. It is the end of civil society.
> It has been and ever will be pursued until it be obtained, or
> until liberty be lost in the pursuit.

This last sentence suggests that justice means much more than the "protection of economic interests." Indeed, it more than suggests that justice ranks above liberty in the hierarchy of ends or values. Of course, against this it could be argued that liberty is but a means of pursuing "justice"—justice understood as the protection of economic interests. If so, the third sentence would have to be translated to read: "The protection of economic interests has been and ever will be pursued until it be obtained, or until liberty be lost in the pursuit." Whether this translation does justice to the author of *Federalist 51*, the reader may decide for himself. Here the question arises: What ends, or what vision of the good life, did the Founders fail to pursue?

According to Diamond:

> So far as concerns those ends of government on which
> *The Federalist* is almost wholly silent, it is reasonable to
> infer that what the Founders made no provision for they did

not rank highly among the legitimate objects of government. Other political theories had ranked highly, as objects of government, the nurturing of a particular religion, education . . . moderation, individual excellence in the virtues, etc. On all of these *The Federalist* is either silent, or has in mind only pallid versions of the originals. . . .[39]

What Diamond is trying to prove here is that the Founders lowered the ends of government (to accommodate, of course, a "profoundly democratic" society). This he attempts to do by contrasting *The Federalist* with the political theories of pre-modern philosophers, theories which emphasized the noble ends on which *The Federalist* is "silent." From this "silence" Diamond infers that the regime established under the Constitution is essentially democratic. Now it may be noted in passing that at least one pre-modern philosopher, again Aristotle, would have questioned such an inference. For this philosopher thought that even in regimes which do not make the encouragement of excellence a matter of law or public policy, there may still be found individuals who are of good repute and esteemed to be of high quality; so that a regime which pays regard to wealth and numbers, but which also recognizes excellence, may be called "aristocratic."[40] Yet Diamond overlooks more pertinent facts. For while it is true that *The Federalist* is silent about education, it is also true that during the debates of the Federal Convention, James Madison and Charles Pinckney proposed to invest Congress with the power to establish a *national university;* that the motion was supported by James Wilson; that it came very close to being adopted; and that it failed of adoption perhaps because some delegates agreed with Gouverneur Morris that the motion was unnecessary, unnecessary because, in his opinion, Congress could establish a university, the "silence" of the Constitution notwithstanding.[41] Furthermore, Diamond forgets that this Constitution does not explicitly reflect the *entire* character of the American regime. For the people of that regime were also to be

governed under the *constitutions of the several states*, many
of which provided for education and religion—some of the
very ends of government on which *The Federalist* is silent![42]
Finally, let it be said here, awaiting the evidence of later
chapters, that *The Federalist* is *not* silent—not silent at all—
on some of the noble ends to which Diamond refers.[43] But
however this may be, to contrast such a work, which in part
is a work of political *rhetoric*, with the *theoretical* disquisi-
tions of political philosophers, and to conclude from the
"silence" of the former concerning the noble ends of the
latter, that the Founding Fathers intended to establish a
mitigated democracy, is a dubious method of constitutional
exegesis. Let me therefore offer an alternative method, one
which has led me to conclude that the Founders intended
to establish a *mixed regime*.

§

The Dialectical Method of Interpreting the Constitution

The Constitution is not a political treatise. Its philosophic
principles are not evident; its key terms are not defined.
This obviously applies to the *Records of the Federal Convention*. To be sure, any serious inquiry into the philosophy
of the Constitution must begin with, and depend largely
upon, the material contained in these records. This material,
however, appears to convey the divergent views of the
Founders' rather than the meaning of their agreement. Shall
we then look for guidance in *The Federalist* papers? Indispensable as these are for a comprehensive inquiry, they
constitute neither an exposition of the debates of the Convention, nor a philosophic treatise on government. True,
they contain many important statements about the inten-

tions of the Convention, as well as many informative arguments pertaining to political philosophy. Nevertheless, these statements and arguments are controlled and colored by the practical or rhetorical purpose of persuading men to a common course of action. As a consequence, the language of *The Federalist* may be intentionally deceptive, at least in part. Indeed, *this may also be true of the language of the Constitution.* But let me elaborate upon some of these difficulties.

When I said that the key terms of the Constitution are not defined, I had primarily in view its ideal ends or purposes. The meaning of these ideal ends or purposes is far from being evident in the *Records of the Federal Convention* (or even in *The Federalist*). In the Preamble of the Constitution, and again in the Virginia Plan, the Founders begin with a statement of purposes. From there they proceed to discuss, for the most part, institutions. In other words, a statement of *ends* is followed by a statement of *means*. This is quite understandable; for political deliberation—and the Constitution evolved out of such deliberation—is concerned mainly, or rather explicitly, with legal and institutional means by which certain ends are to be realized. But it is precisely these ends which must be elucidated if we are to fully comprehend the philosophy of the Constitution. This difficulty would be insoluble were it not for the fact that any intelligent discussion of means tacitly involves an elaboration of ends, the meaning of which may be elicited by dialectical analysis. Here we are most fortunate in that the Founders discuss means in three distinct ways, each of which reveals and mutually confirms the meaning of the ends we are seeking. In the first place, they discuss the various characteristics required of different institutions. These are indicative of the character of the ends to be secured by these institutions. Second, they frequently refer to the various qualities required of statesmen. These are suggestive of the ends to be served by these statesmen. Third, they discuss both the characteristics required of institutions and the qualities required of statesmen in relation to certain *political evils*. The elaboration of these evils is especially significant for understanding the ideal ends or values which the Constitution was intended to foster. There remains, however, one further difficulty which must be overcome in the process of elucidating these ideal ends or values. Again I refer to the divergent views or intentions of the Founders as evidenced in the *Records of the Federal Convention*.

Consider. The Constitution is the result of literally hundreds of resolutions or propositions which were debated and voted upon during the long procedings of the Convention. On most of these resolutions the delegates expressed different opinions. Many agreed to various propositions for *different reasons*. This, by the way, is one reason why it may be unwise (and perhaps fallacious) to reduce the political character of the Constitution to any single formula, whether democratic, oligarchic, or aristocratic. But it may also be unwise to reduce to such formulas any of the institutions of government which the Constitution prescribes. Since each of these institutions derives its character from a multiplicity of propositions—for example, the mode of election, the duration of tenure, the powers of office—it is possible, as just suggested, that each of these propositions was decided by different political principles. Thus, during the course of the debates, a delegate might express democratic views with respect to one proposition, and oligarchic or aristocratic views with respect to another. In addition, he might express such views with different intentions in mind: perhaps he wished the issue to be decided on grounds of principle, or perhaps he was governed by considerations of expedience. Furthermore, a delegate might express contradictory views on the same issue, or he might alter his views on one issue in virtue of the outcome of another. Finally, a delegate might defend his position by the use of rhetorical argument, argument concealing ulterior purposes. To grasp his intentions it is necessary to have in view the debates as a whole—and much more besides. These are by no means the only difficulties and complexities involved in analyzing the intentions of the Founders. But they suffice to indicate how I shall proceed in this analysis. First and foremost, I shall try to elucidate the *collective* intentions of the Founders vis-à-vis the *general* character of each branch of government, and with a view to the ends or purposes which each branch was intended to represent or foster. This will require a dialectical analysis of the manner and way in which the Founders discussed and resolved their differences. Second, I shall try to elucidate the *individual* intentions of the Founders insofar as these are fundamentally consistent with, or explanatory of, their collective intentions. Third, I shall examine these various intentions at *different levels:* at the level of expedience, at the level of principle, and at the level of aspiration.*

---

*Before commencing this inquiry, the reader should understand that I include under the category of the *Founders* only (1) those delegates at the Federal Convention who signed the Constitution; and (2) those delegates who did not sign the Constitution, but who, like Randolph, contributed positively and significantly to its formulation. (Excluded, therefore, are (a) the countless members of the state ratifying conventions, who cannot seriously be regarded as *authors* of the Constitution; and (b) men like John Adams and Thomas Jefferson whose influence would have to be viewed in the light of my critique of the analogical method of interpreting the Constitution.) As for the *intentions* of the Founders: in addition to what I have already said, this term is to be understood to mean (1) their immediate objectives; (2) their long-range objectives or ultimate purposes; and (3) their understanding of various concepts and principles, and the relative importance they attached to different values. (But cf. C. Herman Pritchett. *The American Constitution* (New York: McGraw-Hill Book Co., Inc., 1959), pp. 43-48; Clinton Rossiter, *1787 The Grand Convention* (New York: The Macmillan Co., 1965), pp. 333-334; and my critical comment on Rossiter, *infra,* p. 293, *n.* 3.

2

The Rules of the Federal Convention

O N FRIDAY, the twenty-fifth of May 1787, delegates from seven of the thirteen American states have convened at the State House in the city of Philadelphia for the purpose of reconstituting the government of the United States.[1] George Washington is unanimously elected President, William Jackson is chosen Secretary, and a committee is appointed to draw up rules of procedure for the guidance of the Convention. In the balloting for this committee, the following men are selected: George Wythe of Virginia, Alexander Hamilton of New York, and Charles Pinckney of South Carolina. With the appointment of the committee, the House is adjourned. On Monday, the delegates reconvene. Their numbers are increased by new arrivals including delegations from two additional states. The day is devoted to a reading and discussion of the rules prepared by the appointed committee. Some sixteen rules are reported. With two exceptions, all the rules are adopted—some with amendment. In addition, six other rules are proposed. These are referred back to the committee for the purpose of restatement. They are reported and approved the following morning. And so the delegates adopt a body of rules which are to govern their deliberations until they complete the work of drafting a Constitution for the United States of America. Whatever be the differences among these men, these rules of procedure bear witness to a common ground of agreement. Let us inquire into the spirit of these rules. Perhaps we may learn from them what it means to engage in political deliberation. Perhaps, from this hitherto unrecognized beginning, we may discern a preview of the end.

One of the two rules rejected by the Convention would have allowed any delegate to call for the yeas and nays and have them recorded in the minutes.[2] Why did the delegates reject this rule? Rufus King, a delegate from Massachusetts, opposed the rule on these grounds: " . . . as the acts of the Convention were not to bind the Constituents, it was unnecessary to exhibit the evidence of the votes; and improper as changes of opinion would be frequent in the course of the business and would fill the minutes with contradictions."[3] George Mason, a delegate from Virginia, seconded Mr. King's objection. He urged that "such a record of the opinions of members would be an obstacle to a change of them on conviction; and in case of its being hereafter promulged must furnish handles to the adversaries of the Result of the Meeting."[4] It was for these reasons that the rule was rejected, and not only without dissent, but without any substitute

motion having been proffered. But these very reasons suggest that the delegates had come to *deliberate;* that whatever their political opinions were at the outset of the Convention, they wished to feel free to change them should
these opinions be shown, in the course of deliberation, to
be unsound or deficient. If so, this means that the Founding
Fathers wished to be governed by the unfolding reason of
their discourse and not simply by the counting of hands.
This commitment to rational inquiry is confirmed by a number of rules adopted by the Convention, and it is to these
I now turn.

As an introduction to the first of these rules, consider
a motion made by Richard Spaight, a delegate from North
Carolina. Mr. Spaight urged the Convention "to provide,
that, on the one hand, the House may not be precluded by
a vote on any question from revising the subject matter of
it when they see cause nor, on the other hand, be led too
hastily to rescind a decision which was the result of mature
discussion."[5] As a consequence of this motion, the following
rule was adopted: "That a motion to reconsider a matter,
which had been determined by a majority, may be made,
with leave unanimously given, on the same day in which
the vote has passed, but otherwise not without one day's
previous notice; in which last case, if the House agree to
the reconsideration some future day shall be assigned for
that purpose."[6] Because their deliberations must terminate
in a decision, the Founders acknowledge the practical necessity of being bound by the majority. Nevertheless, they also
suggest a higher standard: in the course of their deliberations they must also be free to reconsider their decisions if
they are to decide wisely. To minimize the possibility of
unwise decisions even further, it was provided that: "The
determination of a question, although fully debated, shall be
postponed, if the Deputies of any State desire it, until the
next day."[7] In this rule may be seen a kind of suspensive

veto—here a way of preventing perhaps heated debate from issuing forth in precipitous decisions. We may even regard this rule as a "check" to insure more "balanced" judgment. This desire of the Founding Fathers to conduct their proceedings as free men open to reason may be characterized by the term *candor* (of which, more later). And it was precisely to foster this candor that the delegates adopted the followilng three rules, which will hereafter be referred to simply as *the rule of secrecy*.

> That no copy be taken of any entry on the journal during the sitting of the House without the leave of the House.
>
> That members only be permitted to inspect the journal.
>
> That nothing spoken in the House be printed or otherwise published, or communicated without leave.[8]

Because the delegates wished to be candid or open with each other, and because they wished to feel free to change their opinions without embarrassment, they thought it prudent to be closed off from the possibility of untoward influences beyond their doors.

Now to appreciate the significance of the rule of secrecy (which, so far as I know, is the only rule to have received the notice of commentators), it is necessary to examine sources other than the records of the Convention, the rule having been adopted without debate. Thus, in a letter to Jefferson, dated June 6, James Madison had this to say about the rule in question: "It was thought expedient in order to secure *unbiassed* discussion within doors, and to prevent misconceptions and misconstructions without, to establish some rules of caution which will for no short time restrain even a confidential communication of our proceedings."[9] Contrast Madison's words with those contained in a letter written by William Johnson to his son on June 20: "It is agreed that for the present our deliberations shall be kept secret, so that I can only tell you that much information and eloquence has been displayed in the introductory speeches, and that we have hitherto preserved great temperance, *candor*, and moderation in debate, and evinced much solicitude for the public weal."[10] Madison of course, was a delegate from Virginia, then the largest state of the Union. Johnson, on the other hand, was a delegate from Connecticut, a considerably smaller state. Now whereas Madison says that the rule of secrecy was adopted to secure unbiased discussion, Johnson does not explicitly state why the rule was adopted. However, in the sentence in which he refers to the rule of secrecy, he notes, among other things, that the debates of the Convention had thus far been conducted with "candor." In the language of the eighteenth century, to be candid is to be free from bias.[11] So it would be reasonable to infer that Madison of Virginia and Johnson of Connecticut agreed that the rule of secrecy was conducive to candid or unbiased deliberation.

The same may be said of George Mason. Thus, anticipating the adoption of the rule of secrecy on May 27, Mason wrote his son:

> It is expected our doors will be shut, and communications upon the business of the Convention be forbidden during its sitting. This I think myself a proper precaution to prevent mistakes and misrepresentations until the business shall have been completed, when the whole may have a very different complexion from that in which the several crude and indigested parts might in their first shape appear if submitted to the public eye.[12]

Notice that Mason supports the rule of secrecy with very much the same reasons he advanced against the rule which, it will be recalled, would have allowed for the recording of the votes. In both cases he suggests that he has not come to the Convention with fixed or unalterable views. In the first, he says that recording the opinions of delegates is not conducive to a change of them on conviction; in the second, he says that opening the debates to the public is not conducive to a refinement of the delegates' opinions during the course of their deliberations. In a word, he suggests that neither is conducive to candor.[13] Now contrast Mason's views with those expressed by Alexander Hamilton some years after ratification of the Constitution.

> Had the deliberations been open while going on, the clamours of faction would have prevented any satisfactory result. Had they *been afterwards disclosed,* much food would have been afforded to inflamatory declamation. Propositions, made without due reflection and perhaps abandoned by the proposers themselves on more mature reflection, would have been handles for a profusion of ill-natured accusation.[14]

Here, then, is a delegate from New York, one often called an "aristocrat," who agrees with a delegate from Virginia, a man generally regarded as a "democrat"—here, we see, are two men of different political persuasions who agree on the purpose and propriety of the rule of secrecy.

It should be evident from the above discussion that the principal object of the rule of secrecy was to promote a virtue essential to political deliberation, namely, the virtue of candor. But what is "candor"? More precisely, what is its ultimate significance for the deliberations of the Founding Fathers? In answering this question, it may be helpful to consider, first, its implications for a theory prevalent among contemporary political scientists. The theory I have in mind is one which, simply stated, would reduce politics to nothing more than a struggle between various interest groups.[15] Now if this theory were sufficient to explain the conduct of the Founders, the question of candor would lose all seriousness—indeed, all meaning. Viewed in the light of this theory, the Founders were merely the spokesmen of diverse interest groups. They had come to the Convention motivated by the mentality of the marketplace; that is, they sought to get as much as possible for as little as possible, in which case, their proceedings must have been governed not by candor, but by artful deception. Of course, proponents of the group-interest theory do not draw, nor wish us to draw, this ultimate conclusion. But we can hardly avoid it if we accept their premise. This is not meant to suggest that the group-interest theory is without political relevance, or that it does not raise questions significant for political life. Indeed, precisely because it is preoccupied with the massive fact of group conflict, it has raised, perhaps to exaggerated preeminence, the question of *how* such conflicts are resolved. Now when this question is applied to the proceedings of the Federal Convention, the most general and widespread reply is that these proceedings were governed by "the spirit of compromise." But again, for the many who hold this belief—and they need not be avowed exponents of the group-interest theory—the significance of candor for political deliberation does not arise. And this is one reason why generations of students have been taught to regard the Constitution as a "bundle of compromises." There is no reason, however, why we must remain forever bound to this superficial truth, for there are *different kinds* of compromises. Some have in view only immediate or temporary interests; others have in view long-range or permanent interests. Both involve mutual concessions. Both will be found in the debates of the Convention. But it is especially the second kind of compromise that requires candor, for here the differences among men involve the permanent interests of the community. But again, what is "candor"?

Consistent with the rules of the Convention, candor may be defined not as the disposition to state one's views so much as the disposition to *alter* one's views on *important* matters should they be shown, in the course of discussion, to be unsound or inadequate. As Madison commented on the debates of the Convention:

Disinterestedness and candor [were] demonstrated by mutual concessions and frequent changes of opinions. Few who
did not change, in the progress of discussions, the opinions
on *important* points which they carried into the Convention.
Few who, at the close of the Convention, were not ready to
admit this change as the enlightening effect of the discussions.[16]

It is precisely this kind of candor that made the deliberations of the Founders so profoundly serious an enterprise.
For such candor makes possible genuine inquiry into questions of political *right*—questions of principle as well as of
policy. But if the Founders did indeed exhibit such candor,
consider the discipline which it imposes on their commentators. No longer can we regard the Constitution as a "bundle
of compromises." Instead, we are called upon to elucidate
the dialectical process out of which the Constitution evolved.
To do this with some measure of the seriousness which
apparently inspired the Founders, it will be necessary to
consider their deliberations as an inquiry into this fundamental question: What is the best kind of regime to which
the American people can reasonably aspire?

3

The Formative Principle of the Virginia Plan

THE RULES of procedure having been adopted, the Convention turned to the problem of reconstituting the government of the United States. Governor Edmund Randolph, on behalf of the Virginia delegation, opened the inquiry. In a candid yet cautiously drawn speech, Randolph addressed himself to the following order of questions. First, what properties ought a federal government possess? Second, what were the defects of the existing Confederation? And third, what was the chief cause of these defects?[1] He then inquired into the remedy, and this he elaborated in the fifteen resolutions comprising the Virginia Plan. In this chapter I shall try to elucidate the formative principle of the Virginia Plan apart from the debates it occasioned. I propose to do this by following the order of Randolph's opening speech and by analyzing those portions of it which bear directly on the principle in question. This analysis will reveal the *ruler-ruled relationship* underlying the legislative provisions of the Virginia Plan, as well as the kinds of men intended to hold the offices prescribed therein.

Consider, first, Randolph's views concerning the properties of a *federal* government. Such a government, he said, should (1) provide for the common defense; (2) prevent dissensions between members of the Union, or seditions in particular states; (3) procure to the several states various blessings which each could not achieve by itself; (4) be able to defend itself against encroachment; and finally, (5) be paramount to the state constitutions.[2] That Randolph should first ask what properties a federal government ought to possess already implies the magnitude with which he conceived the task confronting the Convention. Already he seems to be suggesting that the present form of government must be fundamentally altered. But notice that Randolph does not indicate by the aforementioned properties of a federal government the *kind* of federal government he has in mind. A government having these properties could be a democracy as well as an oligarchy or aristocracy—or even some mixture of the three. In other words, Randolph cautiously begins by setting forth certain properties of a federal government without suggesting the kinds of men whom he believes should exercise the powers of such a government. He does not *begin* with the more fundamental and controversial question, the question of *who should rule*. Nor does this question come to the surface when he discusses the defects of the existing Confederation. But what were those defects?

According to Randolph, the Congress under the Confederation was impotent. Specifically: (1) it could neither prevent the states from violating international treaties, nor secure their safety in the event of war; (2) it could not prevent them from engaging in rivalrous and harmful commercial and fiscal policies; (3) it lacked the power to undertake internal improvements in agriculture and manufactures, or to secure freer intercourse among citizens; (4) it was internally divided and largely at the mercy of local views and interests; and (5) it was the juridical creature of the state legislatures.³ In a word, the Confederation lacked all of the properties which a federal government ought to possess. Notice again, however, that Randolph does not indicate by the defects he attributes to the Confederation, what, in his opinion, is the political character of this Confederation or of the member states. But if the Confederation was so manifestly defective, how did it come to be established in the first place?

After acknowledging the wisdom of those who had framed the Articles of Confederation, Randolph reminded the delegates that, when that system was founded, the states had just won their independence from Great Britain. It should occasion no surprise, therefore, that their knowledge of government should then be in its infancy. Besides, at that time the states were exceedingly jealous of their newly won rights, and men had too recently escaped the evils of tyranny to fear the evils of anarchy. But now, he went on to say, the prospect of anarchy was everywhere in evidence. Still, wherein lay the precise cause of this condition? At this point, Randolph offered the following explanation:

> Our chief danger arises from the democratic parts of our constitutions. It is a maxim which I hold incontrovertible, that the powers of government exercised by the people swallow up the other branches. None of the constitutions have provided sufficient checks to the democracy.⁴

Randolph then concluded by saying that the remedy must be based on the "republican principle." Before examining his elaboration of this remedy in the Virginia Plan, let us analyze and try to grasp the significance of his closing remarks.

When Randolph declares that the "chief danger arises from the democratic parts of our [state] constitutions," this implies that there are parts of these constitutions which are *not* democratic. Or when he says that "the powers of government exercised by the people swallow up the other branches," this indicates that the powers of these other branches are not exercised by the people *de jure,* and that, in his opinion, they should not be. But what is the intended political character of these other branches? What kind of men are supposed to exercise the constitutional powers of these branches? Randolph does not say. We only know that these other branches are not democratic, and that their constitutional powers have been usurped by the democracy. Nevertheless, Randolph proposes to establish a federal government able to resist democratic encroachment, and this government is to be based on the *republican* principle. What does he mean by this? If it be answered that the republican principle is nothing more than the *representative* principle, then the foregoing passage makes little sense. For the "democratic parts" of the state constitutions of which Randolph complained, are none other than the *lower* branches of the state legislatures, and these were based on the same representative principle. The fact that these popular branches were constituted by that principle did not prevent them from encroaching on the other branches of government. Hence, to prevent such encroachment, something in *addition* to the representative principle will be necessary. Stated another way: Randolph proposes a government which is to remedy the defects arising out of what may be called the democratic principle. But if the democratic principle leads to certain defects, these can hardly be remedied by resorting to the identical principle: an effect cannot be nullified by its cause. If, then, a federal government based on the republican principle is to resist democratic encroachment, it must have one or more branches which are not democratic, and these must be constituted in such a way and with sufficient powers so as to ensure their independence. It follows, therefore, that the republican principle, in Randolph's judgment, combines, or permits the combination of, the democratic principle with principles which are not democratic. And we may reasonably suppose that these latter principles, and the branches to which they correspond, are either oligarchic or aristocratic, or perhaps both. Leaving this open, however, let us only say that the republican principle requires the participation, in one or more branches of government, of men who are not *wholly* identified with the democracy. To discover the specific character of these branches, and of the men who are to exercise their powers, I turn now to the Virginia Plan.

I propose to discuss the Virginia Plan in the following way. To begin with, I shall examine those resolutions affecting the composition and character of the national legislature. This will provide a basis from which to analyze, in detail, the debates which these resolutions occasioned. My procedure here is guided by the consideration that these resolutions gave rise to debates not only more detailed and various than those arising from the remaining resolutions, but also more profound in their philosophic import. If these resolutions are first treated apart from the debates, the reader will be able to focus on some of the broad themes which governed the deliberations of the Founders, but which subsequent analysis must elaborate. As for the resolutions related to the executive and judiciary, these will be studied solely within the context of the debates themselves, and their major treatment will appear in later chapters.

The first resolution of the Virginia Plan contains a kind of preamble setting forth the broad objects of government, namely, "common defense, security of liberty and general welfare." Passing over the second resolution, the third provides for a national legislature consisting of two branches. The next two resolutions—and these will concern the remainder of this chapter—elaborate the manner in which the two branches of the national legislature are to be constituted.

> *Resolution 4:* That the members of the first branch of the National Legislature ought to be elected by the people of the several states every ( ) for the term of ( ); to be of the age of ( ) years at least, to receive liberal stipends by which they may be compensated for the devotion of their time to public service; to be ineligible to any office established by a particular State, or under the authority of the United States, except those peculiarly belonging to the functions of the first branch, during the term of service, and for the space of ( ) after its expiration; to be incapable of re-election for the space of ( ) after the expiration of their term of service, and to be subject to recall.

> *Resolution 5:* That the members of the second branch of the National Legislature ought to be elected by those of the first, out of a proper number of persons nominated by the individual Legislatures, to be of the age of ( ) years at least; to hold their office *for a term sufficient to secure their independency,* to receive liberal stipends, by which they may be compensated for the devotion of their time to public service; and to be ineligible to any office established by a particular State, or under the authority of the United States, except those peculiarly belonging to the functions of the second branch, during the term of service, and for the space of ( ) after the expiration thereof.[5]

If the differences between the fourth and fifth resolutions could be summed up in a single word, that word would be *independency.* It is the only term used to signify the purpose of any of the clauses contained in these resolutions. Its inclusion in the fifth, and its exclusion from the fourth, provides an important clue to the respective qualities of the two branches forming the national legislature. The significance of the term becomes apparent so soon as we recall Randolph's earlier remark, namely, that "the powers of government exercised by the people swallow up the other branches." Concerning the character of these other branches (of the state governments), we only learned that they were not democratic and that they did not possess "sufficient checks against the democracy." In other words, these other branches could not "ensure their independency"—to use the language of the fifth resolution. It would seem therefore, that this resolution prescribes a branch of government—soon to be called the Senate—which, in Randolph's opinion, is not democratic, and which is constituted in such a way as to resist, or help resist, encroachment from the democratic branch, namely, the House of Representatives. That this is so will be abundantly substantiated when we study the debates. But now, let us analyze the fourth and fifth resolutions in detail.

Unlike the members of the Senate, those of the House are subject to recall. This implies a fundamental difference in the anticipated relationship of these two branches with their respective constituencies. It may be said that no provision could be better calculated to insure the dependency of a legislator than the provision for recall. For it places in the hands of his constituents the power to remove him from office whenever they think he has not been sufficiently responsive to their wants, or effective in carrying out their wishes. The difficulty, of course, is that the wants and wishes of his constituency may not always be reasonable. Or they may come into conflict with the wants and wishes of other constituencies or with the welfare of the community as a whole. Should this occur, a legislator, acting solely with a view to what he thinks proper, may be removed from office. (Were he not subject to this constant threat, he might have

sufficient time to enlighten his constituents, or they themselves might eventually come to recognize the propriety
of his conduct.) On the other hand, an irresolute legislator
(not to mention an unprincipled one) might conform to
the demands of his constituents against his better judgment.
But even this is no guarantee of his being retained in office.
For he is expected not only to conform to their demands,
but to fulfill them; and this he may not be able to do when
confronting other legislators representing the competing
demands of other constituencies. So whether he holds firmly
to his convictions or compromises them, he may suffer the
same fate. However, this should not obscure the intention
of recall and its probable effect upon the legislator, namely,
to make him subservient to the wants and wishes of his
constituents.

It should be apparent from the foregoing discussion
that the provision for recall increases the likelihood of frequent change in the membership of the first branch. But
the more frequent the change in its membership, the more
difficult it would be for this branch to pursue consistent and
long-range public policies. This difficulty can only be inten-
sified where the prescribed term of office for members of
the first branch is of short duration. And it may be said in
anticipation of the debates that a relatively short term is
intended. When to this we add the provision of the fourth
resolution making the members of the first branch ineligible
for immediate reelection, it is hard to conceive how this
branch of the national legislature would be able to function
at all—particularly in a diverse community! Its members
could hardly acquire any extensive experience in political
affairs. And if they must ever and again appeal to and pla-
cate diverse constituencies, they must either succumb to
inaction or perhaps follow the lead of a more independent
and coherent body of men.

We have seen that the fifth resolution proposes a Senate

whose members are "to hold their offices for a term sufficient to ensure their independency." To anticipate the debates again, it should be noted that the authors of the Virginia Plan had in mind a seven- and as much as a nine-year term for members of the Senate. To preclude interruption of this term, those holding the office of Senator are not made subject to recall. And to give the promise of even greater continuity, they may be reelected as soon as their term of office has expired. All this suggests that the authors of the Virginia Plan wished the members of the Senate to be relatively free to devote themselves to long-range policies of national significance. This they could not do, or do well, unless they possessed the knowledge and political experience afforded by long and continuous public office. But what does this mean for the relationship that is likely to exist between a Senator and his constituency? Given his lengthy term of office and his not being subject to recall, a Senator is in a better position (than is a member of the House) to restrain any unreasonable demands which may be pressed upon him by his constituency, or which, in his opinion, are contrary to the general welfare. In other words, the Senator is invested with an office conducive to the exercise of independent judgment, and one, moreover, which enables him to exert an educative influence on his constituents.

Thus far I have been speaking of the Senate as if it had a clearly distinguishable constituency. But the fifth resolution, it will be recalled, provides that members of the second branch of the national legislature be chosen by those of the first from among persons nominated by the state legislatures. Nevertheless, what was said concerning the relationship between a Senator and his constituency still holds. Indeed, precisely because the above method of election *obscures* his constituency, it may very well increase his independence. Since those responsible for the appointment of a Senator do not constitute a single group, it is more difficult for them to exert a concerted influence on the conduct of his office. Similarly, because he is not directly elected by the people of his state, the people have no direct "access" by which to importune him. Besides, even if the fifth resolution of the Virginia Plan had provided for a Senate elected by the state legislatures, this would not be decisive for the question of its intended constituency. Of greater importance is the term of the Senate in relation to the term of the various state legislatures. If a Senator's term of office were shorter than, or even concurrent with, the term of those who elected him, it might then be inferred that the Senate was meant to represent, primarily, the interests of the several states. For the effect of this would be to increase the influence which members of the state legislatures could exert over their appointees; or the general tendency would be to make the Senate subservient to local interests. However, at the time of the Federal Convention, all save one of the states had annual elections for the first (or only) branch of their legislatures—the exception being South Carolina which had biennial elections.[6] And as concerned those states having a second branch, the average term was approximately two-and-a-half years, the longest being Maryland's, which had a five-year term.[7] So in view of the much longer term of office intended for the Senate, it is evident that the members of the state legislatures would not be in a very favorable position to influence their senatorial appointees—indeed, this influence might even be reversed. That this is the intention of the Virginia Plan becomes strikingly clear when we compare the fifth resolution of this plan with the Fifth Article of Confederation. For the Fifth Article provides for a Congress whose members are (1) to be appointed annually; (2) to hold office for no more than three years in any term of six; and (3) to be subject to recall! The obvious intention of this article is to bind the members of Congress to their constituents, that is, to the state legislatures which appoint them. How sharply does this contrast with the Senate intended by the authors of the Virginia Plan. By virtue of its lengthy and uninterrupted term of office, the Senate is to have as its constituency, not the individual states, so much as the nation as a whole.[8]

From the preceding discussion it will be evident that the character of the Senate is in marked contrast with the character of the House. With the House, the emphasis is not on the whole but on the parts. We have seen that the manner in which it is constituted can hardly be better calculated to bring about the subordination of its members to local views and interests. They are to represent the democracy, or democratic values. They are to be restrained, however, by one or more branches of government—here the Senate—having the capacity to promote the general welfare. But the Senate cannot restrain the democracy by promoting democratic values. The Senate must therefore promote other values, values which are not democratic, but which, by exercising a corrective influence on democratic values, can contribute to the good of the whole community. What these values may be is not evident from the fifth resolution of the Virginia Plan. But there is one thing that is evident, and it bears upon those values.

It will have been noticed that the fifth resolution provides for monetary compensation for members of the Senate. From this it follows that the authors of the Virginia Plan did not intend the Senate to consist simply of men of independent wealth. This is further confirmed by the absence of any property qualification for Senators. Nevertheless, we must set against the provision for monetary compensation, as well as against the absence of a property qualification, the fact that the fifth resolution provides for a Senate *nominated* by the state legislatures. With few exceptions, the state constitutions prescribed a property qualification for office, and a rather high one for the upper branches of those states having a bicameral legislature.[9] In view of this, did the authors of the Virginia Plan expect the state legislatures to nominate for the Senate men who were moderately wealthy or at least friendly to the interests of property? And insofar as higher education in those days was largely confined to the middle and upper classes, did they expect the men so nominated to possess considerable learning? If so, why were men like Randolph so concerned about the dangers stemming from the state legislatures? This concern is the more remarkable when we consider that the members of the Federal Convention were themselves appointed by these very legislatures. Generally speaking, they themselves were moderately wealthy and, as an assemblage of statesmen, their breadth and depth of learning is probably unsurpassed in recorded history.[*] It could be argued, however, that the authors of the Virginia Plan did not expect the future Senate to be composed of men comparable to those who attended the Convention. Perhaps; yet against this it could be said that some of the leading members of the Convention did in fact become Senators.[†] The question arises, therefore: Was the Senate intended to be the aristocratic branch of the national legislature? To answer this question with any degree of confidence, it will be necessary to turn to the debates, but first, to those on the House of Representatives.

[*] The French chargé wrote that "if all the delegates named for the Philadelphia Convention are present, one will never have seen, even in Europe, an assembly more respectable for talents, knowledge, disinterestedness and patriotism than those who will compose it." Cited in Pritchett, *op. cit.*, p. 16.
[†] For example, Gouverneur Morris, Rufus King, Pierce Butler, and Roger Sherman.

4

On the Mode of Electing
the House of Representatives

O N MAY 31, the Convention took up the third resolution
of the Virginia Plan.* This resolution, it will be recalled,
envisioned a national legislature consisting of two branches.
The existing legislature, of course, had only *one* branch—in
which the states were represented as politically autonomous
entities. Now unless the states were no longer to remain
autonomous, or unless their autonomy was to be significantly
diminished, why should the third resolution call for the es-

---

* To facilitate analysis of the debates, I shall hereafter conform to the
following method of citation. Unless otherwise indicated, all references to
the debates will be taken from Madison's notes *under the date in question.*

tablishment of a *bicameral* legislature? What is remarkable however, is that despite its profound implications, the third resolution was adopted without debate or dissent![1] This was hardly the case with the first clause of the fourth resolution. For this clause provided that the first branch of the legislature be elected *by the people*. Thus, no sooner was the clause introduced than Roger Sherman of Connecticut rose to speak against its adoption. "The people," he declared, "should have as little to do as may be about the [new] Government." Not only are they uninformed, but they are too easily misled by demagogues. Accordingly, Sherman proposed that the first branch be elected by the state legislatures—evidently he thought they were better qualified to choose men of distinguished character.

Seeing that "the evils we experience flow from the excess of democracy," Elbridge Gerry of Massachusetts concurred in Sherman's proposal. He himself, he confessed, had been "too republican" in the past, though he wished it to be understood that he was "still republican." Does this mean that Gerry regarded the terms "democracy" and "republic" as synonymous? Leaving this open for the present, let two things be borne in mind. First, Gerry opposed popular election of the first branch partly because he thought the people were "the dupes of pretended patriots." Second, he preferred to have the first branch elected by the state legislatures partly because he thought these would advance men of merit to the national government.

Without joining issue as to what mode of election is more favorable to the appointment of good men, Mason argued in behalf of popular election of the House of Representatives. The first branch, he said, ought to be the "grand depository of the democratic principle." It ought to be, "so to speak . . . our House of Commons." Accordingly,

It ought to know and sympathise with every part of the community; and ought therefore to be taken from not only the different parts of the whole Republic, but also from different districts of the larger members of it, which had . . . different interests and views arising from difference of produce [and] habits.

Unlike Gerry, Mason admitted to having been—not too republican—but "too democratic." Nevertheless, he firmly believed that "we must preserve a portion of democracy."[2] Indeed, he feared that the Convention might "incautiously run to the opposite extreme." Evidently Mason thought that election of the first branch by the state legislatures (as proposed by Sherman and Gerry) would be a step toward this opposite extreme. In the present context, the opposite extreme of democracy would be an oligarchy. Mason preferred a middle course. But a middle course could only be one which either combined democratic and oligarchic institutions, or which united, in a single institution, democratic and oligarchic characteristics. That Mason preferred something like the former arrangement is implied by his expressed desire to "preserve a portion of democracy," and by his conception of the first branch of the national legislature as the "grand depository of the democratic principle." From this it may be inferred that he wanted the *second branch* to represent the oligarchic principle—at least in some significant respect. In this way Mason hoped to strike a mean between two extremes, between democracy and oligarchy. The mean would be a *republic*.

There is evidence, however, of other reasons, more profound and more subtle, why Mason wished to "preserve a portion of democracy" in the new government. "We ought to attend," he said, "to the rights of every class of people." And, he went on to say:

[I have] often wondered at the indifference of the superior classes of society to this dictate of humanity and policy, considering that however affluent their circumstances, or elevated their situations might be, the course of a few years, not only might but certainly would, distribute their posterity throughout the lowest classes of Society. Every selfish motive therefore, every family attachment, ought to recommend such a system of policy as would provide no less carefully for the rights and happiness of the lowest than of the highest orders of Citizens.

No doubt Mason is here anticipating the consequences of laws abolishing primogeniture and allowing for the division of family estates. These laws foreshadowed the demise of a society organized according to fairly distinct and stable classes. Mason does not say, however, that America will become a classless society. Classes will continue to exist; but their composition will be less stable, the distinctions between them less clear. Nor does he say that the laws of the emerging society will hinder men of wealth from acquiring political power and influence.[3] Great wealth will very likely remain in the hands of the few. But the membership of the few will be more mutable (perhaps also because of the greater mutability of the rising commercial class, of commercial property as compared to the old landed estates). Though Mason envisions a greater degree of equality in American society, he does not say that men of distinguished character will not be advanced to positions of high office in this society. The point is we ought not exaggerate the democratic tone of Mason's speech by abstracting his genuinely democratic sentiments from the whole. He earnestly wished to secure the rights of the humble by popular election of the first branch. But he justified this, not only as a "dictate of humanity," but as a matter of "policy" or expediency. It would be a mistake to think that this reference to expediency has in view simply the status of posterity, that is, the posterity of the superior classes. Securing the rights of the lower classes, by popular election of the first branch, is expedient because the rights of the superior classes will be endangered to the extent they disregard this "dictate of humanity." To repeat what Mason said: "We must attend to the rights of *every* class of people."[4] But we are not to infer from this that the rights of the superior classes will be attended to solely by the other branches of the government. The first branch itself, by representing the different interests and views of the *whole* republic, is to represent not only the poor and the unenlightened, but the wealthy and the wise.[5] In short, Mason wishes to establish a balanced government able to protect the rights and promote the happiness of all citizens regardless of their station.

In support of Mason's position, James Wilson of Pennsylvania expressed the desire "to see the new Constitution established on a broad basis, and rise like a pyramid to a respectable point."[6] But while certain branches or institutions should endow the new government with respectability, a popular branch was necessary to endow the entire edifice with *durability.* "No government," Wilson declared, "could long subsist without the confidence of the people." And "in a republican government," he continued, "this confidence was peculiarly essential." Now had Wilson said that the confidence of the people is peculiarly essential in a *democracy,* he would have uttered a mere truism. In a *republic,* however, the confidence of the people is peculiarly essential because this form of government has certain institutions which are not democratic, or which are not simply so.[7] But there was yet another reason why Wilson favored popular election of the House of Representatives.

The provision for popular election of the House involves not only the general issue of democracy versus oligarchy, but also the particular issue of *state* versus *federal* authority. We have seen that the Virginia Plan sought, among other things, to make the federal government paramount to the states. In his introductory speech, Randolph had spoken of the need to resist encroachment from the state legislatures. Now according to Wilson, "the opposition of States to federal measures has proceeded much more from the Officers of the States, than from the people at large." This helps to clarify why Wilson preferred election of the first branch by the people rather than by the state legislatures. As a matter of principle, the first branch should derive its authority from the people. This would accomplish three things. First, the proposed government would be more readily acceptable to the people. Second, *federal policies* would be more apt to receive *popular support.* Third, and as a consequence of the preceding, the obstructive influence of state officers would be minimized. For should the officers of the states seek to oppose federal policies, it would be more difficult for them to claim or secure the full support of their citizens. Thus, like Mason before him, Wilson favored popular election of the House, not only as a matter of principle, but as a matter of expediency.

Both Wilson and Mason refer to principle in support of their position. But they also refer or allude to the practical consequences of alternative positions. The principle provides a sense of form. But its relevance depends on the extent to which it is compatible with existing conditions and anticipated developments. This should caution one against a doctrinaire approach to the debates ahead. In trying to understand the political problems and alternatives confronting the Federal Convention, we ought not think of the delegates as mere "democrats" or as mere "oligarchs." Such labels obscure the complexity of the issues and the subtlety with which they were treated. They hinder us from understanding why a delegate like Hamilton voted with Wilson and Mason in favor of popular election of the first branch.

Let us now examine Madison's response to Sherman's proposal. Madison considered "popular election of one branch of the national legislature as essential to every plan of free Government." Popular election, of course, is equivalent to *direct* election. However, if direct election of one branch of the national legislature is essential to free government, it follows that a government based solely on *indirect* election is not consistent with free government. Evidently such a government would be an oligarchy. Hence, any branch of government based on indirect election would be oligarchic.[8] Stated another way, a system of indirect election favors the *few* as opposed to the *many*.[9] Yet it is this very system of election which Madison would use in forming the other branches of the new government. Perhaps for the purpose of assuring Sherman and Gerry that he and they could find a common ground of agreement, Madison suggested that the indirect mode of election be used in "refining" the second branch of the legislature, as well as the executive and the judiciary. In suggesting this, Madison conceded the relevance of Sherman's and Gerry's position. Nevertheless, he thought they were going too far in proposing indirect election of the first branch. He pointed out that "in some of the states one branch of the Legislature was composed of men already removed from the people by an intervening body of electors." If the Convention were to accede to Sherman's proposal, "the people would be lost sight of altogether and the necessary sympathy between them and their rulers and officers [would be] too little felt." Besides, Madison believed that the new government "would be more stable and durable if it should rest on the solid foundation of the people themselves, than if it should stand merely on the pillars of the Legislatures." Accordingly, Madison's response to Sherman and Gerry may be reformulated as follows. In deciding upon the mode of electing the *first* branch of the national legislature, primary emphasis should be placed, not on the *refinement* of its membership, but on the *stability and durability* which this branch might lend to the government as a whole.[10]

In reply to the proponents of popular election of the House, Gerry argued along two lines. First, he differed with

Wilson on the question whether direct election would secure popular support of the government. He remarked that
the state legislatures drawn immediately from the people
did not always win their confidence. In response to Mason,
he said that it was often fallacious to apply the principles
of the British constitution to what, in his opinion, were the
very different conditions affecting the American people.
Unfortunately, Gerry did not elaborate this statement, or
its elaboration is not recorded. Nevertheless, it may be inferred that he had in mind America's extensive territory, its
diverse interests, and the fact that there existed thirteen
autonomous states. So while he differed with Wilson on the
interpretation of certain historical events, he differed with
Mason on the application of certain principles to the American condition. (These kinds of differences recur throughout
the debates and, when possible, will be analyzed for their
political significance.) Nevertheless, Gerry proposed a way
of resolving the major difference between himself and the
proponents of popular election of the first branch. Perhaps
reassured by Madison's position respecting the other
branches of the government, he recommended that the state
legislature choose representatives from persons nominated
by the people. In this way, he thought, "men of honor and
character . . . might be joined in the appointments." In this
way, however, Gerry would construct the first branch on
both democratic and oligarchic principles.

On this note, a motion was raised for a vote on the first
clause of the fourth resolution—which passed in the affirmative, six states voting for popular election, two voting
against, while the delegations of two states were divided.
Nevertheless, this did not dispose of the issue, for it was
again the subject of debate on June 6. But before turning
to the debates of that date, it will be helpful to contrast
the different points of emphases reflected in the debates
thus far.

Both Gerry and Sherman emphasize the need to infuse wisdom into the process of appointing the first branch. Mason, on the other hand, emphasizes the need to have this branch closely bound in sympathy with all classes of society so that the rights of all citizens will be safeguarded. Madison agrees with Mason and points up the need to secure a stable and durable government. Meanwhile, Wilson emphasizes the importance of gaining popular support and the need to minimize the obstructive influence of state politicians on federal policies. These differences of emphases begin to expand and complicate the inquiry. They convey different concerns and qualities of government. They proceed from reflection on contemporary sentiments and tendencies of American society. All this is informed by reference to certain political principles. But the different emphases mentioned above suggest that men may agree to a given principle for different reasons—the reasons being in the realm of practical judgment involving immediate and long-range considerations. Some aspects of this problem may be illustrated by reformulating the debates of May 31 in view of the last chapter.

Without excluding Wilson, all agree, tacitly or otherwise, that it is necessary to refine the electoral process so as to promote the appointment of distinguished men to one or more branches of the government. Excepting Wilson, all agree that the states provide a ready means of accomplishing this end. Appointments to the federal government may be refined by having the state legislatures join in the election of certain federal office-holders. This method of election, we saw earlier, could serve to insulate these officers from their constituents and so promote their independence. The states could thus function as an instrument for advancing the *oligarchic* principle. But in exercising this function, the influence of the states on the federal government might become excessive. Hence, indiscriminate use of the oligarchic principle of election could frustrate the federal plan of union. For this reason, the introduction of the *democratic* principle as a mitigation of the oligarchic one can also be justified on grounds of expediency. By establishing the federal government on both oligarchic and democratic principles, its authority would be derived from two distinct though related sources: the states on the one hand, the people on the other. And yet, the government so formed would be neither the creature of the states, nor of the people, nor of both (for reasons adduced in the last chapter). Such a government would be a *federal republic.* It would possess the services of distinguished men. It would be united in sympathy with the people and thus gain their confidence. It would be stable and enduring. But notice that all this is consistent with Gerry's modified position. For, as already noted, Gerry proposed to combine the oligarchic and democratic principles in the same institution (instead of their being separately embodied in different institutions). On its face, this proposal appears to resolve the differences between Gerry and his opponents. But this is not entirely true in view of the fact that included among these differences were different evaluations of popular sentiment. Unresolved was the question of whether the people would support the new government by virtue of having elected the first branch of the national legislature. As a consequence of this alone (that is, apart from any question of principle), one could reject Gerry's proposal on the following grounds. First, it was more important to secure popular support for the new government than to infuse wisdom into the appointment of the *first* branch. Second, popular support was more likely to be won if the first branch was elected directly and simply by the people. Third, a system of indirect election could be used to promote the election of reputable persons to *other* branches of the federal government. Thus, gradations of relevance and evaluation of existing sentiments may qualify the application of abstract principles.

As already mentioned, the issue respecting popular election of the first branch of the national legislature was reopened on June 6. The rule of procedure which made it possible to reconsider majority decisions now made it possible to further elaborate and deepen the issue in question. Like Sherman before him, Charles Pinckney of South Carolina moved that the first branch be elected by the state legislatures. Again like Sherman, Pinckney said that the people were not as capable as the state legislatures of making a wise choice. But now he added that the state legislatures would be less likely to promote the adoption of the new government if they were excluded from the election of the first branch. On the one hand, good government would not be established unless good men were appointed to its offices—and the appointments were less apt to be good if made by the people. On the other hand, the adoption of the new government would depend largely upon the approval of men holding positions of state power. Again to principle is added the factor of expediency. Both claim attention. Both argue for election of the House by the state legislatures.

At this point, Gerry further elaborated his last-stated position. Addressing himself first to Mason's remarks of May 31, he disclaimed any disposition to run to political extremes: "[I am] as much principled as ever against aristocracy . . ." Does this mean that a branch of government elected by the state legislatures would not be aristocratic? Certainly this would be the case if the term aristocracy were defined simply as a government controlled by an hereditary nobility. Gerry readily disclaimed any inclination for such a government. Nevertheless, he did not limit the qualities of an aristocracy to those contained in the above definition. In the debates on the Senate, he spoke of certain state legislatures as having upper branches which are "somewhat aristocratic," and there he associated aristocracy with *wealth* and *merit*.[11] To Gerry, this was a compelling reason for having the Senate elected by the state legislatures. In the present context, however, Gerry conceded the necessity of having the people appoint one branch of government as a means of gaining their confidence. Nevertheless, he persisted in his desire to have the election of this branch "so modified as to secure more effectually a just preference for merit." Accordingly, he proposed that "the people should nominate certain persons in certain districts, out of whom the State Legislatures should make the appointments." From this it is evident that Gerry regarded election by the state legislatures as being "somewhat aristocratic" in its consequences.

By proposing popular nomination by districts, Gerry is responding to Mason's plea for a branch of government representing the diverse parts of the whole republic. Yet Gerry wants something more than representation of "different interests and views": He wants *merit*. And though it is not recorded in the debates, we may infer from Wilson's immediate response that Gerry also wants *vigor*. Hence, looking back to his fear of the evils of democracy, Gerry believes that one of the remedies for these evils is a vigorous and enlightened government or—to suggest the equivalent —a government capable of exercising *leadership*.

Wilson agreed that the new government must possess vigor. But he wished "that vigorous authority to flow immediately from the source of all legitimate authority," namely, the people. Presumably, Gerry meant, by vigor, independent action, the kind we associate with leadership. Wilson, on the other hand, shifts the argument toward *legitimacy*, as if to say it is legitimacy upon which vigor or leadership will ultimately depend. Thus, whereas Gerry emphasizes the need for certain kinds of *men* in government, Wilson emphasizes the need for a *principle* of government that will endow these men with authority. Of course, Wilson and Gerry may have different kinds of men in mind. For Wilson, "The Legislature ought to be the most exact transcript of the whole Society." But this society consisted of different classes: to simplify, the rich and the poor. Hence, a legislature representing the rich and the poor might not be radically different from the legislature envisioned by Gerry. True, an exact transcript of the different elements of society need not, of itself, issue forth in vigorous and enlightened government, or in leadership. But Wilson does not say that the government *as a whole* should be an exact transcript of society as a whole. He refers only to the legislature. He does not exclude the exercise of leadership, say on the part of the executive.[12] In short, perhaps Wilson is suggesting that in discussing the character of the *legislature,* Gerry's emphasis on vigor is misplaced.

But Wilson was not concerned merely to enunciate general principles. He also alluded to the necessity of reducing the powers of the states. To this, Sherman responded by positing two extreme alternatives confronting the Convention:

> If it were in view to abolish the State Governments, the elections ought to be by the people. If the State Governments are to be continued, it is necessary in order to preserve harmony between the national and State Governments that the elections to the former should be made by the latter.

These alternatives, it should be noted, conform to two kinds of government: the first, a *unitary* government, the second, a *confederation.* A unitary government is one whose acts operate directly on individuals (without any intervening authority other than administrative ones). A confederation, on the other hand, has a central organ whose acts operate on the member states, while the relationship between the states and their own citizens is one of almost complete autonomy. Now the Virginia Plan combines these two alternatives. Accordingly, the government so formed would have a central organ whose acts would be divided between those which operate directly on individuals and those which act on the member states. This arrangement leaves to the states some degree of autonomy with respect to their own citizens, while it may also involve certain areas of concurrent jurisdiction between the central and state governments.[13] It is this system of government which I have called the "federal plan of union"; and it is precisely such a plan which Sherman rejects in favor of a confederation.[14] This helps to explain his opposition to popular election of the House of Representatives: Sherman saw that this mode of election would result in a fundamental change in the existing Confederation. But to defend the form of the existing Confederation, he would have to argue on grounds other than those respecting electoral modes of constituting a government. He would also have to address himself to the ends or purposes of government, in this case, of the present Union.

In Sherman's opinion, the purposes of union are relatively few, namely: "(1) defense against foreign danger; (2) [defense] against internal disputes and a resort to force; (3) treaties with foreign nations; (4) regulating foreign commerce, and drawing revenue [there] from." This enumeration of the purposes of union should be compared with the five properties which Randolph attributed to a federal government.[15] It will be recalled that Randolph had included among these properties the supremacy of the federal government over the state constitutions. Sherman omits this. In addition, Randolph had also included the security of "various blessings," without specifying, however, their character.[16] Sherman substitutes for these unspecified blessings *commerce*. Perhaps Randolph had in mind, as included in such blessings, certain civil rights or liberties which he thought inadequately protected by the state governments. For Sherman went on to say that "matters civil and criminal would be much better in the hands of the States" than in the hands of the national government. He admitted that faction and oppression were more likely to occur in small states; but it was his opinion that in large states, the powers of government could not effectively pervade the whole so as to prevent or remedy these evils. So here Sherman injected into the debates over popular election of the House two new problems. On the one hand, he placed in question the very purposes of the Union. On the other, he placed in question the very *form* of this Union as this bears on its purposes. The issue over popular election of the first branch has thus eventuated in questions of the first magnitude.

In a speech foreshadowing his celebrated *Federalist 10*, Madison took up the defense of popular election of the first branch and, at the same time, attempted to resolve the problems introduced by Sherman. He agreed that the objects of union mentioned by Sherman were very important. But he would combine with these objects "the security of private rights, and the steady dispensation of Justice." The violation of these, he thought, "were evils which had more perhaps than anything else, produced this Convention." Madison is thus posed with the task of defending the democratic principle of popular election despite the general recognition that this same principle has contributed to the evils in question. It should be recalled, however, that he also regards popular election of one branch of government as essential to every play of free government, or as a necessary means of avoiding the evils, say, of an oligarchy. But what evil does Madison especially seek to avoid?

Madison approaches this problem in the following way:

All civilized Societies would be divided into different Sects, Factions, and interests, as they happened to consist of rich and poor, debtors and creditors, the landed, the manufacturing, the commercial interests, the inhabitants of this district or that district, the followers of this political leader or that political leader, the disciples of this religious sect or that religious sect.

Diversity is essential to all civilized societies. Yet this very diversity may occasion discord and oppression. Productive good, it may also lead to evil, especially the evil of *faction.* In *Federalist 10,* Madison defines faction as follows:

> By a faction, I understand a number of citizens, whether amounting to a majority or minority of the whole, who are united and actuated by some common impulse of passion, or of interest, adverse to the rights of other citizens, or to the permanent and aggregate interests of the community.

From this definition of faction three kinds of evils may be distinguished: (1) infringement of the rights of private citizens; (2) infringement of the rights of various groups whose interests comprise the aggregate interests of the community; and (3) infringement of the *permanent* interests of the community which in some way transcends the particular interests of any citizen or group. Now what Madison proposes as a remedy for these evils is nothing less than a new conception of union. We have seen that he wishes to enlarge the purposes of union so as to include "the security of private rights." The security of these rights applies to individuals and to such groups as those enumerated. As *private* rights they may be understood to vary from time to time according to changing economic and social conditions. But Madison wishes to provide for "the steady dispensation of Justice." What Madison may have in the background of this phrase could be stated as follows: The administration of justice disposes men to respect the rights of others insofar as it habituates them to resolve their differences through due processes of law. Conceived in these terms, justice makes civilized life possible, that is, it makes possible the *diversity* which Madison attributes to all civilized societies. But justice is also an end to be pursued, an end which men seek in seeking a more perfect union. Conceived in this light, justice may be numbered among, and may even embrace, the *permanent* interests or concerns of the community.[17]

Whether having as its object the security of private rights or the achievement of a more perfect union, justice is endangered by faction. In his speech of June 6 (as in *Federalist 10*), Madison refers to two kinds of faction: majority and minority. To understand what he means by majority faction, it is necessary to understand what he means by "the majority." Though Madison does not spell this out, it is reasonable to assume that by the majority he means primarily the "poor." However, in American society, it would be more accurate to regard the poor, not as the poverty-stricken, but as those who must *and* do earn their livelihood by some form of manual labor. Majority faction would then be the organized attempt by the poor (or their leaders) to control the government for their own ends, which attempt, if successful, would deprive the minority of its economic and political rights. The minority, in this case, would be primarily the rich. Hence, minority faction would be the organized attempt by the rich (or men identified with the interests of property) to control the government for their own ends, which attempt, if successful, would impair the rights of the majority. Both majority and minority faction thus implicate the question of *who should rule* and the purposes or ends of government. From this emerges the question of justice, whether justice be conceived in terms of private rights or in terms of the right ordering of political society. Faction brings this question to the foreground, particularly when it involves conflict between the governed and their governors. According to Madison, when one or the other are activated by interests which they deem separate from those of the whole community, oppression is the result. Faction thus presents a twofold problem requiring a twofold solution. On the one hand, the government must be constituted in such a manner that those exercising its offices will conceive of their interests as consistent with their lawful duties and with the permanent interests of the community.[18] On the other hand, the community itself must be organized in such a way that the members of the majority are not likely to become united as a faction. Addressing himself to the second problem, Madison says:

> The only remedy is to enlarge the sphere, and therefore divide the community into so great a number of interests and parties, that in the first place, a majority will not be likely at the same moment to have a common interest separate from that of the whole or of the minority; and in the second place, that in case they should have such an interest, they may not be apt to unite in the pursuit of it.[19]

From this it is evident that Madison wishes to prevent the majority, or the poor, from controlling the government so as to impair the rights of the minority, namely the rich; and he proposes to do this by fostering a multiplicity of diverse interests within the community. Now here let us not read into Madison's proposal our contemporary infatuation with *pluralism*. For Madison regards "pluralism" not as an unqualified good, so much as a check against an evil, the evil of majority faction. Furthermore, he fully realizes that "pluralism" is itself a cause of faction. Essential to civilized society, it may nevertheless shatter the bonds of society. And while it may hinder men from becoming united by some interest opposed to the common good, it may also hinder them from becoming united in behalf of the common good. In other words, "pluralism" is a mixed blessing. It is not Madison's formula for the Good

Society. This said, Madison's remedy for majority faction may now be elaborated.

Madison brings to bear on the problem of majority faction three remedial and related factors: (1) a multiplicity of diverse interests extending over (2) a large territory governed in part by (3) the representative principle. In Madison's opinion, majority faction is less likely to occur in a community composed of many diverse interests. But what kinds of interests does he have in mind? Earlier, he referred to the landed, the manufacturing, and the commercial interests. But these are to be identified with the wealthy and moderately wealthy, and it would be rather absurd to think that they might constitute a *majority* faction. It is not the men who own or manage these interests, but the men who are *employed* by them who might unite in majority faction. Hence it is primarily the fragmentation of the *working class* that would be accomplished by dividing the community into a multiplicity of diverse interests. This fragmentation, of course, would make it extremely difficult for the working class to become *organized*, politically or otherwise. But this means that Madison would be opposed to monopoly in any of its forms. On the one hand, concentrations of economic wealth would facilitate minority faction or control of the government by the rich. On the other, such concentrations would facilitate the organization of the majority and might thus lead to control of the government by the poor.[20] It may be said, therefore, that Madison favored a diversified and decentralized economy as a check against majority (and minority) faction. Such an economy would encourage the growth of a large middle class, a class which would hold the balance between the very rich and the very poor.[21]

The danger of majority faction is further diminished by the problem of communicating over a large territory. It is difficult enough to pursue a course of action whose success requires the cooperation of a large number of diverse groups. But the difficulty is compounded when these groups are widely separated in space and lack facilities for timely communication. Such factors have profound political consequences. The more remote an object, the less inclined are men to pursue it. Furthermore, since more time is required for a faction to spread its influence over a large territory, more time is available for the constituted authorities to stem its progress, either by force or by peaceful remedies. It may be said, therefore, that "space-time" has a "conservative" tendency proportionate to its extent.

This tendency is also exemplified by the effects of the representative principle. One effect of this principle is to discourage the majority from acting independently. Another effect is that it serves to insulate the government from the governed. (Again this is particularly so in a large republic.) It was Madison's opinion that the principle of representation would tend to "refine and enlarge the public views"; that representatives, removed from local influences, would more likely be motivated by a "love of justice" and by the "true interest of their country."[22] Thus, when the representative principle is conjoined with Madison's conception of a large republic composed of many and diverse interests, it becomes evident that the likelihood of majority faction is minimal indeed.

Now at this point it may be argued that Madison's solution to the problem of faction is in fact reducible to, or depends ultimately upon, the representative principle. For it is precisely this principle which is to facilitate the establishment of an extended republic with many diverse interests. Furthermore, it could be argued that it is the representative principle alone which is to distinguish this republic from a democracy. Certainly this is the impression conveyed by

Madison both in *Federalist 10* and *14*. Nor is this all. During the debates of June 6, Madison declared, in effect, that the establishment of a large diversified republic, by means of the representative principle, is "the only defense against the inconveniences of democracy consistent with the democratic form of government."[23] From this it appears that, contrary to my earlier interpretation, Madison regards his proposed republic as *generically* indistinct from a democracy. Permit me, therefore, to digress a moment to resolve this difficulty.

The problem before us involves Madison's understanding of what constitutes a republic. So far it would appear that the representative principle alone is what distinguishes a republic from a democracy. Consider, however, *Federalist 39* where Madison writes:

> If we resort for a criterion to the different principles on which different forms of government are established, we may define a republic to be, or at least may bestow that name on, a government which derives all its powers directly or indirectly from the great body of the people, and is administered by persons holding their offices during pleasure, for a limited period of time, or during good behavior.

Now if, among "the different principles on which different forms of government are established," the representative principle alone is what distinguishes a republic from a democracy, we should then have to conclude, from the above definition of a republic, that a government *wholly* "administered by persons holding their offices . . . during good behavior" is consistent with the democratic form of government so long as these persons derive their "powers directly or indirectly from the great body of the people." True, there is no logical inconsistency. But surely we need not be deceived by the prudence and caution of a statesman whose primary purpose is not to expound upon what he means by a republic, but to persuade men to adopt the Constitution. Suppose, however, that Madison privately conceived of this Constitution as exemplifying some kind of *mixed regime* (one consisting, say, of democratic and aristocratic branches). This supposition might be countered by again referring to *Federalist 14*. For in that essay Madison would not only have some readers believe that the representative principle alone is what distinguishes a republic from a democracy but also that the republic he is proposing for the United States is an "unmixed" one.[24] Certainly that republic could be regarded as "unmixed" in light of the fact that its various branches are not to correspond to *legally* distinct classes of citizens. But despite the absence of class distinctions *de jure,* Madison might still have intended the Constitution to preserve a *de facto distribution of power* comparable to that which existed in mixed regimes of the classical variety. And that he would not publicly avow such thoughts is understandable when we ask (as we must when examining all rhetorical works): To what kind of audience is *The Federalist* addressed? It is a mixed audience, of course. But as will become apparent from the debates of June 12, Madison's deeper thoughts are addressed not to what he there calls the "unreflecting multitude," but to "the most enlightened and respectable citizens," that is, to the "influential class" of society. Presumably it is this class which will see through Madison's various definitions of a republic, and who will consequently approve of the Constitution while persuading "others" to do likewise. And yet, perhaps I am being overly subtle. Perhaps the difficulty can be explained by saying that Madison simply has failed to draw adequate or even consistent distinctions between the terms republic and democracy. To confirm this I need only observe that he frequently applies the term republic to governments partly ruled by hereditary nobles and princes!* From this it would follow that the generic factor uniting these various kinds of republics is that the people had some share in the appointment of their rulers. All republics would then conform to what Madison calls "free government," or to what he calls a "free constitution" when referring, as he does in *Federalist 47*, to the government of Great Britain.[25] Nevertheless, Madison's generic use of the term republic does not dispose of the fact that he refers to the government of the United States as some kind of democracy (and this *during the debates of the Convention*). But let us examine things in context. After all, when Madison speaks of the representative principle as distinguishing a republic from a democracy, he is trying to allay the fears of those who oppose a branch of government elected by the people. Furthermore, let us examine things with a view to the government *as a whole*. Hence, leaving the problem open to the elucidation of subsequent chapters, let us return to and reformulate the issue dividing Madison and Sherman.

It will be recalled that Sherman had injected into the debates over the first branch of the national legislature two fundamental and related questions, one concerning the very purposes of union, the other concerning the form of this

---

* In *Federalist 63*, which must be largely attributed to Madison, he speaks of Sparta, Carthage and Rome as republics. These states had a hereditary nobility and were generally recognized as *mixed regimes*. Cf., also, *Federalist 18* and *39*. In the debates of June 19, Madison speaks of the Belgic confederacy as a republic, even though it had a hereditary prince for its executive. Cf., also, *Federalist 20*. On the character of Sparta and Carthage, cf. *The Politics of Aristotle* (Oxford: Clarendon Press, 1952; Ernest Barker, trans.), pp. 60, 84-87. On the Roman constitution, cf. Polybius *Histories* vi 11. For various discussions of the terms democracy and republic, cf. Rousseau, *The Social Contract*, I, 4, II, 6, III, 3-4; Montesquieu, *The Spirit of the Laws*, (New York: Hafner Publishing Co., 1949; Thomas Nugent, trans.), pp. 8-15; Machiavelli, *Discourses*, I, 2; Edward Dumbauld (ed.), *The Political Writings of Thomas Jefferson* (New York: Liberal Arts Press, 1955), pp. 51-52; and cf., also, Locke, *Second Treatise of Civil Government*, chap. x; William Blackstone, *Commentaries on the Laws of England* (2 vols.; Chicago: Callahan & Co., 1876), I, 28; Spinoza, *Tractatus Politicus*, chap. xi.

union. His position with respect to these questions may be arrived at in the following way. To begin with, we have seen that Sherman preferred election of the first branch by the state legislatures. He thought that these were better fitted than the people to make a wise choice of representatives. Election by the people, he feared, would lead to certain evils. Demagogues would get into office, and the rights of property would be endangered. These rights, he believed, could not be well protected by the proposed government because its powers could not effectively pervade the entire Union. For this reason the powers of the states should be left essentially intact. Hence the form of the existing Confederation should be preserved along with its present division of purposes. The most palpable difficulty besetting this argument is that the evils feared by Sherman had admittedly occured, and under the existing Confederation. Madison was quick to point this out. Sherman had also admitted that faction was more apt to occur in small states—though, as already noted, he thought this evil could not be prevented if a state were so large that the powers of government could not effectively pervade the whole. Madison responded to this objection by saying, in effect, that the representative principle made it possible to enlarge the sphere—really the power—of government. But what I omitted to point out earlier is that Sherman professed the opinion that "the people are more happy in small than in large states." Perhaps he thought that political liberty had its home in small republics, where the individual citizen could exert greater influence on political decisions affecting not only his own life but the life of his community. Or perhaps he felt that the governments of small states were closer to the people, more responsive to their interests and opinions. But it is precisely these characteristics of small states that make them more prone to faction. For while it may be true that political liberty has its home in small republics, it is also true that such republics are not likely to have much economic diversity, so that one interest or one political party may more readily become dominant and thus endanger liberty.

Madison was fully aware of this. The state governments, he felt, were indeed close to the people—too close. Liberty had already been endangered, precisely because some of the state governments were too responsive to the people. Hence we can understand why Madison proposed to enlarge the sphere or power of the federal government on the one hand, and to encourage greater diversity on the other. Both, we have seen, would depend on the representative principle. But for Madison, the main purpose of this principle was to enable the federal government to act on individuals. Given the authority to do so, the federal government could then prevent or suppress faction, whatever its form. That is, it could then provide more effectively for "the security of private rights, and the steady dispensation of Justice." This does not mean that the states would be precluded from exercising original jurisdiction in these matters when only their own citizens were involved. Nevertheless, the adoption of the representative principle could not but reduce the powers of the states, as Sherman well understood. On the other hand, and as was generally admitted, these powers had, to some extent, been subverted by the democracy. What Madison is therefore proposing is to employ a democratic principle as a check against democratic vices.[26] It should be obvious, however, that Madison is not depending solely upon the operation of this principle. That is, he is not depending solely upon the adoption of the fourth resolution of the Virginia Plan to accomplish the purposes of union.

It would seem from the preceding discussion that Sherman's interpretation of the fourth resolution is somewhat exaggerated—perhaps deliberately. For there is nothing in this resolution which involves the merging of the states into a unitary form of government. Besides, it was already clear from the proceedings of May 31 that the Convention would very likely adopt a Senate elected by the state legislatures. Apparently to remind Sherman of that Senate, John Dickenson of Delaware declared that while he favored popular election of the House, he thought it both expedient and wise to have the Senate elected by the state legislatures. "In the formation of the Senate," he said, "we ought to carry it through such a refining process as will assimilate it as near as may be to the House of Lords in England." On the one hand, he wished to assure Sherman of his desire to leave to the states "a considerable agency in the System." On the other hand, he agreed with Sherman that the state legislatures could perform an important role in securing to the Senate men who will "speak and decide with becoming freedom." Unlike Sherman, Dickenson does not reduce the character of the whole to one of its parts. Along with Madison, he does not reduce the character of the proposed government to that of the first branch of its legislature.

The outcome of the debates of June 6 sustained the decision of May 31. The motion to have the House elected by the state legislatures was rejected by a vote of eight states to three. Whereas the Delaware and Connecticut delegations had been divided on May 31, Delaware, the smallest state of the Union, voted, in effect, for popular election of the House, while Connecticut, a much larger state, voted for election by the state legislatures. At the same time, New Jersey and South Carolina reversed their earlier position and now voted with the majority. Hence, between May 31 and June 6, political deliberation persuaded certain delegates to alter their views with respect to the first branch of the national legislature. A broader basis of agreement had been established.[27]

5

On the Mode of Electing the Senate

W E MUST now return to the debates of May 31 at the point where the majority had just voted in favor of the first clause of the fourth resolution.[1] Having decided that the first branch of the national legislature should exemplify the democratic principle, clearly the next problem was to determine what principle should be exemplified by the second branch. Accordingly, the delegates postponed consideration of the remaining clauses of the fourth resolution to take up the first clause of the fifth. It will be recalled that this clause provided for election of members of the second branch by

those of the first from persons nominated by the state legislatures. However, motion for amendment was raised by
Richard Spaight of North Carolina, who urged that the
second branch be chosen simply by the state legislatures.

At this point, Pierce Butler of South Carolina (who concurred with Spaight) called upon Randolph to elaborate his
views on the proposed Senate, particularly as to the number
of members he meant to assign to this body. Randolph
replied by saying that the second branch of the national
legislature ought to be smaller than the first: "so small as
to be exempt from the passionate proceedings to which
numerous assemblies are liable." A good Senate, he continued, would be necessary to check "the turbulence and
follies of democracy." To do this, it would have to be a
small one. In addition, Randolph thought that the Senate
should be appointed by the House from persons nominated
by the state legislatures. Were the Senate appointed simply
by the latter (as proposed by Spaight), the check against
the democracy would not be complete. Evidently, Randolph
believed that the danger of democratic encroachment would
stem mainly from the states. But why should he believe that
a *popularly* elected House would choose, from among persons nominated by the state legislatures, a body of men
able and willing to resist democratic encroachment? I shall
consider this difficulty at the close of the present chapter.
It was a difficulty, however, which Mason and Sherman
were quick to perceive. Both thought that a Senate appointed by the House would be too dependent on that
body. So here were a number of men agreeing that the
Senate should be independent, while disagreeing as to the
best manner of securing this independence. Of course, they
may have had somewhat different notions as to the meaning
of an independent Senate; they may have been agreeing to
a principle for somewhat different reasons.

Though Spaight withdrew his motion (for reasons noted

below), the Convention rejected the first clause of the fifth resolution by a vote of seven states to three. The debates of May 31 thus left open the mode of appointing the Senate.

It will be recalled that, on June 6, the Convention had adopted the first clause of the fourth resolution providing for popular election of the House. On the following day, June 7, John Dickenson proposed that the Senate be elected by the state legislatures. In this way, he claimed, the views of the states would be better represented, and men of talent and distinguished character would more likely be appointed. While agreeing with Dickenson, Pinckney pointed out that if the small states should be allowed one Senator, then, on the basis of *proportional representation,* the Senate would consist of at least eighty members, a number he thought much too large for this body.[2] This did not disturb Dickenson. Though he was opposed to proportional representation, he did favor a numerous Senate, and for this reason: Given the likelihood of distinguished men being appointed to the Senate by the state legislatures, then, "by enlarging their numbers you increase their consequence and weight; and by combining [with the popularly elected House, a Senate representing] the families and wealth of the aristocracy, you establish a balance that will check the democracy."[3]

In a speech which merits close and extensive treatment, Madison joined issue with Dickenson. For convenience, I shall divide this speech into two parts, the second part being an elaboration of the first. In the first part, Madison said:

> If the motion of Mr. Dickenson should be agreed to, we must either depart from the doctrine of proportional representation, or admit into the Senate a very large number of members. The first is inadmissable, being evidently unjust. The second is inexpedient. The use of the Senate is to consist in its proceeding with more coolness, with more system, and with more wisdom, than the popular branch. Enlarge their number and you communicate to them the vices which they are meant to correct.

We see here a conflict between the just and the expedient. The political problem raised by Madison is this: How can we unite the two? Proportional representation is the just idea that equal numbers of men should have equal numbers of representatives, while unequal numbers of men should have unequal numbers of representatives in strict proportion to their numerical inequality. From this it should be apparent that the idea of proportional representation is derived from the principle of *political equality,* that is, the political equality of all men as individuals. It is this principle from which proportional representation derives its justice. But in the present context, proportional representation, though just, is inexpedient. Hence, in the same context, political equality, though just, is inexpedient. Now what is inexpedient is such because it leads to undesirable consequences. Proportional representation is inexpedient because a Senate based on this idea will be too numerous. It will not be able to deliberate wisely and dispassionately. Its deliberations will lack system, that is, rationality and consistency of purpose. This being so, the acts of this body, whether of omission or of commission, will result in certain vicious consequences. Hence, strict application of proportional representation will lead to certain vicious consequences. But as the vicious is also unjust, strict application of proportional representation and therefore, of political equality, is unjust. What this means is that political equality does not exhaust the requirements of justice. Justice is a higher or more *architectonic* principle, a principle which may require different degrees of political *inequality* under different conditions of society. The determination of this is a problem for men of practical wisdom, of men who can unite philosophy and action. But still, how can we unite the just and the expedient? How can we make proportional representation expedient?

Obviously the only way to render proportional representation expedient is to formulate a schema whereby the larger states will have fewer representatives than they would under strict proportionality, but more than they would if all the states were represented as equals. (Such a schema is later proposed.)⁴ To entitle all states to equal representation is *oligarchic*. It violates the democratic principle of the political equality of all men as individuals. The democratic principle is satisfied by the idea of strict proportionality. Hence, the schema suggested combines the democratic and the oligarchic principles of representation.

There are two things to be noted with respect to Madison's position on proportional representation. First, his attitude is not one of doctrinairism. He does not believe that the vast complexities of political life can be ordered according to neat formulas. Second, Madison does not approve of strict proportional representation, despite the fact that he is a delegate from Virginia, the most populous state of the Union. This should caution us against oversimplifying the controversy between the large and the small states. This controversy will not be fully understood if reduced to the politics of self-interested groups.°

We have seen that Madison opposed a large Senate on grounds similar to those expressed by Randolph on May 31.

°On the initial vote over equal representation of the states in the Senate, the Georgia delegation divided, and the remaining states were aligned as follows:

For		Against	
New York	(233,000)	S. Carolina	(150,000)
Maryland	(218,000)	N. Carolina	(200,000)
Connecticut	(202,000)	Massachusetts	(360,000)
New Jersey	(138,000)	Pennsylvania	(360,000)
Delaware	(37,000)	Virginia	(420,000)

Notice the population figures in parentheses. These indicate that New York, Maryland, and Connecticut each had *larger* populations than either South Carolina or North Carolina. So here were three "large" states that voted *for* equal representation of the states in the Senate, while two "small" states voted *against* such representation! Notice also that slave as well as nonslave states were divided on the issue. But the very fact that the Georgia delegation was itself divided confirms the inference to be drawn from the above data, namely, that questions of *principle* played a significant part in the issue and in its outcome. Cf. *Farrand*, I, 510; III, 253.

Both thought that a large Senate would be prone to the vices of democracy. What might they have had in mind here? Very likely it is this: The larger the assembly, the greater its diversity of interests and opinions. The greater this diversity, the greater the likelihood of factious rivalry —or at any rate, the more difficult it would be for such an assembly to unite in recognition of the common good and to pursue a consistent course of public policy. Again, the larger the assembly, the weaker the sense of individual responsibility. Or as Madison said on June 6 when speaking of faction: "Respect for character is always diminished in proportion to the number among whom blame or praise is to be divided."[5] And yet, are not these the very vices which may be attributed to the first branch of the national legislature? Both Madison and Randolph were obviously aware of this implication, for which reason they wanted a small Senate. If a large assembly is required to represent the diverse interests of a pluralistic society, a small assembly is required to represent the common good of this society. And if a large assembly is prone to the defects mentioned, the greater is the need for a small assembly to restrain the larger one, and to infuse system and wisdom into the proceedings of the whole.

But still, according to Dickenson, a Senate composed of distinguished men will have greater weight the greater their number. While Madison agrees with this in principle, he questions the extent to which it should be applied to an institution like the intended Senate. He says:

> When the weight of a set of men depends merely on their personal characters, the greater their number the greater their weight. When it depends on the degree of political authority lodged in them, the smaller their number the greater their weight. These considerations might perhaps be combined in the intended Senate; but the latter is the material one.

To grasp the subtlety and profundity of this statement, it must first be recalled that Dickenson favored election of the Senate by the state legislatures partly because he thought the latter were more likely to choose men from "the families and wealth of the aristocracy." Though Madison does not deny the likelihood of such appointments,[6] he does not think it prudent to constitute the Senate primarily on this basis. If the Senate were to consist solely of gentlemen, that is, if its membership were confined to the aristocracy, it would then be proper to increase their number. A Senate so constituted would be united by such aristocratic qualities as civility and liberality, as well as by a common interest in protecting property. In other words, such a Senate would not be prone to faction. But this must be qualified by two considerations. First, though the aristocratic class would have a common interest in protecting property, there are different *kinds* of property, such as landed and commercial. Second, as Dickenson admits, or implies, the Senate is not likely to consist *entirely* of men from the aristocracy. The Senate is to be chosen, not by an aristocratic class, but by the various state legislatures whose composition is only partly aristocratic. Stated another way, the members of the Senate are to exercise political authority delegated to them, indirectly, by society *as a whole*. In view of these considerations, the membership of the Senate will be somewhat heterogeneous. Increasing its number would therefore increase the likelihood of internal faction. It would weaken the Senate and undermine its intended purposes. Thus, Madison could say, in agreement with Dickenson, that while "the Senate ought to come from, and represent, the Wealth of the nation . . . delegated power will have the most weight and consequence in the hands of the few."[7]

It is still not sufficiently clear, however, why, in Madison's opinion, a small Senate, though less prone to faction than a large one, is better calculated to fulfill the purposes intended for this branch of the national legislature.[8] One of these purposes is to check the vices of democracy. Another is to protect the rights of property. But what is there about a small Senate that will disincline its members from aligning themselves with the democracy? On the other hand, what is to prevent them from unduly favoring the wealth of the oligarchy? In other words, what does Madison see in the smallness of the Senate that will foster the independence of its members and so incline them to serve the common good? The answer to this question contains one of the fundamental principles underlying the American Constitution. To grasp this principle, one must assess the probable effects of a small Senate on the attitudes and conduct of its members. All this is implied in that statement of Madison's wherein he says, in effect, that the proper functioning of the Senate will depend more on its smallness than on the *personal character* of its members. This can only mean that the smallness of the Senate will somehow induce its members to act in conformity with the purposes of this institution even if they should be otherwise inclined. What follows is the explanation of Madison's statement.

The smaller the body of men possessed of political authority, the greater the power possessed by each member. But the greater the power of each member, the greater his *prestige,* his status. *The effect of this is to deepen his loyalty to the institution itself vis-à-vis the will of popular majorities as well as any particular minority. Esprit de corps,* a sense of aloofness, a heightened feeling of personal responsibility—such are the qualities which a small Senate will foster among its members.[9] Stated somewhat differently, the members of a small Senate will be more jealous of their constitutional prerogatives, and as these are to be of great importance, their personal ambitions will very likely be aligned with their public duties.[10] The guiding principle here is to unite, in the conduct of office, *self-interest and the common good.* To do this, the size of the Senate must be such as to endow a Senator with great dignity and honor, the preservation of which will require his adherence to the ends of the institution. But what many men possess in common is less esteemed by each and, indeed, by others. Consequently, a small Senate is necessary to enhance the pride and prestige of its members and to thereby secure their loyalty to the institution and its intended purposes.

It might appear from this that Madison did not expect the future Senate to consist, for the most part, of men of distinguished character. This is not the case. What Madison wished to provide for were the worse contingencies. The work of a Senate composed of distinguished men should not be undone in the event that less than distinguished men are elected to this office. Indeed, the Senate should hold the promise of serving the common good even in the event that bad men are elected.[11] Even such men (in view of the above discussion) will have a strong interest in preserving the integrity of the Senate vis-à-vis the House of Representatives or any other group seeking to impair its independence. The political character of the Senate is thus to compensate for defects in the personal character of men. It is to moderate, if not elevate, their conduct. It is to bend future statesmen to the intentions of the Founders. As Montesquieu has written: "At the birth of societies, the rulers of republics establish institutions; and afterwards the institutions mould the rulers."[12]

This attempt to formulate Madison's intentions concerning the size of the Senate has removed us from the controversy over the mode of electing the Senate. It will be recalled that Dickenson had proposed election by the state legislatures. Wilson (who, by the way, also opposed a large Senate) took issue with Dickenson. According to Wilson, a Senate elected by the state legislatures would suffer from three defects: First, it would represent neither the number nor the wealth of the nation. Second, it would be too dependent on the state governments. Third, it would conflict with the House of Representatives in view of the fact that the two branches would rest on different foundations. This last "defect" Dickenson regarded as one of the merits of his proposal. He thought that by constituting the two branches "like the British House of Lords and Commons, whose powers flow from different sources . . . [the two will check] each other, and will thus promote the real happiness and security of the country."[13] Wilson rejoined by saying that it was erroneous to apply the principles of the British constitution to the American condition. "We have no laws in favor of primogeniture, no distinction of families, [and] the partition of Estates destroys the influence of the Few."[14] Of course, Dickenson appears to have been drawing only an analogy with the British constitution. The aristocracy he wished to have represented in the Senate would not be hereditary; it would be based largely on wealth and merit. In any event, Wilson proposed, as a substitute for Dickenson's motion, that the Senate be elected by the people. He recommended that the Union be divided into a small number of large districts, though solely for electoral purposes. This method of election, he said, "would be most likely to obtain men of intelligence and uprightness." Presumably Wilson thought that in large districts the most reputable citizens would have the best chance of gaining the votes of the people.[15]

Wilson's electoral scheme had already been advanced by him on May 31. At that time, Madison opposed the scheme on the ground that it "would destroy the influence of the smaller states associated with the larger ones in the same district; as the latter would choose from within themselves, although better men might be found in the former."

In the present debate, Dickenson and Gerry argued in a similar vein. In addition, they pointed out the impracticality of combining different states, or parts of distinct states, into a single electoral district. Following this, Wilson's substitute motion was rejected by a vote of ten states to one (Pennsylvania being the exception). Dickenson's motion was thus left open.

In support of election of the Senate by the state legislatures, Mason of Virginia adopted part of Sherman's defense of the same method of electing the House of Representatives. Thus, because he believed that one power could not effectively pervade the entire Union, he felt that the states should be left sufficient power to administer local justice. No doubt Mason feared that this power would be swallowed up by the federal government if the states were deprived of a direct voice in the national legislature. He pointed out —what Sherman had apparently failed to—that the state governments ought to have some means of defending themselves from possible encroachments of the federal government. So, to the mutual restraints between the first and second branches of the national legislature, Mason would add mutual restraints *between* the federal and state governments.

The debates of June 7 closed with a unanimous decision of eleven states in favor of election of the Senate by the state legislatures.[16] This should be contrasted with the vote of May 31 on the first clause of the fifth resolution which would have had the state legislatures nominate, and the House elect, the members of the Senate. At that time, this clause received at least majority support from the Virginia, Massachusetts, and South Carolina delegations. Perhaps the decision of June 6 favoring popular election of the House inclined these states, on June 7, to reverse their earlier position. But what is striking by its absence is that the debates of June 7 contain no clear argument, certainly no persuasive one, in support of the first clause of the fifth resolution. How, for example, would the House make the appointments from the lists of nominees submitted by the state legislatures? Presumably the House would not divide up into committees representing each of the various states. For then the choice of Senators, in some instances, would devolve upon a single man, that is, in the event that some states might be limited to a single representative. The more practical alternative would be for the House to sit in committee as a whole. This would induce the state legislatures to nominate men having some national reputation—which is not to say they would not be so inclined in any event. Perhaps Randolph and Madison had this in mind, but the record is silent on this point. Still, what advantages would this mode of election have over that finally adopted? The state legislatures would offer their nominees, say two or three times the number to be chosen by the House. How would this materially affect the quality of the Senate? True, the representatives of the people would choose the Senators. But the appointments would be severely limited by the state legislatures. It may be said, however, that the House would have greater influence on their appointees. Though this cannot be denied, the influence of the House would be minimized in view of the longer term of office intended for the Senate. Nevertheless, how could Randolph and Madison defend this mode of election after arguing, in effect, that the more numerous House would tend to exhibit the turbulence and follies of the democracy? Of course, having in mind the defects of the Articles of Confederation, perhaps they thought the influence of the states should be reduced to the extent of depriving them of exclusive choice over the membership of the Senate. They would then have to depend on the size and tenure of the Senate to compensate for the defect connected with its appointment. But so involved are these considerations that they provide no clear defense for Madison's and Randolph's position with respect to the mode of electing the Senate.

What has just been said is also relevant to the position maintained by those favoring appointment of the Senate by the state legislatures. The main reason given in its defense is that the state legislatures were more likely to appoint distinguished men. But if they would *appoint* such men, would they not also *nominate* such men? Hence, what difference would result if the first branch were to make the final choice? To this it may be replied that the Senate would be too dependent on the House, notwithstanding its longer term of office. But against this it could be argued (as Randolph suggests), that election of the Senate by the state legislatures would make the former dependent on the latter. After all, there was unanimous agreement that the Senate ought to be an independent body. In view of these considerations, what factors may then be said to have determined the decision in favor of having the Senate appointed, rather than nominated, by the state legislatures?

To begin with, recall Pinckney's warning to the effect that the state legislatures might not adopt the new government if deprived of exclusive choice of Senators. No doubt they would regard the new plan as too radical a departure from the Articles of Confederation. They might fear, as Mason implied, the ultimate absorption of all power by the central government.[17] Exclusive choice over the membership of the Senate would therefore provide greater assurance to the state legislatures of a firmer bond of sympathy between themselves and their appointees. Another probable factor influencing the decision of June 7 is this: There can be little doubt that a Senate appointed by the state legislatures would have greater prestige than one elected by the House of Representatives. Once again it must be noted that a number of the state legislatures were, in Gerry's words, "somewhat aristocratic," namely those whose constitutions required a high property qualification for office. Besides, it was generally understood that the Senate would be more aristocratic the further it was removed from the suffrages of the people. Indeed, it may well be that a number of distinguished men of the time might have felt some· what reluctant to enter the Senate if this depended on the suffrages of the lower House. To be nominated by the state legislatures only to be rejected by the House of Representatives is a thought which might have disturbed the sensibilities of some eighteenth-century aristocrats. Such men preferred to be *appointed*—and by their peers. But all this aside, the decision in favor of having the Senate appointed by the state legislatures rested on a broad and clear basis of agreement. For despite their differences, the delegates wished to constitute the Senate in such a way as to favor the election of distinguished men, to foster their independence, and to facilitate the exercise of wisdom. A number of delegates expressly declared that the Senate should represent the wealth of the nation, though they frequently associate wealth with merit or talent. They intend the Senate to exert restraint over the popular branch—more generally, to check the vices of the democracy. In short, they speak of the Senate in terms which more than suggest that this is to be the aristocratic branch of the national legislature.

Let me now summarize the results of the debates over the mode of electing the national legislature. Thus far, two related principles have governed the decisions of the Convention. The first is the *federal* principle, one which combines the unitary and confederative forms of government. This principle is fulfilled by having the first branch of the national legislature elected by the people, while having the second branch elected by the state legislatures. As a consequence of this, the federal government can act directly on individuals as well as on the several states, while leaving the states some measure of autonomy. Moreover, the federal principle provides the basis for a union of diverse loyalties: loyalty to a whole, in a sense transcending, in a sense only consisting of, distinct parts. The second principle is the *republican*. This principle is fulfilled by combining the democratic and oligarchic principles in the national legislature by the electoral methods indicated above. As a consequence of the republican principle, the basis is prepared for a *union of diverse values* reflected in the democratic House and oligarchic Senate. These two branches constitute a *single* legislature—for the present, a whole consisting of two parts exercising mutual restraint, but therefore mutual influence, upon each other's conduct and character. The Senate, however, is to be the more permanent and the more independent body. Nevertheless, it is through being a "one" and a "many" that the national legislature is to foster a more perfect union of diverse values.

6

On the Tenure of
the House of Representatives

ONE OF the most important factors shaping the character of a political institution is the prescribed term of its members. In Chapter 3 it was pointed out that the tenure of the first and second branches of the national legislature is indicative of the relationship which was meant to exist between the members of these branches and their respective constituents. It was also said that the term of legislators is significant for the kinds of men intended to be elected. In the present chapter I shall examine the debates on the tenure of the House of Representatives, and the reader shall want to keep the foregoing considerations in mind.

On June 12, the business of the Convention commenced with the second clause of the fourth resolution. This clause, it will be recalled, left open the term of office for members of the first branch of the national legislature. To fill in the deliberate omission, Sherman and Rutledge proposed, respectively, one- and two-year terms; whereas Daniel Jenifer, a delegate from Maryland, proposed a three-year term. Jenifer advised his colleagues that the great frequency of elections which then existed "rendered the people indifferent to them, and made the best men unwilling to engage in so precarious a service." On the one hand, Jenifer wished to arouse greater popular interest in the election of Representatives; on the other hand, he wished to encourage the best men to become Representatives. To accomplish these two aims, Jenifer suggested, in effect, that the term of the House of Representatives must be longer than those prescribed for the lower branches of the state legislatures, for this would heighten, in the public mind, the comparative importance of the lower branch of the national legislature. At the same time, it would give this branch greater stability, the effect of which would be to attract superior men to the seat of the national government. The reasoning implied here is this: If the tenure of an office is too short, then, given the indifference with which it is apt to be regarded by the electorate in general, and by men of caliber in particular, the greater the likelihood of inferior men getting into office. The very same principle was later suggested by Hamilton (on June 21). Thus, speaking of his own state of New York, Hamilton declared that frequent elections engendered public "listlessness," as a consequence of which electors did not "in general bring forth the first characters to the legislature."[1] Indeed, it was Hamilton's opinion that the apathy produced by frequent elections tended "to facilitate the success of little cabals."[2]

What is perhaps most striking about Jenifer's and Hamilton's position on the issue before us is that both employ democratic arguments in behalf of ends which are not democratic, or at least which are not simply so. Both wish to reduce the frequency of elections partly on grounds that this will increase popular interest in the election of Representatives. Notice, however, that neither Jenifer nor Hamilton speak of increasing the people's *influence* over Representatives. Quite the contrary! For to reduce the frequency of elections is to extend the term of Representatives, and the effect of this is not only to attract Representatives of higher caliber, but to increase their *independence vis-à-vis the electorate*. But this indicates a somewhat aristocratic attitude on the part of Jenifer and Hamilton toward the *democratic* branch of the national legislature. It represents a subtle attempt to elevate the character of this popularly elected assembly, an attempt, we shall now see, which is also evident in Madison's defense of Jenifer's motion.

Whereas Madison had argued, at an earlier date, that popular election of the House of Representatives would give greater stability to the government as a whole, he now argued that the desired stability could not be achieved if elections were too frequent or if the term of Representatives was too short. "Three years," he said, "will be necessary, in a Government so extensive, for members to form any knowledge of the various interests of the States to which they do not belong . . ." For elaboration of this statement, consider *Federalist* 53. Thus:

No man can be a competent legislator who does not add to an upright intention and a sound judgment a certain degree of knowledge of the subjects on which he is to legislate. A part of this knowledge may be acquired by means of information which lie within the compass of men in private as well as public stations. Another part can only be attained, or at least thoroughly attained, by actual experience in the station which requires the use of it. The period of service, ought, therefore, in all such cases, to bear some proportion to the extent of practical knowledge requisite to the due performance of the service.

Politics is preeminently a practical science. Academic knowledge of government may inform and facilitate, but it cannot obviate, the need for long and intimate experience in public affairs. This does not mean that practical experience alone is sufficient for the proper conduct of public affairs, or that any citizen is capable of political deliberation. For as the above passage is careful to point out, a legislator must possess, *to begin with,* "an upright intention and a sound judgment," that is to say, good moral and intellectual qualities. He must bring these qualities to his office if the knowledge or experience he acquires while in office is to serve the common good.[3] But what are some of the subjects with which a Representative will have to become familiar? Again consider *Federalist 53.*

Some knowledge of the affairs, and even of the laws, of all the States, ought to be possessed by the members from each of the States. How else can foreign trade be properly regulated by uniform laws, without some acquaintance with the commerce, the ports, the usages, and the regulations of the different States? How can the trade between the different States be duly regulated without some knowledge of their relative situations in these and other respects? . . . In regulating our own commerce [a Representative] ought to be not only acquainted with the treaties between the United States and other nations, but also with the commercial law and policies of other nations. . . . And although the House of Representatives is not immediately to participate in foreign negotiations and arrangements, yet from the necessary connection between the several branches of public affairs, those particular branches will frequently deserve attention in the ordinary course of legislation, and will sometimes demand particular legislative sanction and cooperation.

Whereas Jenifer says that the best men will be unwilling to

serve in too mutable an office, Madison says, in effect, that such an office can hardly be well served even by the very best men.[4] Regardless of the caliber of those elected to the House of Representatives, more than one year will be required for them to become acquainted with the many diverse interests and complex problems, not only of the states individually, but of the nation as a whole. Only having acquired such knowledge can they best "discern the true interest of their country."[5]

Now at this point the question may arise as to whether Madison's views on the House of Representatives can adequately be described as democratic. But what does one mean by the term "democratic" as applied to a political assembly such as the House of Representatives? For example, would it be sufficient to say, from a legal point of view, that a political assembly is democratic if (1) its members are elected under universal manhood suffrage, and (2) those having the right of suffrage have also the right of becoming members? That this is not an adequate definition of a democratic assembly becomes apparent as soon as we recall *Federalist 39*, where Madison's definition of a republic logically allows for an elected assembly having a permanent tenure. Clearly, given the conditions of such a tenure, the electorate would have almost no legal control over the conduct of its Representatives. Of course, in speaking of the tenure of an office, no precise line can be drawn between one which is democratic and one which is not. For the Founding Fathers, the problem is a matter of prudence. It involves practical judgment as to what duration of office is required given (1) the kind of legislator which is wanted, and (2) the kind of relationship which is to exist, or which ought to exist, between him and his constituents—to mention only two of the more important considerations. The whole point of this argument is that even though the House of Representatives is to be elected by the people, it does not follow that it is to be governed by popular opinion. And surely the latter is a decisive factor in determining the intended character of this branch of the national legislature. To return, however, to Madison's intentions, we shall presently see that he repudiates even the suggestion that the House of Representatives be constructed simply with a view to satisfying popular opinions or sentiments. But to learn of this, consider, first, Gerry's position with respect to the tenure issue.

In opposition to a three-year term for the House, Gerry declared that annual elections were "the only defense of the people against tyranny." He warned the Convention that the people of New England would never consent to anything but annual elections, and that it was "necessary to consider what the people would approve." Yet it was as recently as May 31 that Gerry had not only opposed popular election of the House, but had done so on grounds that the people are "the dupes of pretended patriots"! Rather than point out this apparent change of attitude (of which more later), Madison thought it more pertinent, and perhaps more urbane, to address himself to this very question of popular opinion. In a most candid statement, Madison declared:

> . . . if the opinions of the people were to be our guide, it would be difficult to say what course we ought to take. No member of the Convention could say what the opinions of his Constituents were at this time; much less could he say what they would think if possessed of the information and lights possessed by the members here. . . . We ought to consider what was right and necessary in itself for the attainment of a proper government. A plan adjusted to this idea will recommend itself. The respectability of this Convention will give weight to their recommendations . . . and all the most enlightened and respectable citizens will be its advocates. Should we fall short of the proper and necessary point, this influential class of citizens will be turned against the plan, and little support in opposition to them can be gained to it from the unreflecting multitude.[6]

Of course, Gerry had not said that the Convention ought to be guided solely by popular opinion, but rather that it should take popular opinion into account.[7] On the other hand, Madison does not deny the propriety of considering the opinions of the people. He simply contends that no one could say what the people's opinions were on the matters before the Convention. Indeed, even if their opinions on these matters were known—were known and were *unambiguous*—still it would not follow that popular opinion ought to determine the decisions of the Convention. It is not that Madison would ignore, say, the findings of a Gallup Poll (assuming, of course, that such polls really ascertain what people think beyond a "yes" and a "no" to a given question). It is only that such a poll would not relieve him and the other delegates of their responsibility, namely, to recommend what they themselves regard as "right and necessary in itself for the attainment of a proper Government." Nor by this does Madison deny the importance of securing popular approval of the Convention's recommendations. Rather, he deems it of greater importance to win the approval of "all the most enlightened and respectable citizens"—citizens, he suggests, who in turn will influence the "unreflecting multitude" in favor of the proposed government. But what light does this shed on the intended character of this government and of the lower branch of its legislature?

Madison says, in effect, that to win general approval, the proposed government must recommend itself to the educated and wealthy, for they constitute the most "influential class of citizens." This does not mean that the new government must be an aristocracy; but it does mean that it must possess certain aristocratic characteristics. One of these characteristics is *political independence,* and what is this but that which makes it institutionally possible for legislators to act according to what they themselves deem right and necessary? I do not mean to suggest by this that the proposed House of Representatives was to exhibit the same degree of independence which Madison claimed for the Federal Convention. Unlike a member of that Convention, one charged with the task of reconstituting a government—of formulating a body of fundamental laws shaping the destiny of a people—a member of the popularly elected House would be guided by these very fundamental laws while representing the changing wants and needs of a fairly small constituency. But insofar as these wants and needs might conflict with each other, as well as with those of other constituencies, a Representative would have considerable latitude in which to exercise independent judgment. Furthermore, problems were bound to arise which would not directly or significantly affect his constituents, or concerning which they would have formed no opinion. Here again a Representative would have to act according to what he himself deems right and necessary, at least if he were to fulfill his office properly and not "sacrifice it to temporary or partial considerations."[8] Indeed, a major reason for investing a Representative with a three-year term is to facilitate the exercise of independent judgment, and this, by somewhat insulating him from his constituents. To strengthen the spirit of detachment rather than the feeling of dependency; to increase the efficacy of knowledge rather than the pressures of public opinion—it is aristocratic thoughts such as these which influenced Madison's position respecting the tenure of the House of Representatives. Not that the popularly elected branch was to be other than democratic *in principle.* But that principle is not only susceptible to different degrees of exemplification, but for this very reason it can shade into principles of another nature. For example, the decision of the Convention on this same day of June 12 to reject the ineligibility clause on reelection, as well as the provision for the recall of Representatives, rendered the popular branch less democratic.[9] That is, the

decision made Representatives less dependent on their constituents. Similarly, a three-year term of office is less democratic than a one-year term—again because it affords Representatives a greater degree of political independence.
And that we are to understand this independence as falling
within what may be termed a "democratic-aristocratic
continuum" is evidenced by Madison's response to Gerry.
For surely Madison would not deny to members of the
House of Representatives some measure of the very independence he claimed for members of the Federal Convention. And that this independence was not to be exercised
simply for the sake of the democracy—if indeed this were
possible—is the only reasonable inference one can draw from
his expressed desire to have the recommendations of the
Convention accepted by "all the most enlightened and
respectable citizens," that is, by those who would recognize
"what is right and necessary for the attainment of a proper
Government."

Though Jenifer's motion was adopted by a vote of seven
states to four, the issue over the tenure of the House of
Representatives was reconsidered on June 21.[10] It was Edmund Randolph, the spokesman for the Virginia Plan, who
proposed, on this date, to substitute a two-year term for
that which had already been approved. He himself would
have preferred annual elections were it not for the burden
they would impose on Representatives from far-flung parts
of the Union. It was then noted by Dickenson that the idea
of annual elections had been borrowed from England, a
country of rather small extent. For a country as large as
the United States, he thought triennial elections were more
appropriate. But to avoid the possibility of too great a
change in the membership of the House at any one time,
Dickenson suggested a rotation of Representatives by annual elections of one-third. Wilson, however, did not regard
the size of the Union as a reason for objecting to annual

elections. It was his opinion that there would be no necessity for Representatives to convene for more than three to six months of the year. Mason disagreed, at least in part. He thought the size of the Union should be considered in deciding the issue in question. As the states would be differently situated from the nation's capitol, the term of office, he felt, should place them as nearly as possible on the same level. If elections were annual, however, the middle states would have a great advantage over the more distant ones, where four months might elapse before the election returns could be known—a period during which the remote states would be deprived of representation. To minimize the discrepancy, Mason, though from Virginia, favored biennial elections.

While still preferring annual elections, Sherman threw his support in favor of a two-year term. He professed the belief that Representatives "ought to return home and mix with the people" lest they acquire "habits" and "interests" which "might differ from those of their constituents."[11] A three-year term, he thought, might instill in them a dangerous detachment, a certain *"esprit de corps."* So now Sherman (like Gerry) appears to have harbored democratic sentiments, in striking contrast with those expressed by him on May 31. For at that time, it will be recalled, he advised the Convention that the people "should have as little to do as may be about the [new] Government." It must also be remembered, however, that Sherman wished to preserve the general balance of state versus federal authority. It would therefore be wrong to attribute to him (or to Gerry for that matter) inconsistency of purpose—which is not to say that his intentions with respect to the political character of the government as a whole were not "mixed." Again we ought not be deceived by the occasional rhetoric. Like the problems confronting them, the motivations and thoughts of these men are too complex to be explained by means of simple formulas. But this, only in passing.

Perhaps in elaboration of a hint dropped by Dickenson, Madison again took up the defense of a three-year term. Again he pointed out that considerable time would be required for Representatives to gain sufficient knowledge of public affairs. But now he added (what is indeed necessary to his argument) that the House, after each election, would always consist of a large proportion of new members. (If, to the contrary, the membership of the House were not materially altered as a result of each election, it would be difficult to justify a three-year term over a shorter one on grounds that the longer was necessary for Representatives to gain sufficient political experience.)[12] Clearly, Madison anticipated a rather precarious career for members of the lower branch of the national legislature. Indeed, he continued:

> none of those [Representatives] who wished to be re-elected would remain at the seat of Government confident that their absence would not affect them. The members of Congress had done this with few instances of disappointment. But as the choice was here to be made by the people themselves who would be much less complaisant to individuals, and much more susceptible of impressions from the presence of a Rival candidate *than the Legislatures had been,* it must be supposed that the members from the most distant states would travel backwards and forwards at least as often as the elections should be repeated.[13]

Unlike a Senator, a Representative will be dependent upon, that is, will have to campaign for, the suffrages of the people—an impressionable body of electors less fitted than the state legislatures to evaluate the official conduct of public officers. To increase the frequency of elections is to increase this dependency of Representatives on the changing sentiments of their constituents. It is to subject the House to excessive mutability in its membership. And as *Federalist 62* points out—though in connection with the tenure of the Senate—such mutability will make it extremely difficult for the new government to develop and carry out long-range and consistent plans of public policy. In short, the very fact that the House of Representatives is to be elected by the people necessitates the institution of a three-year term, that is, if the House is to contribute to the political stability, maturity, and independence of the government as a whole.

Although the Convention had decided in favor of triennial elections on June 12 by a vote of seven states to four, the decision was now reversed by an almost identical margin. Indeed, Randolph's subsequent motion for biennial elections was carried without comment. What produced this change of sentiment is difficult to say with confidence. One can only speculate that the introduction of the New Jersey Plan on June 15 influenced the decision of June 21. Before the introduction of this plan, the Convention had agreed on a number of issues (which have yet to be examined) affecting the basic character of the proposed government, and representing a radical departure from the Articles of Confederation. It may be that the submission of New Jersey's plan, *as an alternative* to Virginia's, persuaded a number of delegates that it would be prudent not to force the decision in favor of triennial elections. More important issues were at stake, and they may have felt that little was to be gained by imposing this decision on what after all was a rather large minority. Be this as it may, the question arises as to whether the decision in favor of biennial elections reflects a change of intentions with respect to the character of the House of Representatives. With the possible exception of Sherman, whose motives on this issue are not simple, no delegate ever spoke of the House as if it were merely to represent the wants and wishes of its constituents. None of these men professed a political philosophy of the "grass roots" variety. All agreed with Hamilton that "a Representative ought to have full freedom of deliberation, and ought to exert an opinion of his own"; that there "ought to be neither too much nor too little dependence on popular sentiments." To be sure, biennial elections have the effect of making the House more democratic and more subject to local influences than would be the case if elections were to be held every three years. (Interestingly enough, however, Madison still felt compelled, in *The Federalist*, to justify the departure from *annual* elections, which were held for all but one of the lower branches of the state legislatures.) So, granting that the House was to exemplify the democratic principle, nevertheless it was hoped and intended that Representatives would "refine and enlarge" the views of their constituents, and that they would be governed not by "temporary and partial considerations," but by "the true interest of their country."

7

On the Tenure of the Senate:

THE HAMILTONIAN VISION

WHAT ROLE was the Senate intended to play in shaping the character of American society? To answer this question we should have to know what the Founding Fathers thought of American society. We should have to know their hopes and fears as to the future course of this society. Consider, then, the following statements:

> Society naturally divides itself into two political divisions
> —the *few* and the *many*, who have distinct interests.
>
> ALEXANDER HAMILTON
June 18, 1787

The people of the United States are perhaps the most singular of any we are acquainted with. Among them there are fewer distinctions of fortune and less of rank than among the inhabitants of any other nation.

. . . however distinct in their pursuits . . . [they] have but one interest.

CHARLES PINCKNEY
June 25, 1787

In all civilized Countries the people fall into different classes having a real or supposed difference of interests. There will be creditors and debtors, farmers, merchants and manufacturers. There will be particularly the distinction of rich and poor.

JAMES MADISON
June 26, 1787

In the speeches from which the foregoing statements are taken may be found three distinct and fundamental ideas of American society.* To grasp the significance of these ideas for the political philosophy of the Constitution, it will be necessary to examine them in connection with the Senate. In this and in the following chapter, the central thesis of my inquiry will be tested and elaborated in conjunction with the debates of the Founding Fathers on the tenure of the Senate. The present chapter will be mainly devoted to an analysis of Hamilton's celebrated speech of June 18. The analysis is undertaken with a view to elucidating a particular idea or vision of American society which the Senate was intended to foster.

On June 12, the Convention took up for the first time that portion of the Virginia Plan concerning the tenure of the Senate. After a rather brief debate, the Convention voted by an overwhelming majority for a senatorial term of seven years. Now for the purpose of this chapter, it will be sufficient to consider only Randolph's reasons for voting with the majority.

* The distinction between Hamilton's and Madison's statements will be clarified at the conclusion of the next chapter.

As on former occasions, Randolph emphasized the dangers which necessitated the institution of a firm and independent Senate. Again he warned of the "democratic licentiousness" of the state legislatures and the turbulence which might be expected from the democratic branch of the national legislature. But now he added that a firm and independent Senate was necessary to "guard the Constitution against the encroachments of the Executive who will be apt to form combinations with the demagogues of the popular branch." From this it is evident that Randolph wished to institute a Senate capable of resisting the will of the people whenever, in the judgment of the Senate, that will is licentious or in conflict with the laws of the Constitution. It is also evident that such a Senate is not, or at least was not intended to be, a democratic institution—if by democratic is meant the unqualified rule of the people or of popular majorities. Finally, in view of the fact that Randolph regarded a senatorial term of seven years *as a means* by which the Senate was to check the democracy, it is clear that the means proposed was not thought to be democratic by this statesman.[1]

With the close of the meeting of June 12, the Convention, after two weeks of deliberation, had reached agreement on nineteen propositions which, taken together, present the outline of a constitution very much in conformity with the Virginia Plan. Accordingly, on June 13, a report of these propositions (many of which remain to be examined) was read and submitted to the Convention. Consistent with a decision which had been reached two days earlier, the eighth proposition of the report provided for a Senate drawn according to the rule of proportional representation specified for the House. This, of course, was a radical departure from the rule of equal representation of the states under the Confederation. Hence it is not surprising that the morning of June 14 would see William Paterson move to postpone further consideration of the committee's report— this, to afford him and some of his colleagues sufficient time to prepare what would later become known as the New Jersey Plan. The next day, Friday, June 15, the plan, consisting of nine resolutions, was read and referred forthwith to committee. Saturday, June 16, the New Jersey and Virginia plans were compared. The main topic concerned the representation of the states in the Senate; but the very nature of the American Union, and the extent of the Convention's authority to alter it, also came under debate. No decision was taken on any point, and the Convention adjourned till Monday. The stage was now set for Hamilton's speech of June 18.

The progress of the Convention had come to an abrupt halt. The delegates now had before them a second plan of government, a plan very different from the first. The two plans proceeded from different conceptions of the American Union. Should the Union be a confederation of more or less sovereign states? Or should it have a *national* government with more or less sovereign powers? The New Jersey Plan leaned toward the former, the Virginia Plan toward the latter. This being so, whatever influence the New Jersey Plan might have on the deliberations of the Convention, that influence could only serve to perpetuate the existing regime. To preclude or nullify that influence was the least that Hamilton set out to do. But how? For one thing, by outlining a *third* plan of government, a plan which, in contrast to that of New Jersey's, would make the plan of Virginia appear as a mean between two extremes, a mean toward which the Convention might be drawn. Whether or not Hamilton had precisely this strategy in mind, it is a fact that the day following his speech of June 18, the New Jersey Plan was killed in committee.[2] True, one of the principal objects of those who had advanced the New Jersey Plan was later achieved when the Convention agreed upon equal representation of the states in the Senate; and this was certainly significant for the character of the American Union. But quite apart from anything else, and at least so far as Hamilton was concerned, even more significant for the character of the Union, *in the long run*, was the *tenure* of the Senate. But this will appear in his speech of June 18 to which I now turn.*

It should be noted at the outset that Hamilton's speech of June 18—a speech, by the way, lasting some five or six hours—comprehended a range of topics extending far beyond the issue over the Senate's tenure.[3] The state of the American Union, the history and character of ancient and modern regimes, the political doctrines of ancient and modern philosophers, the motives of men and public bodies—these and other subjects were treated by Hamilton, and all as an introduction to a general plan of government for the United States.[4] Now to elucidate those portions of Hamilton's speech which bear directly on the Senate, I propose the following order of inquiry: (1) What *kind* of government did Hamilton wish to establish? (2) What was his conception of the society for which this government was intended? (3) What was his position with respect to the tenure of the Senate? (4) What did he conceive to be the role of the Senate in the life of American society? Before commencing this inquiry, however, I should like to offer a brief introduction to Hamilton's speech and to his political philosophy.

Conscious of his youth—he was no more than thirty-two years of age—Hamilton begged the indulgence of his senior colleagues before addressing himself to the crisis which

* Unless otherwise indicated, all references to Hamilton in this chapter appear in his speech of June; but cf. *infra*, p. 302, *n*. 3.

then confronted the American Union. He said, in apology, that this crisis was "too serious to permit any scruples whatever to prevail over the duty imposed on every man to contribute his efforts for the public safety and happiness." In contributing his efforts for the public safety and happiness, he deemed it necessary, at this time, to have recourse to fundamental principles, that is, to political philosophy. Hamilton had studied the political philosophers of ancient and modern times with an interest that can only be regarded as *serious*. It was serious because he felt that what these philosophers had to say about the various kinds of good and bad regimes or constitutions was pertinent to the choice one made of an American Constitution, and hence, to the safety and happiness of his own country.[5] By this seriousness, Hamilton attests to the principle, upheld by these philosophers, that men can *rationally* choose between the politically *better* and the politically *worse*.[6] Of course, this principle was attested to *by every one of the Founding Fathers*. But for that very reason, is it not evident that this is one of the cardinal principles underlying the American Constitution? And yet, though the significance of that principle can hardly be overestimated, the politically decisive question is this: *Who* is to judge between the politically better and the politically worse? The Founding Fathers provide an answer to this question. Here is Hamilton's.

Not content with the Virginia Plan, and strongly opposed to the plan of New Jersey, Hamilton nevertheless agreed that, given America's vastness and diversity, it would be unwise to recommend any other than a republican form of government for the United States. But within the republican form itself Hamilton saw a number of alternatives. The task of the Convention, he thought, was to choose the best possible one. To do this, the delegates should have clearly in view two questions: first, what is the best form of government per se, and second, to what extent could this form of government be approximated in America. These are Hamilton's words, taken from his notes of June 18:

> Here I shall give my sentiments of the best form of govern-
> ment—not as a thing attainable by us, but as a model which
> we ought to approach as near as possible.

Immediately following this statement appears the notation: "British constitution best form." Now what moved Hamilton to prefer the *form* of the British constitution over all others is that it exemplified a *mixed regime*.[7] Here was the model which he thought the Convention should look to in framing a government for the United States. But what was Hamilton's *generic* conception of a mixed regime? Unfortunately, the various accounts of his speech are silent on this question. Nevertheless, in his notes of June 18, directly after the notation "British constitution best form," Hamilton cites the names of Aristotle, Cicero, and Montesquieu, all of whom regarded a mixed regime if not as *the* best form of government at least as the best *practical* one. Inasmuch as Hamilton appeals to the authority of these philosophers, we may do the same for a generic description of the regime in question.[8]

It is common to regard a mixed regime as being composed of monarchy, aristocracy, and democracy. While this conforms to the ideas of Cicero and Montesquieu, Aristotle regarded a mixed regime as consisting of democracy and oligarchy. Now without wishing to minimize the differences between these philosphers, I shall draw together certain basic ideas which they held in common, but which, at the same time, are illustrative of Hamilton's views on government. Thus, according to these philosophers, a mixed regime (which, bear in mind, is a *republic*) requires a division of political power between different bodies of men. This power is the power to make *laws*, a power which involves three distinct though inseparable functions, namely, the formulation of laws, their enforcement, and their interpretation. In a mixed regime, then, the power of making laws is divided into legislative, executive, and judicial functions, and these are distributed among different bodies of men. It is to be noted, however, that so important is the legislative function—for more than any other, it determines the ends or purposes of the laws—that this function may also be divided and placed in the hands of different men. But this is not all; for in a mixed regime, these different bodies of men may represent different *classes* of citizens, for example, the rich and the poor. Generally speaking, the rich and the poor have distinct interests. And such is their bias that, did either class possess the sole power of making laws, the laws would be made to serve the interests of the one to the detriment of the other. However, because this power is divided in a mixed regime, laws cannot be made without the cooperation and agreement of those who represent the two classes. As a consequence, the laws reflect some adjustment of their diverse interests. A mixed regime may then be thought of as a government based on law; and as the laws have been agreed to by the various classes, it may be thought of as a government based on *consent*. This being so, a mixed regime would seem to be well calculated to promote justice and domestic tranquility. While it protects property, it secures to all liberty, and because it secures liberty, all may acquire property. But everything hinges on respect for law.

Now if emphasis is placed on the division of powers or functions, a mixed regime exemplifies a particular way of making laws. On the other hand, if emphasis is placed on the representation of the different classes, and thus, on the diverse ends of the laws, a mixed regime exemplifies a particular way of life. Aristotle and Cicero, and, to a lesser extent, Montesquieu, emphasize the representation of the different classes more than the division of powers or functions. For while the questions of *how* laws ought to be made was deemed extremely important by these philosophers, they regarded the question of *who* ought to participate in the making of laws as more decisive for the way of life or character of the community. As we shall see, Hamilton agreed.

Having presented to the Convention a model of government exemplified by the British constitution and recommended by ancient and modern authorities, it was incumbent upon Hamilton to explain why some version of that government or constitution would be viable in America, and how it would promote the safety and happiness of the American people. Obviously Hamilton must have thought that there was something about American society—something decisive for the proper choice of its government—that was analogous to British society, or to those ancient societies which prospered under mixed regimes. The task, in other words, is to elucidate Hamilton's conception of society in general, and of American society in particular. Only having done this will it be possible to understand why Hamilton wished to establish a republican form of government patterned after a mixed regime.

After citing the names of Aristotle, Cicero, and Montesquieu, Hamilton penned the following statements:

> Society naturally divides itself into two political divisions—the *few* and the *many,* who have distinct interests. If government [is] in the hands of the *few,* they will tyrannize over the many. If in the hands of the many, they will tyrannize over the few. It ought to be in the hands of both; and they should be separated.

Notice that Hamilton speaks of the political division between the few and the many as a *natural* one. Why "natural?" To answer this question it would be necessary to know what Hamilton conceived to be the cause or causes which give rise to the political division between the few and the many.

Fortunately, Madison's notes of June 18 provide a clue. There, Hamilton is reported as saying: "In every community where industry is encouraged, there will be a division of it into the few and the many." But why should this be? Why should the political division between the few and the many be caused by the encouragement of *industry*? The word "industry" is ambiguous. It may mean the various branches of productive and systematic labor. If this is Hamilton's intended meaning, one may infer that the political division between the few and the many is coextensive with the growth of commerce, or better, of *cities*. Indeed, it is with cities that we ordinarily associate political divisions. But having defined industry in these terms, it may be thought that the division between the few and the many corresponds to a division between the rich and the poor. This, however, is not quite the case; for in Yates's notes it appears that Hamilton included in the category of the few, not only the rich, but the "well born." Usually, the term denotes persons born into old and distinguished families, perhaps families having a tradition of public service, but in any event, families with whom we often associate moral and intellectual refinement. Perhaps it should be said, therefore, that the division between the few and the many is characteristic of what we call *civil* or *civilized* society.[9] But still, why should this division be a *natural* one? And why should it have been caused by the encouragement of "industry"? Is it possible that Hamilton means by the term "industry," not only the various branches of productive and systematic labor but also such human qualities as *skill* and *diligence*—qualities in which men differ, partly by virtue of the class to which they belong, but also by virtue of the *unequal gifts of nature*? Can it be that the natural division between the few and the many has its origin in the *natural* inequality of men or of men's faculties?

If so, it may be said that whereas the encouragement of "industry" is the *efficient* cause of the division between the few and the many, this division has its *material* cause in the inequality of men's natural endowments.[10]

To repeat, Hamilton sees in all civilized societies a natural division between the few and the many. He sees this division existing in America, and because it is a *natural* division, and not simply a *conventional* one, he accepts it. Indeed, it is precisely because he regards and accepts this division as a natural one that he feels justified in recommending the form of the British constitution (or the mixed regime of antiquity) as a model of government for the United States. But this means that the division between the few and the many is the foundation upon which Hamilton would establish a republican form of government! The proposal is even more challenging once it is recognized that· the republic envisioned by Hamilton would ultimately be rooted, or so I have inferred, in the natural inequality existing among men.[11]

Now at this point, let us not commit the error of measuring or labeling Hamilton according to present standards or prejudices. While it is true that he saw in American society a natural division between the few and the many, it should not be thought that he saw in such a division a fixed order of classes; nor did he propose that such an order be established.[12] To recommend the form of the British constitution as a model for the government of the United States is one thing; to suggest that American society be patterned after the British is another. A fixed order of classes cannot exist without hereditary institutions, institutions which Hamilton deemed incompatible with the genius of the American people. What is more, when it was once proposed to Hamilton that membership in the *Cincinnati* be made hereditary, he rejected the idea, saying it was contrary to a society based on friendship.[13] Hence it would be a grave error to think that Hamilton wished to alter the class structure of American society. Quite the contrary: he regarded the social order as basically sound, and only wished to bring it to *political* maturity. This is clearly evident in *Federalist 35*.

In that essay, Hamilton takes up for consideration the problem of representing the different classes of American society. He states, to begin with, that "the idea of an actual representation of all classes of the people, by persons of each class, is altogether visionary." He continues: "Unless it were expressly provided in the Constitution, that each different occupation should send one or more members, the thing would never take place in practice." Whether the Constitution does not otherwise favor the *actual* representation of certain classes, as opposed to the *virtual* representation of others, has been considered in connection with the mode of appointing the Senate.[14] Leaving this aside, however, there are three classes, according to Hamilton, which may be expected to receive an actual representation in government, namely, the *merchant or mercantile class,* the *learned professions,* and the *proprietors of land.* These three classes may be said to comprise the "few." But what classes comprise the "many," and what description of persons may be expected virtually to represent these classes? Strange as it may seem, Hamilton includes in the category of the "many" not only mechanics or artisans but *manufacturers* as well. Of course, we are not to confuse the manufacturer of Hamilton's time with that of our own—industry then having been conducted on a rather small scale. But as for the persons who are to represent the mechanic and manufacturer, Hamilton expects them to be drawn mainly from the mercantile class. Here is what he says:

Mechanics and manufacturers will always be inclined, with few exceptions, to give their votes to merchants, in prefer-

ence to persons of their own professions or trades. Those discerning citizens are well aware that the mechanic and manufacturing arts furnish the materials of mercantile enterprise
and industry. Many of them, indeed, are immediately connected with the operation of commerce. They know that the
merchant is their natural patron and friend; and they are
aware, that however great the confidence they may justly
feel in their own good sense, their interests can be more
effectually promoted by the merchant than by themselves.
*They are sensible that their habits in life have not been such
as to give them those acquired endowments, without which,
in a deliberative assembly, the greatest natural abilities are
for the most part useless;* and the influence and weight, and
superior acquirements of the merchants render them more
equal to a contest with any spirit which may happen to infuse itself into the public councils, unfriendly to the manufacturing and trading interests. (Italics added)

Notice that "natural abilities" are said to be almost useless
in a deliberative assembly unless adorned, as it were, by
"acquired endowments." But consider first the "superior
acquirements" of the mercantile class. Obviously this class
is composed of the wealthier members of the community.
They are men of affairs. They are engaged in commercial
and financial transactions. They are familiar with domestic
and foreign markets. They are knowledgeable about such
matters as banking and taxation. But surely these merchants
—and perhaps they ought to be called "entrepreneurs"—
surely they would also have acquired, in virtue of their
wealth, a formal education superior to that of most citizens.
Without such education they could hardly be very effective
in a *deliberative assembly.* What is more interesting to
contemplate, however, is the condition of mechanics and
manufacturers. Their "habits in life" reduce them to an
inferior status. They lack the leisure necessary for the
cultivation of the mind. Unlike the entrepreneur, they lack
the freedom and opportunity to engage in political affairs.
Their occupations narrow their horizons and render them

incapable of promoting their own interests in public councils. Such, then, is the situation of the "many," as may be inferred from *Federalist 35*. Their situation, however, need not prevent the "many" from choosing representatives from their own ranks. This consideration is taken up by Hamilton in *Federalist 36*.

Again Hamilton observes that the government "will consist almost entirely of proprietors of land, of merchants, and of members of the learned professions." These three classes will represent the different views and interests of the entire community. Hamilton continues:

> If it should be objected that we have seen other descriptions of men in the local legislatures, I answer that it is admitted there are exceptions to the rule, but not in sufficient number to influence the general complexion or character of the government.

Presumably, by "other descriptions of men," Hamilton again has in view persons included in the category of the "many." This notion is borne out in the sequel.

> There are strong minds in every walk of life that will rise superior to the disadvantages of situation, and will command *the tribute due to their merit*, not only from the classes to which they particularly belong, but from society in general. *The door ought to be equally open to all*; and I trust, for the credit of *human nature*, that we shall see examples of such vigorous plants flourishing in the soil of federal as well as of State legislation; but *occasional instances* of this sort will not render the reasoning, founded upon the *general course of things*, less conclusive. (Italics added)

"The door [to political advancement] ought to be equally open to all [citizens who] command the tribute due to their merit." Nevertheless, we are told not to expect more than "occasional instances" of persons of humble origin rising "superior to the disadvantages of [their] situation." To paraphrase Hamilton's earlier remark regarding mechanics and

manufacturers; The greatest natural endowments are ineffective without certain acquired endowments, that is,
without education and the habits cultivated in urbane society. Hence the "general course of things" will be such as
to insure the predominance in the national legislature of
merchants, landholders, and members of the learned professions. It is the weight and influence of these three classes
that will preserve "the general complexion or character of
the government." (But of course the Constitution of government will foster the ascendency of these classes.)

Now it would be erroneous to conclude from the preceding discussion that *wealth* rather than *merit* is intended
by Hamilton to be the mainspring of political advancement.
Even ignoring the role of the learned professions (of which
more later), it should be evident that the rule of mere
wealth is contrary to Hamilton's intentions. It is not wealth,
but the "superior acquirements" afforded by wealth, that
he wishes to see predominate in the councils of government.
Above all, Hamilton is a *political* man, but a political man
of aristocratic temperament. In favoring the wealthier
classes of the community, he is guided by the reasonable
assumption that superior education and political abilities
will generally be found among the rich than among the
poor. As a matter of principle, however, he would surely
contend that *merit,* rather than wealth or class, should be
the mainspring of political advancement. This principle,
it should be noted, is in perfect accord with *liberalism.* It
reflects the liberal's skeptical attitude especially toward
the propertied classes—their pretension to rule on the basis
of wealth or family connection. It should be understood,
however, that the true liberal does not identify himself
with any class of society, knowing as he does that each class
has its peculiar prejudices, indeed, its own vices. It should
also be understood that this detachment of the liberal need
not prevent him from weighing the character of the various

classes as well as their relative importance in the political scale. Consider, for example, this remarkable statement which Hamilton addressed to the New York ratifying convention.

> Experience has by no means justified us in the supposition that there is more virtue in one class of men than in another. Look through the rich and poor of the community. . . . Where does virtue predominate? The difference indeed consists, not in the quantity, but kind of vices, which are incident to the various classes; and here the advantage of character belongs to the wealthy. Their vices are *probably* more favorable to the prosperity of the state than those of the indigent, and partake less of moral depravity.[15]

In denying that there is more virtue in one class than in another, Hamilton probably means something like this: If one class excels, say, in knowledge, another may excel in courage, while yet another in industry. Hence, while the distribution of the virtues varies from class to class, the balance of virtue favors none. The balance is altered, however, when character is considered as a whole, that is, when, in addition to their virtues, the vices of the different classes are thrown into the scale. For example, assume, to begin with, that Hamilton would attribute to the rich, more than to the poor, an immoderate desire for wealth, in other words, the vice of *avarice*. (This assumption might have been made quite apart from his saying that the vices of the rich may be more conducive to the prosperity of the state than those of the poor.) Now what vice might Hamilton ascribe to the poor more than to the rich? For reasons which will soon become apparent, assume it is *envy*. But why should envy be more vicious than avarice? Indeed, in its neutral form, envy is simply a longing for another's superior advantages, so that it might well be regarded as no worse than on a par with avarice. However, when envy assumes *class proportions* (it need not), it readily passes from its neutral to its negative form.[16] Then it is that the longing for another's superior advantages is mingled with ill will or *resentment*. It is therefore understandable why the character of the rich—if their vice is avarice—partakes less of moral depravity. But there is yet another vice which Hamilton would no doubt ascribe to the rich more than to the poor, a vice of greater significance for his thoughts on politics, namely, the vice of *ambition*.[17] This vice may also serve to clarify the foregoing passage, and more besides. As ambition, or the inordinate desire for place or honor, will often turn toward enterprise or political office, again it is understandable why, in Hamilton's opinion, the advantage of character belongs to the wealthy. But this also explains why Hamilton regards the vices of the rich as probably— but notice he says only "probably"—more conducive to the prosperity of the state than the vices of the poor. For whatever benefits society may derive from the ambitions of the rich, this very vice constitutes one of society's great dangers: the danger of *oligarchy*. To paraphrase Hamilton's earlier remarks: If the rich have sole control of the government, they will oppress the poor. On the other hand, such is the envy of the poor that, did they have sole control of the government, they would despoil the rich. But it is precisely because neither class has a monopoly of *virtue* that neither should have a monopoly of political power. Furthermore, because virtue is to be found "in every walk of life," it is not class but merit or excellence that Hamilton prefers to see as the mainspring of political rule. This detachment of Hamilton's, his refusal to identify himself with any class of society, cannot be emphasized too often. The recognition of this is the key to understanding his conception of a republic founded upon the natural division of society between the few and the many. But now I must turn to consider in greater detail the character of this republic, in particular, that part of it which is to represent the *few*, namely the Senate.

It will be recalled that the few and the many, according to Hamilton, have "distinct interests." Presumably, the interest of the few is to protect or extend their "property" as well as the advantages which such property may afford. Meanwhile, the interest of the many is to achieve a comfortable and independent station in life, which is to say, to become rich. Ambition, avarice, and envy thus have fertile ground on which to thrive, and the statesman must know how to turn these vices or passions to public advantage. Interest must not only be weighed against interest, but brought into harmony with the common good. Now it is precisely in the way in which the British constitution adjusted the interests of the few and the many that Hamilton saw its particular excellence.

> Their House of Lords is a most noble institution. Having nothing to hope for by a change, and a sufficient interest by means of their property, in being faithful to the National interest, they form a permanent barrier against every pernicious innovation, whether attempted on the part of the Crown or of the Commons.

Quite apart from any other motives, the interest of property is sufficient to secure the fidelity of the House of Lords to the interests of the nation. It should be borne in mind, however, that Hamilton would not confine the meaning of the term "property" to material possessions. For as we have seen, and as even the above passage suggests, the term property once included the possession of rights or privileges, particularly those of office.[18] Be this as it may, a Senate patterned after the House of Lords will have to be founded partly on property. Accordingly, Hamilton's plan of government provides that:

> The Senate shall consist of persons to be chosen . . . by the Electors for that purpose by the Citizens and inhabitants of the several States comprehended in the Union who shall have in their own right, or in the right of their wives, an

estate in land for not less than life, or a term of years, whereof at the time of giving their votes there shall be at least fourteen years unexpired.[19]

Notice that while Hamilton proposes a property qualification for senatorial electors—a property qualification which is in *land*—he proposes none for Senators themselves. Indeed, his plan even prescribes "a reasonable compensation for their services"! To appreciate the significance of this, consider a message of President Washington to Congress dated December 7, 1796, the draft of which is in Hamilton's hand. Though the subject concerns the salaries of public officers, it is pertinent to the present inquiry.

> No plan of governing is well founded, which does not regard man as a compound of selfish and virtuous passions. To expect him to be wholly guided by the latter, would be as great an error as to suppose him wholly destitute of them. Hence the necessity of adequate rewards for those services of which the public stand in need. Without them, the affairs of a nation are likely to get sooner or later into incompetent or unfaithful hands.
>
> . . . If the rewards of the government are scanty, those who have talents without wealth, and are too virtuous to abuse their stations, cannot accept public offices without a sacrifice of interest; which, in ordinary times, may hardly be justified by their duty to themselves and their families. If they have talents without virtue, they may, indeed, accept offices to make a dishonest and improper use of them. The tendency then is to transfer the management of public affairs to wealthy but incapable hands, or to hands which, if capable, are as destitute of integrity as of wealth.[20]

Without pausing to reflect on this most interesting document, it is clear that the Senate proposed by Hamilton was not intended to represent mere wealth. But this is only consistent with a principle enunciated earlier, namely, that the door ought to be equally open to all who command the tribute due to their merit. Recall that, in *Federalist 36,*

Hamilton made the prediction that the new government "will consist almost entirely of proprietors of land, of merchants, and of members of the learned professions." Referring to the learned professions in *Federalist 35*, Hamilton says they "form no distinct interest in society, and according to their situation and talents, will be indiscriminately the objects of the confidence and choice of each other, and other parts of the community." Because they form no distinct interest, the learned professions, Hamilton continues, will likely prove to be an "important arbiter" between the various interests of society. Not identified with the rule of wealth, nor with the rule of popular majorities, the members of the learned professions will be inclined by their very character to promote those interests which are conducive to the good of the entire community. But since this is essentially the character and role which Hamilton intended for the Senate, it may reasonably be assumed that he expected the learned professions to be well represented in that branch of the government.[21]

That Hamilton should contemplate a Senate wherein members of the learned professions would play a decisive role becomes more understandable once it is recognized that, by the learned professions, Hamilton meant primarily, but not exclusively, the then highly educated profession of law. It was precisely because that profession was identified with the rule of law that it formed no distinct interest in society. It was because that profession had a certain *esprit de corps* that it was not identified with the rule of wealth nor with the rule of popular majorities. But this must be spelled out, bearing in mind that it is the legal profession of Hamilton's time that is under review.

It may be admitted, at the outset, that the legal profession is not simply an aristocracy. As Tocqueville points out, it stands between aristocracy and democracy and partakes of the character of both. By interest, the legal profession is bound to the preservation of democratic institutions. But by training and disposition, it constantly thwarts the tendencies of democracy. On the one hand, it necessarily follows the law of precedents. This insures continuity and stability; it acts to restrain majority will in the interest of deliberation and justice. On the other hand, the general dependence of all classes of people upon the legal profession insures the lawyer a superior status in society. He is jealous of his privileges and ever mindful of the deference accorded him. This, coupled with the peculiar cultivation of his mind, makes him somewhat disdainful of the "layman" or of the unenlightened "many"—be they rich or poor.

Though the legal profession is not identified with the rule of wealth, it is nevertheless bound, by duty and inclination, to protect the rights of property. But these rights, in Hamilton's view, cannot be wholly identified with the interests of any particular class. Indeed, the rights of property, he has written, cannot be severed from the *"rules of morality and justice"* which underlie these rights. Through these rules—rules involving good faith, fulfillment of promises or contracts—men are schooled in some of the most distinct ideas of right and wrong, of justice and injustice. By the discipline of these rules do men secure their liberty and the rewards of their labor. Only fail to honor the clear and abiding rules of morality and justice upon which the rights of property are founded and "everything," says Hamilton, "must float on the variable and vague opinions of the governing party of whomsoever composed." And though these rights, for Hamilton, are not absolute, so intimately are they connected with liberty and public morality, that their protection ranks among the first objects and blessings of constitutional government.[22] It is thus for the most profound reasons that Hamilton wished to establish a high-toned Senate.

I have been describing a Senate so constituted as to

unite self-interest and justice. In this union is to be found a notion especially prevalent in modern thought, namely "enlightened self-interest." As an ideal of human conduct, it is perhaps the highest to which most men and all public bodies can attain. A Senate embodying this ideal may not be noble, but it will certainly be honest and respectable.[23] Higher ideals are reserved to "the *very* few" indeed, as Hamilton was aware.[24] But to insure its integrity and respectability, Hamilton proposed a *permanent* Senate, one whose members would hold office during good behavior. Permanence of tenure would serve to satisfy their political ambitions and so secure their loyalty to the Constitution. It would also serve to protect the interests of wealth, with which some Senators would no doubt be identified. Moreover, as a new government was about to be formed, Hamilton wanted to turn the ambitions of the best men away from the state governments toward the seat of the national government. More generally, and with a view to the future, he wanted to attract the "first characters" of the nation. Many of the most talented and virtuous members of the community, he thought, might be reluctant, during ordinary times, to sacrifice their private station for a temporary public office. Thus, while the permanence of the Senate was calculated to unite self-interest with justice, it was also calculated to bring to the public the leadership of its most distinguished citizens.

In view of the above, it will not surprise the reader that what Hamilton most objected to in the Virginia Plan was its provision for a temporary Senate. No temporary Senate, he declared, can serve the purposes which the authors of such a body have in mind. "Gentlemen say we need to be rescued from the democracy."[25] But what means, asks Hamilton, do they propose? "A democratic assembly is to be checked by a democratic senate . . ."[26] Now as the reader will immediately see, Hamilton's evaluation of this Senate is in striking conflict with the intentions I have attributed to its authors—suffice to mention only Randolph. I must therefore take time to consider this conflict more closely.

Prior to any other consideration, a distinction must be made between what a thing *is* and what it is *intended* to be. That is, an institution may be one thing while its authors may have intended it to be another. The proposed Senate may correctly or incorrectly be judged to be democratic. In neither case, however, is the judgment determinitive of the *intended* political character of this institution. The second point to be made is this: At no time did Randolph (or anyone else for that matter) declare to the Convention that he wished to establish a democratic Senate. Quite the contrary. His expressed intention is to form a Senate that will check the democracy, or as noted earlier, a Senate capable of resisting the will of the people whenever, in the judgment of the Senate, that will is licentious or unlawful. To be sure, Randolph said, in effect, that the Senate he proposed is consistent with the republican form of government. But a republic is one thing, a democracy another; and between the two is a difference which, for Randolph, made all the difference between a good and bad form of government. This difference, it must again be emphasized, cannot be confined or reduced to the representative principle—though the importance of this principle is not to be underestimated. The representative principle is a formal or legal principle having substantive implications for the character of the government such as those discussed in an earlier chapter. But we have seen that Randolph would have the Senate check the very branch of government embodying this principle.[27] If the difference between a republic and a democracy is to be formulated in precise yet comprehensive terms, it may be said: Whereas a democracy serves only the interests of the many, a republic serves the interest of both the many *and* the few—hence, the interests of the entire community. This distinction between a democracy and a republic is consistent with Randolph's stated intentions. To check the democracy is to check the many, a function to be performed by the few, i.e., the Senate, and for the sake of the common good. It is precisely to this end that Randolph favored a senatorial term of seven years, a term which he believed sufficient to give the Senate the necessary firmness and independence with which to check the democracy. For Hamilton, the means proposed by Randolph were incommensurate with this end: the means, in his opinion, were themselves democratic. Hamilton may or may not have been correct in his opinion. But in no way does this decide the character of Randolph's intentions.

It may be, however, that Hamilton was engaging in a bit of rhetoric when he characterized Randolph's plan as democratic.[28] For consider how he characterized his own plan of government, a plan, by the way, which included not only a permanent Senate, but a permanent Executive as well. Thus, in Madison's notes, Hamilton is quoted as saying: "But is this a Republican government it will be asked?" And to his own question he answers: "Yes, if all the Magistrates are appointed, and vacancies are filled, by the people or a process of election originating with the people."[29] Contrast, however, Hamilton's own notes: "The democracy," he writes, "must be derived immediately from the people." And, he continues: "The aristocracy ought to be entirely separated. . . ." To whatever extent Hamilton's criticism of the proposed Senate is rhetorical, it is clear that the ambiguity of the term republic readily lends itself to rhetorical usage. Recall, for example, Gerry's profession of being a "republican," while opposing popular election of the House of Representatives. Yet the same Gerry, when later opposing ratification of the Constitution, characterized the Senate as "aristocratical."[30] This, of course, is very much the same Senate which Hamilton now characterizes as democratic! Strange indeed is the republican form of government. It admits of so many diverse qualities and institutional combinations that, while from one vantage it appears democratic, from another it appears aristocratic, or as some might prefer, oligarchic. But however strange this may be, I venture to say it would not have appeared so to Aristotle, as the following may indicate.

> We may add that it is a good criterion of a proper mixture of democracy and oligarchy that a mixed constitution should be able to be described indifferently as either. When this can be said, it must obviously be due to the excellence of the mixture. It is a thing which can generally be said of the mean between two extremes: both of the extremes can be traced in the mean, [and it can thus be described by the name of either].[31]

For this philosopher, by the way, a Senate indirectly elected by the people for a term of seven years is unquestionably oligarchic, and, depending upon the character of its members, may or may not be aristocratic. Hamilton, who cited Aristotle in support of his own plan of government, must be presumed to have understood this—which is not to say he necessarily agreed.

Returning, however, to Hamilton's objection to a temporary Senate, it was noted that he did not believe such a Senate could be depended upon to check the democracy. Those who thought otherwise, he said, "suppose seven years a sufficient period to give the Senate an adequate firmness, from not duly considering the amazing violence and turbulence of the democratic spirit." The firmness they desired would not be forthcoming for two principal reasons: First, it would be lacking to the extent that the Senate lacked *character;* and a temporary Senate would lack character to the extent that it discouraged some of the most distinguished members of the community from accepting this office. "Will not the power, therefore, be thrown into the hands of the demagogue or middling politician, who, for the sake of a small stipend and hopes of advancement, will offer himself as a candidate . . . ?"[32] Men of this stamp, Hamilton was to write in defense of the Constitution, "will enflame the minds of the well-meaning, tho' less intelligent parts of the community, by sating their vanity with that cordial and unfailing specific, that *all power is seated in the people*."[33] Second, a temporary Senate, even if moderately well composed, would lack firmness to the extent that it lacked *independence;* and it would lack independence to the extent that its members would be subject, periodically, to the changing sentiments and attachments of their electors. To be sure, it may be objected that the electors in question would not be the people but the separate state legislatures. But to this Hamilton would very likely rejoin that the state legislatures were themselves too much under the sway of the people. Furthermore, because the membership of each of the state legislatures was mutable, so too would be the membership of the Senate.[34] Indeed, even if the Senate's membership were to remain relatively constant (its incumbents having been reelected a number of times), still it would not follow that the Senate's *policies* would remain relatively constant. For too often, Senators seeking reelection would succumb to temptations, or sacrifice principle for popularity. Compelled more by ambition than by virtue, they might yield to the importunities of this group or that group, or trade one vote for another, so that in the end, legislation might become a patchwork of compromises reflecting the changing and disorganized interests of the community. Stable as its membership might be, a temporary Senate, according to Hamilton, would be incapable of formulating wise, consistent, and long-range plans of public policy. And failing this, America could hardly achieve unity and greatness of purpose.

Having examined Hamilton's views on the tenure of the Senate, one thing remains before this chapter is concluded, and that is to draw together certain aspects of the preceding inquiry in order to project Hamilton's designs for the future course of American society, in particular, the role of the Senate in shaping the character of that society.

No doubt the reader will have been aware of a certain tension or difficulty in Hamilton's thoughts. On the one hand, Hamilton wished to divide the government between the few and the many, the few comprising the rich and the well born, the many comprising the poor. On the other hand, he wanted merit or excellence to be the mainspring of political advancement, such that the door would be open equally to all regardless of wealth or class. I shall try to resolve this difficulty while further elaborating Hamilton's political philosophy.

Hamilton accepted the existence of classes. There will always be the *few* and the *many*, at least so long as societies remain civilized. This division between the few and the many is inevitable given the natural inequality of men's faculties. Recognizing this, the wise statesman, in founding a new government, will provide an avenue for the political advancement of the few. This is just as well as prudent. The few—the rich and the well born—do contribute, in no ordinary way, to the progress of society, and their support and services are indispensable for the proper functioning of government. If there is no place in the political order set aside for the few, too many will follow other callings, some less noble than the political. Government will thus be deprived of much talent and fall more into the hands of mediocre men. But while a place in the political order should be set aside for the few, no person should be barred from this place on the basis of wealth or class. Again: "The door ought to be equally open to all," that is, to all who "command the tribute due to their merit." It may therefore be said that Hamilton regarded merit or excellence as the *ideal* principle of political rule; but since the conditions of society are less than ideal, prudence dictates the addition of lesser principles in the constitution of government.

Now let us suppose one branch of government, a Senate, reserved for the few. No doubt some members of this branch will have risen to office not by way of merit, but by way of "influence," especially through the influence of wealth. But is this less likely to happen where the government is not divided between the few and the many? Bear in mind that Hamilton is speaking within the context of a free society, and he is assuming certain permanent facts of human nature. Men of ambition will ever find a way to high places, and wealth will always smooth the path. If the division of society between the few and the many has no political or *institutional* counterpart, the influence of wealth will only retire to the back door. The cost to the community will be great, for the very tone and character of political life will be degraded. Indeed, "Who gets what, when, and how?" —this will become the science of politics. But this may be the political science of a society in process of disintegration. Given, however, a Senate reserved for the few—the rich *and* the well born—the development of a more perfect union is possible. For that Senate—and here I turn to Hamilton's speech before the New York ratifying convention—that Senate, said Hamilton, would constitute "the center of political knowledge." Unlike the House, it would distinguish between "apparent" and "real" interests, between "local" and "general" interests. Unlike the House, it would represent the interests of the whole over and above those of the parts. Furthermore, such a Senate would "correct the prejudices, check the intemperate passions, and regulate the fluctuations of [the] popular assembly." As a council of wisdom, it would help to mature comprehensive and long-range national policies; that is, it would facilitate the exercise of

Presidential leadership.[35] It would do these things because it would attract and bring together the talents of the nation.

Having supposed one branch of government, a Senate, set apart for the *few*, let us now omit from that branch, as Hamilton does not, the well born. In other words, project a Senate which is solely and specifically designed to represent wealth. What kind of society would be compatible with such a Senate? What impact would such a Senate have on the political life of that society?

Imagine a society which not only places high value on wealth, but which even acknowledges the contribution of the wealthy to the nation's prosperity. Shunning hypocrisy on the one hand, and acting under prudent counsel on the other, this society accords to the wealthy separate representation in one branch of government, the Senate. This, in itself, tends to encourage men of independent means to enter upon a political career: they have a place in the Senate for the exercise of their ambitions. But now their ambitions are under greater public scrutiny, checked by other branches of government, and even modified by the *political* or *constitutional* order.[36] Not to say that interest groups no longer seek special favors, or utterly cease to exercise undue and out-of-public-sight influence on the course of legislation. But having received representation in the Senate, the interests of wealth are more inclined to operate in public view. Furthermore, since the members of the Senate owe their position not simply to wealth, but to the *public* and *publicly* recognized benefits of wealth—this being so, they have a personal interest in preserving the integrity of the government, indeed, of economic life itself. Profound consequences have thus followed upon the institution of this Senate. The distribution of power in the community has shifted from the *de facto* to the *de jure*. This means, among other things, that the government has more control over the economic and competitive forces of society.

Such control is precisely what Hamilton deemed indispensable for the establishment of a true political union. Consider what he wrote in 1782 concerning the regulation of trade:

> Perhaps it will be thought that the power of regulation will be best placed in the governments of the several states, and that a general superintendence is unnecessary. If the States had distinct interests, were unconnected with each other, their own governments would then be the proper . . . depositories of such a power; but as they are parts of a whole, with a common interest in trade, as in other things, *there ought to be a common direction in that as in all other matters.*[37]

Among the "other matters" which Hamilton contemplated and for which he sought a *common direction,* may be mentioned industry or manufactures, banking and currency, labor and agriculture.[38] Though private enterprise would still flourish in the economic system, the system itself would be guided, more or less, by *national* goals or purposes. In other words, economic activity would become more of a *public* concern. And lest it be thought that Hamilton's vision of a common directing power was focused simply on a national Executive, it should be noted that the passage cited is contained in a paper whose stated purpose is to have the power in question vested in *Congress.* But now it becomes more evident why Hamilton wanted the Senate to represent "wealth." Only by bringing together, in one political assembly, men representing the wealth of the nation, can the economic and competitive forces of society be *politically* structured and directed toward national ends or purposes.

Let us now draw this chapter to a close. We have seen that Hamilton acknowledged the necessity of establishing in America a republican form of government, a government drawn from and representing the parts of a whole. To this end he proposed a popularly elected assembly, a "House of

Commons." But such is America's vastness and diversity that the government so formed must be capable of uniting the whole. To this end Hamilton proposed (in part) a permanent Senate, a non-hereditary "House of Lords." This permanent Senate (with the aid of a permanent Executive) was to endow the government and the community with what Hamilton called a *permanent will*.[39] Here is the one thing lacking in American society. In Hamilton's opinion, it is folly to suppose that a permanent will can be found in the people. The people, he warned, are fickle, are too easily played upon by the flattery and deceits of demagogues. Though well-meaning, they are ill-qualified to judge for themselves on the great and complex issues of government. "[N]or is this to be wondered at. The science of government is not easily understood."[40] But if the nation be lacking a permanent will, it must ever float upon the changing opinions of the governing party, of whomsoever composed. Lacking a permanent will, America, according to Hamilton, can hardly aspire to lofty ideals of national purpose.

8

On the Tenure of the Senate:

THE MADISONIAN VISION

I T WAS SAID at the outset of the last chapter that, to understand the intended role of the Senate in American society, we should have to understand what the Founding Fathers thought of the character of that society, as well as their hopes and fears concerning its future. With this in view I cited the following statements:

> Society naturally divides itself into two political divisions —the *few* and the *many*, who have distinct interests.
>
> Alexander Hamilton
June 18, 1787

The people of the United States are perhaps the most singular of any we are acquainted with. Among them there are fewer distinctions of fortune and less of rank than among the inhabitants of any other nation.

. . . however distinct in their pursuits . . . [they] have but one interest.

CHARLES PINCKNEY
June 25, 1787

In all civilized Countries the people fall into different classes having a real or supposed difference of interests. There will be creditors and debtors, farmers, merchants and manufacturers. There will be particularly the distinction of rich and poor.

JAMES MADISON
June 26, 1787

By itself, the third statement may appear to be but an elaboration of the first. In its proper context, however, it might be recognized as a mean between two antithetical conceptions of American society. When Madison uttered that statement on June 26, he was about to call into question a view—say rather a vision—of America which Charles Pinckney had portrayed the previous day. The specific issue was the tenure of the Senate. But involved in that issue, as Madison saw, was the future course of American society. To understand how Madison addressed himself to this issue, it will be necessary to consider first Pinckney's speech of June 25.

Although we have only the introductory pages of this speech, they provide the clearest, and perhaps the only clear, antithesis to the Hamiltonian conception of American society. Because he agreed with Hamilton on the superior merit of the British constitution, Pinckney was compelled to argue that that constitution was adapted to a society whose character differed greatly from our own. "Great Britain," he declared, "contains three orders of people distinct in their situation, their passions and principles."[1] On the one hand was the Commons, on the other the Crown, and holding the balance between the two was the order of the Peers. This order, said Pinckney, was founded on hereditary rights and privileges the origin of which dated far back into antiquity. No class comparable to this existed in America and the materials for forming such a class were utterly lacking. Primogeniture had been abolished and landed estates could be divided and disposed of with hardly any limitation. Hence a landed aristocracy was out of the question. Would an order comparable to the British Peers emerge from commerce? To this question Pinckney replied: "I believe it will be the first Nobility that ever sprung from merchants." Why then a Senate patterned after the House of Lords? What class of citizens would such a body represent? Between what "orders" would it stand balancing one against the other? No, said Pinckney, we must form a government suitable to the character and condition of our own people. "These are, I believe, as active, intelligent and susceptible of good government as any people in the world." The American people, he continued,

> . . . are perhaps the most singular of any we are acquainted with. Among them there are fewer distinctions of fortune and less of rank than among the inhabitants of any other nation. Every freeman has a right to the same protection and security, and a very moderate share of property entitles them to the possession of all the honors and privileges the public can bestow. Hence arises a greater equality than is to be found among the people of any other country, and an equality which is more likely to continue. I say this equality is likely to continue; because in a new country, possessing immense tracts of uncultivated lands—where every temptation is offered to emigration and where industry must be rewarded with competency, there will be few poor and few dependent. Every member of the society, almost, will enjoy an equal power of arriving at the supreme offices and consequently of directing the strength and sentiments of the community. . . . The whole community will enjoy in the

fullest sense that kind of political Liberty which consists in
the power which the members of the state reserve to themselves of arriving at the public offices, or at least of having
votes in the nomination of those who fill them.

Here, lucidly portrayed, is Pinckney's vision of American
society—a vision as idyllic on the one hand, as it is equalitarian or democratic on the other. We shall look in vain among
the debates of the Constitutional Convention for a more
felicitous portrayal of this vision. And this is why I feel some
embarrassment in informing the reader that, although Pinckney's vision of American society is undeniably democratic,
his specific recommendations for the government of that
society are undeniably *oligarchic.* For unless Pinckney expected that most Americans would acquire wealth or property to the value of fifty thousand dollars, I can in no other
way explain his having proposed, on August 10, that such
a sum be made a qualification for holding office in the
legislature of the United States!* I would have preferred a

* I blush to add that, not only did Pinckney propose the same qualification
for the Judiciary, but *twice* that amount for the Executive! Hence it is
remarkable that Professor Hans Morgenthau, in his book *The Purpose of
American Politics* (New York: Alfred A. Knopf Inc., 1960), pp. 11-18,
should have chosen Pinckney, among others, to exemplify his belief that
the historic purpose of America is "equality in freedom." This purpose, he
says, is "intangible, shapeless, and procedural"; it does not consist in any
"substantive ideal and achievement" (p. 21). This may well be true *if*
"equality in freedom" *is* the historic purpose of America. But I wonder
that Professor Morgenthau should not have weighed the significance for
America's historic purpose of the Preamble of the Constitution, or the domestic policies initiated by Washington and Hamilton. Nevertheless, Professor Morgenthau does hit upon the dilemma of American politics. For
while the American government has now the power which Hamilton would
have conferred upon it, that power is purposeless precisely because "equality in freedom" has become the accepted dogma of the day. I would point
out, however, that other ideals were represented at the Constitutional Convention, indeed, that the Founding Fathers were particularly concerned to
check the tendencies of the very ideal which Professor Morgenthau translates into America's historic purpose. Still, it is to Professor Morgenthau's
credit that he vacillates between accepting the dogma of "equality in freedom" and seeing in this dogma the purposelessness and degradation of
American politics (pp. 236-238, 243-252, 298-300).

more straightforward consistency. But this ought not prevent us from taking Pinckney's vision of America seriously.

Abstractly considered, Pinckney's vision was inspired by the promise of the New World, the promise of *equality of opportunity*. The vast tracts of uncultivated land, the absence of rigid class distinctions or of a permanent body of rulers, the enjoyment of political liberty and the protection of private property—these were the conditions which gave to each American citizen the opportunity to acquire wealth, to rise above the station of his birth, to attain to the highest public offices, and all this as the fruit of his own labor or as the reward of his own merit. Although Pinckney saw but one order of people in American society, he divided this order into three familiar classes: commercial, landed, and professional. The interests of these classes, according to Pinckney, were not distinct, they were "one." The merchant and the planter necessarily depended upon each other, and both had to rely on the professions in private as well as public affairs. Seeing "no distinctions of rank and very few of fortune" among these classes, Pinckney regarded them as "individually equal in the political scale." Nevertheless, Pinckney would alter the balance against the commercial in favor of the landed interest. "If that commercial policy is pursued which I conceive to be the true one, the merchants of this country will not, or ought not for a considerable time, to have much weight in the political scale." In this country, he continued, the landed interest "ought ever to be the governing principle of the system." From this it is clear that Pinckney's vision of America, like Jefferson's, was decidedly agrarian. In his America most citizens would possess their own land, enjoy nature's abundance, and be their own masters. Few would be poor or dependent because few would live in cities, laboring in factories or engaged in commerce.[2] The solid and self-reliant tiller of the soil, the hardy yeoman, simple and virtuous and free from the artificialities and speculations of moneyed society—this was the ideal citizen of Pinckney's vision.*

If Pinckney's vision of America lacks the interest of complexity, we may be grateful for its noble simplicity. Nevertheless, inasmuch as our task is to understand the political philosophy of the American Constitution, we must understand *why* this vision is simple, and wherein it fails to reflect some of the evident as well as underlying principles of the Constitution. As for its simplicity, there is to be considered: (1) its division of the social order into three undifferentiated classes; (2) its easy assumption that the interests of these classes are "one"; and (3) its utter silence as to the passions of men. These three considerations are elaborated by Madison in his speech of June 26. (The last is reserved for later treatment.)

> In all civilized Countries the people fall into different classes having a real or supposed difference of interests. There will be creditors and debtors, farmers, merchants and manufacturers. There will be particularly the distinction of rich and poor. It was true, as had been observed by Mr. Pinckney, we had not among us those hereditary distinctions of rank which were a great source of the contests in the ancient Governments as well as the modern States of Europe, nor those extremes of wealth or poverty which characterize the latter. We cannot however be regarded, even at this time, as one homogeneous mass, in which every thing that

---

* It is obvious from the above that, contrary to Morgenthau, Pinckney's vision of America did indeed contain a "substantive ideal and achievement." Certainly it was *not* "intangible, shapeless, and procedural." Surely the achievement of *independence,* by means of the ownership of land, is a solid goal. Surely the discouragement of a large-scale factory system is solidly significant for a people's way of life. But that goal, for good or bad, is passé. In its place we have "equality in freedom," the likes of which was never encouraged by the Founding Fathers. But what is lacking in the agrarian vision—and this is more true of Jefferson than of Pinckney —is a *constructive* view of government. How indeed can such a view be forthcoming when, consistent with the democratic vision of Jefferson, "that government is best which governs least." But is a constructive view of government—an *architectonic* view of government—lacking on the part of men like Washington and Hamilton?

affects a part will affect in the same manner the whole. In framing a system which we wish to last for ages, we should not lose sight of the changes which ages will produce.

The changes which Madison anticipated in America will be considered in due time; but perhaps it was mention of these changes that induced Pinckney to propose the enormous property qualification referred to earlier. Be this as it may, one fact remains clear: Pinckney's vision of American society was—or became—colored by oligarchic sentiments, so that even here we find exemplified the principles of a *mixed regime*. But now let us turn to the more complex problems presented by Madison's speech of June 26 on the tenure of the Senate. First, however, I must explain to the reader why the tenure issue was again before the Convention.

On June 25, a number of delegates expressed the desire to provide for partial and periodic rotation of the Senate's membership (their main object: to insure greater continuity of public policy). Because a senatorial term of seven years—the term decided on June 12—was not convenient for the purpose, that decision was voided and the entire issue left open for June 26. Now on this day—the day on which the Senate received its existing tenure—it was proposed by Nathaniel Gorham of Massachusetts, and seconded by James Wilson, that Senators be appointed for a term of six years and that one-third be rotated biennially. Opposing this motion, General Charles C. Pinckney of South Carolina[3] argued that a term longer than four years might detach Senators from the interests of their respective states. It was precisely to foster such detachment, however, that George Read of Delaware proposed that members of the Senate be appointed for nine years and that one-third be rotated triennially.[4] After a seconding motion by Jacob Broome (also from Delaware), James Madison rose to speak in behalf of Read's proposal. And thus do we come to the central concern of this chapter.

It may be helpful to note at the very outset that the form and language of Madison's speech of June 26 makes it virtually certain that he was the principal author of *Federalist 63*—of the five essays devoted to the Senate, one of the two most important ones.[5] Indeed, after reading the notes of his speech and turning to *Federalist 63* (which I shall do later), one soon feels that Madison did the same. And yet, if Madison did in fact have these notes before him when writing *Federalist 63*, he certainly did not fail to use caution in deciding which parts of his speech should be included in this essay and thus be expanded for the general public. But this is mentioned only to indicate that Madison's speech requires particularly close attention.

The issue is the tenure of the United States Senate and Madison is speaking on behalf of a nine-year term. He begins with the following statement: "In order to judge of the form to be given to this institution, it will be proper to take a view of the ends to be served by it." The *form* of the Senate may be regarded as the means of achieving the *ends* of the Senate. The means must be commensurate with the ends, must be of the same character as the ends. These ends are, first, "to protect the people against their rulers," and second, "to protect the people against the transient impressions into which they themselves might be led." The form of the Senate, which is to say its political character, must somehow be elicited from these ends. Now to say that one end or purpose of the Senate is to protect the people from their rulers can only mean that the Senate is to protect the people against a body of rulers *other* than itself. This body of rulers, of course, is the House of Representatives, as may be confirmed in *Federalist 63*. There it is said that the people "may possibly be betrayed by the representatives of the people," that is, by their own elected Representatives.[6] But since Representatives are elected by the people, the Senate, in protecting the people against their Represen-

tatives, would ultimately be protecting them against themselves! This is not to deny a distinction between the people
and their Representatives. Nevertheless, it must be remembered that the Senate is to protect the people against their
own "transient impressions," and such impressions, Madison
said on June 12, may affect, to the people's detriment, their
choice of Representatives. It thus turns out that the two
ends which Madison attributes to the Senate are fundamentally one and the same, namely, *to check the democracy.*[7]

The "two" ends or purposes of the Senate having been
laid down, Madison continued:

> A people deliberating in a temperate moment . . . on the
> plan of Government most likely to secure their happiness,
> would first be aware, that those charged with the public
> happiness, might betray their trust. An obvious precaution
> against this danger would be to divide the trust between
> *different* bodies of men, who might watch and check each
> other.[8]

Here, in brief, is what is known as the principle of "checks
and balances." Now to grasp the fundamental significance
of this principle for the character of the American Constitution, it will be necessary to suppress the tendency to
think of it solely in mechanical or in negative terms. A
more interesting challenge is to elicit the specifically human
qualities and purposes which the principle of checks and
balances is ultimately intended to serve and which give to
this principle the seriousness it possessed for the Founding
Fathers. In the present context, however, we need only consider the principle of checks and balances as it applies to
the legislature. Accordingly, notice that the principle requires a division of the legislature, not between *two* bodies
of men, but as Madison says, between *different* bodies of
men. This use of the term "different" is most significant, as
the following will bear out. In *Federalist 62*, of which Madi-

son was very likely the principal author, the Senate is spoken of as a second branch of the legislature "distinct" from the first, the first being the House of Representatives. How the word *distinct* is to be understood is prepared for a little earlier where Madison alludes to some advantage to be gained from instituting a Senate by "select appointment." The advantage, of course, but one never made explicit in *Federalist 62,* is that appointment by the state legislatures is likely to secure to the Senate men of wisdom and virtue.[9] The term "select" has precisely these connotations, and that such connotations are intended is confirmed in *Federalist 63.* At the very outset of this essay, and once again a few paragraphs later, Madison refers to the Senate as the "select" member of the government. Reading further we learn that the Senate is to be composed of the "temperate and respectable body of citizens" who, without Madison actually saying so, are to be appointed by the state legislatures. Finally, and later still, in warning against the danger of "popular fluctuations," Madison says that this danger will be greater where the legislative power "is lodged in the hands of one body of men, than where the concurrence of separate and *dissimilar* bodies are required."[10] We see, therefore, that the principle of checks and balances requires a division of the legislature between two "dissimilar" or "distinct" or "different" branches—that is, between two branches having different or distinct or dissimilar *forms.* Since the form of one branch, the House of Representatives, is to be democratic, the form of the other branch, the Senate, must be other than democratic. But inasmuch as the Senate is to be composed of men noted for wisdom and virtue, surely its form will have to be aristocratic.[11] How else will the Senate be able to check the democracy? But we have already seen that the *form* of the Senate must be *commensurate* with its *ends.*

It is evident from these considerations that the principle of checks and balances must ultimately be understood in

terms of a relationship between two more fundamental principles: the democratic principle on the one hand, the aristocratic principle on the other. To clarify the relationship
between these two principles, consider again Madison's
speech of June 26, especially as to the character of the
people whose minds lie open before him.

Having divided the legislature between different bodies
of men,

> It would next occur to such a people, that they themselves
> were liable to temporary errors, through want of information
> as to their true interest, and that men chosen for a short
> term, and employed but a small portion of that in public
> affairs, might err from the same cause. This reflection would
> naturally suggest that the Government be so constituted,
> as that one of its branches might have an opportunity of
> acquiring competent knowledge of the public interests.
> Another reflection equally becoming a people on such an
> occasion, would be that they themselves, as well as a numer-
> ous body of Representatives, were liable to err also, from
> fickleness and passion. A necessary fence against this danger
> would be to select a portion of enlightened citizens, whose
> limited number and firmness might seasonably interpose
> against impetuous counsels.

What a remarkable people has Madison drawn for us—a
people so candid, so modest, so uncorrupted by flattery.
Realizing that they are subject to error through ignorance
and through passion, that they may not always understand
their true interests, this people, we are given to believe,
would institute a Senate to stand against them in their
moments of folly. At the same time, they would have this
Senate stand against the occasional follies of their own
chosen Representatives. This is indeed a remarkable people,
for they would willingly impose limits on their own sovereignty! Of course, much of this is but the play of Madison's rhetoric. The people he has presented here as deliberating on a plan of government are not to be confused with

the multitude whose opinions on government, it will be recalled from the debates of June 12, Madison did not profess to know. Nevertheless, here, as there, Madison permits us to see that, any appearances to the contrary notwithstanding, the government or constitution he seeks to establish is not meant to be *organized* according to the principle of *popular sovereignty.*[12] That he would institute a Senate to oppose not only the passions of the people but their misguided opinions indicates that, for Madison, a well-founded government does not exist simply for the people's pleasure; that the art of government does not consist in ministering to all the people's wants and wishes. The people, he so much as said, do not always know what is good for them: they do not always want what they need or need what they want. In other words, the will of the people is not to be identified with the public good. The very same conclusion may be drawn from *Federalist 63.*[13] There Madison points out that it is not the will of the people but rather "the cool and deliberate sense of the community" that ought to prevail over the government. The cool and deliberate sense of the community, however, is to be represented *in* government by the Senate. For the Senate is to be composed of "temperate" and "enlightened" citizens whose task, according to *Federalist 63,* is to uphold the authority of "reason, justice and truth"—to uphold that authority over against the passions and follies of the multitude. It should therefore be evident that however much Madison may affirm, or appear to affirm, the principle of popular sovereignty, he would nevertheless organize the government (and indeed the community) in such a way as to make it extremely difficult for the people to determine the policies of government unless their will conformed to reason, justice, and truth. But now to probe a little deeper into the principle of checks and balances.

Again and again Madison decried the passions of the people. Too often the passions of the people are the rulers of the people. These rulers must be checked and balanced by other rulers, by rulers who are governed by reason, who are motivated by a desire for justice, who, in so being governed and motivated, teach men to seek and honor truth. The people require educators. They require a high-toned Senate. "What bitter anguish would not the people of Athens have often escaped if their government had contained so provident a safeguard against the tyranny of their own passions."[14] But what passion or passions of the multitude is the Senate particularly to check or constrain? A clue to this question may be found in the speech mentioned earlier. The reader will recall that, in criticizing Pinckney's optimistic and egalitarian vision of American society, Madison said: "In framing a system which we wish to last for ages, we should not lose sight of the changes which ages will produce." Immediately following this statement he continued:

> An increase of population will of necessity increase the proportion of those who will labour under all the hardships of life, and *secretly sigh* for a more equal distribution of its blessings. . . . No agrarian attempts have yet been made in this Country, but symptoms of a *leveling spirit* . . . have sufficiently appeared in certain quarters to give notice of the future danger. (Italics added)

Now the question as to what passion or passions require the constraint of the Senate resolves itself into the question: What passion underlies or is identical with the *leveling spirit?* Inasmuch as Madison speaks of the leveling spirit in connection with those who *secretly sigh* for a more equal distribution of life's blessings, it can hardly be doubted that the passion in question is none other than *envy*. Again consider the meaning of this term.

It was said in the last chapter that envy, in its neutral form, is a *longing* for another's superior advantages. In its negative form, however, this longing is mingled with ill will or *resentment* toward the one possessing superior advantages.[15] In either form the object of envy may be another's wealth or his status or even his character. But envy is not simply a phenomenon of mere individuals; it may assume class proportions. Indeed, should envy coexist in the leveling spirit, its ultimate aim would be to render all men equal by reducing them to a level of mediocrity. Can it be that this is what Madison sees in the leveling spirit, an envy of such scope and magnitude as to endanger the very order and diversity essential to civilized society—an envy which I am tempted to call "democratic envy"? If such a conclusion is to stand, however, it will require a foundation of evidence deeper and broader than that provided in Madison's speech of June 26. Fortunately, Madison provides this foundation in *Federalist 10*.

Though the term "leveling spirit" does not appear in *Federalist 10* (or in any of *The Federalist* papers), in this essay will be found its cautiously phrased equivalent, for the leveling spirit is none other than the spirit of *majority faction*.[16] Hence, whatever be the ultimate aim of majority faction, the same will be the ultimate aim of the leveling spirit. But to arrive at this aim, it will be necessary to proceed by way of Madison's analysis of faction per se, its causes and its remedy.

According to Madison, the causes of faction originate in the differences of opinions, passions, and interests which exist among men. But while faction could not arise without these differences, neither could civilization.[17] To remedy the evil of faction by removing its causes would thus be destructive of civilization, that is, of civil society.[18] It would require nothing less than "giving to every citizen the same opinions, the same passions, and the same interests." Not only is such uniformity undesirable, it is also, as a remedy, impracticable. Says Madison:

As long as the reason of man continues fallible, and he is at liberty to exercise it, different opinions will be formed. As long as the connection subsists between his reason and self-love, his opinions and passions will have a reciprocal influence on each other. . . .

To this Madison adds: "The diversity in the faculties of men, from which the rights of property originate, is not less an insuperable obstacle to a uniformity of interests." This diversity in men's faculties would appear to be the fundamental obstacle to *any* kind of uniformity. But leaving this open for a moment, let us consider first what Madison means by "property."

In a letter appearing in the *National Gazette* (March 29, 1792), Madison expounds upon the meaning of property as follows:

This term in its particular application means 'That domination which one man claims and exercises over the external things of the world, in exclusion of every other individual.' In its larger and juster meaning, it embraces every thing to which a man may attach a value and have a right; and which leaves to every one else the like advantage. In the former sense, a man's land, or merchandise, or money is called his property. . . . In the latter sense, a man has property in his opinions and the free communication of them. He has a property of peculiar value in his religious opinions, and in the profession and practice dictated by them. He has property very dear to him in the safety and liberty of his person. He has an equal property in the free use of his faculties and free choice of the objects on which to employ them. In a word, as a man is said to have a right to his property, he may equally be said to have a property in his rights.[19]

Bearing in mind Madison's broad conception of property, and noting that it includes the use of one's faculties, the reader will see in *Federalist 37* that Madison includes among these faculties judgment, volition, desire, memory, and imagination. Now men may differ as to these faculties in two ways. From the viewpoint of common sense, they may differ without being superior or inferior—in which case the differences would lie primarily in the concerns or objects of these faculties. For example, one person may display good judgment on matters of law, another on matters of enterprise; or one man may desire the honors of public office, another this or that form of property. But in addition to such differences, men may differ in the sense of being *unequal* in these various faculties—in which case every difference which follows would be only secondary. Thus Madison speaks of the "different and unequal faculties of acquiring property," from which results "the possession of different degrees and kinds of property." Hence it may be inferred that the rights of property originate not only from the diversity of men's faculties but from the inequality of men's faculties. Indeed, it may also be inferred that this inequality of men's faculties is precisely what constitutes the most fundamental obstacle to a uniformity of opinions, passions, and interests. But such inequality is a cause of faction; and we have seen that Madison regards any attempt to remedy faction by removing its causes as impracticable—perhaps even visionary.

> Theoretic politicians . . . have erroneously supposed that by reducing mankind to a perfect equality in their political rights, they would, at the same time, be perfectly equalized and assimilated in their possessions, their opinions, and their passions.

What these "theoretic politicians" overlook is that *men are not born equal in their natural endowments.* It is this fact, more than any other, which explains why Madison deems it impracticable, if not impossible, to remedy the evil of faction by removing its causes.

> The latent causes of faction are thus sown in the nature of man; and we see them everywhere brought into different

degrees of activity, according to the different circumstances of civil society.

The latent causes of faction are sown in the very nature of man, and among these causes is the inequality of men's faculties. Civil society may influence the degree to which this inequality of men's faculties becomes manifest, but it cannot fundamentally alter this inequality, at least not without destroying the liberty which is essential to civil society. Indeed, "The protection of these faculties," says Madison, "is the first object of government."[20] Negatively stated, this means that the first object of government is to guard against any attempt to remove the latent causes of faction! It means that the first object of government is to prevent any attempt to bring about a massive uniformity of opinions, passions, and interests. But since the first object of government must be commensurate with the principal danger confronting civil society, and since the principal danger, for Madison, is none other than *majority faction*, it follows that to protect the diverse and unequal faculties of men is to protect men of superior advantages from any attempt of the *many* to render all men equal by reducing them to a level of mediocrity. This danger is none other than the danger of the *leveling spirit*, which I have called "democratic envy."

At this point, let us pause and consider some of the philosophical implications of the preceding discussion. We have seen that Madison wished to institute a system of checks and balances to preserve the republic from the leveling spirit. To guard against that spirit is to guard against the degradation of the republican form of government. The cause of this degradation is inherent in one of the constitutive principles of a republic, namely, the principle of *equality*. When that principle supplants every other principle of the regime—when equality, in other words, becomes totalitarian—we have the ascendancy of the leveling spirit. But this only means that the leveling spirit emerges with the extension of equality beyond the limits prescribed by the republican form. These limits may be defined in terms of political equality as opposed to social and economic equality.[21] By political equality I mean the right of each adult person to have some influence on the making of laws. In a republic, however, this influence is limited and modified in a variety of ways. For example, the legislature is divided between two dissimilar branches, and the two branches are dissimilar in virtue of being constituted for different terms by different electors. As a consequence, the influence which citizens may have on the making of laws is for the most part *indirect*. The degradation of this process involves the substitution of *direct* for indirect influence by means of mass demonstrations and pressure groups. What I mean is this: The making of laws requires inquiry and deliberation, the weighing of alternative courses of action, consideration of immediate and long-range consequences—all of which necessitates some distance and detachment of legislators from the public at large—and all of which will not be forthcoming when legislators are subject to gross forms of direct influence. But so much for political equality. As for social and economic equality, neither is prescribed by the republican form of government. True, it is essential to the stability of a republic that there be a fairly prosperous middle class whose members comprise a large majority of the people. Nevertheless, social and economic equality will be limited in a republic primarily by the laws governing property. Private and public property will coexist, each in varying degrees depending partly on circumstances. When the distinction between private and public disappears, so too will the integrity of the republic: it will have succumbed to the leveling spirit.

I have argued that a republic imposes certain limits on the principle of equality; that it prescribes political, but not social and economic equality. This, by the way, is in perfect accord with the equality spoken of in the Declaration of Independence. There it is said that "all men are created equal." Equal in what respects? Equal in their unalienable or natural rights to "Life, Liberty and the pursuit of Happiness." Notice it is not said that men have a natural right to happiness but to the *pursuit* of happiness. The Declaration could not reasonably affirm a right to happiness if only because happiness is very much a personal achievement, something to be won by our own, though not entirely by our own, effort. Furthermore, the extent to which we may achieve happiness depends largely on our physical and moral and intellectual endowments—say also our worth or merit. In these respects all men are not equal, and the Declaration does not suggest the contrary. But as we cannot infer from the Declaration that all men are equal in character, worth, or merit, we cannot infer from this supposedly democratic document that all men have a natural right to social and economic equality. (Here again we enter the realm of personal achievement, at least so far as social and economic equality may be involved in the pursuit of happiness.)[22] Turning from the Declaration to the Constitution, there not the slightest suggestion is made of a right to social and economic equality. Indeed, of the ideal ends enumerated in the Preamble, equality is not even mentioned! (Embodied in the Constitution, of course, is a large measure of political and legal equality.) There is, however, an ideal end which appears in the Preamble and which the leveling spirit would identify with equality, namely, *justice*. And it is precisely when justice is identified and made coextensive with equality that we have the degradation of the republican form of government.

The justice fostered in a republic is a mixture of democratic justice and oligarchic-aristocratic justice. I hyphenate the latter under the assumption that a connection generally exists between wealth and talent. (It is because of this connection, but also because the wealthy and the talented constitute a minority, that the terms "oligarchy" and "aristocracy" are frequently identified.) But to facilitate the exposition, let us say that a republic fosters a mixture of democratic and aristocratic justice, bearing in mind that the latter is not unalloyed. Now as a matter of principle, democratic justice would treat all men as equal regardless of their differences.[23] In contrast, aristocratic justice would treat all men according to their worth or merit.[24] To promote justice —the justice of the Preamble—is to promote the good of men in those respects in which they are entitled to equal treatment and in those respects in which they are entitled to unequal treatment. It is to promote the common good and the common good *par excellence.* The common good requires that government "insure domestic Tranquility, provide for the common defence, promote the general Welfare, and secure the Blessings of Liberty." To "secure the blessings of liberty" (apart from its equalitarian aspects) is to secure those goods which men achieve or acquire by the superior use of their faculties.[25] If these goods be excluded, the common good may then be reduced to the protection of life or to security in general. In contrast, the common good *par excellence* requires that government foster, not merely the life of ease and comfort, but the life appropriate to man *qua* man. That life is the life of human excellence. In the words of James Wilson: "The cultivation and improvement of the human mind [is] the most noble object [of government]."[26] The common good and the common good *par excellence* are not in essential conflict. The conflict arises from the question: What good should constitute the ruling principle of government? It is this question that underlies the controversy as to *who should rule,* a controversy involving justice. Here, the democratic and aristocratic conceptions of justice again confront each other. For the democrat, justice requires the political formula, "one man one vote"—again, equality regardless of wealth or merit. For the aristocrat, political power should be distributed among men according to their capacity to contribute to the common good and the common good *par excellence.* These two conceptions of justice coexist in a republic. Their co-existence is preserved by a system of institutional checks and balances. In the system proposed by Madison, the Senate would uphold aristocratic justice over against the democratic justice upheld by the House of Representatives. The Senate would thereby prevent the principle of equality from overstepping its republican limits or from becoming identified with justice. We see, therefore, that the system of checks and balances is intended to prevent the degrada-tion of the republican form of government, which is to say, to prevent the transformation of a *mixed regime* into a democracy.

Having analyzed the leveling spirit, and having con-sidered its philosophical implications for the republican form of government, we can now more fully appreciate the significance of the Senate in Madison's thoughts. For now it should be evident that one of the main functions of the Senate is to guard against the stultifying uniformity and egalitarianism of a *mass society.* (This may also be regarded as a function of *federalism,* a principle which the Senate alone was to exemplify.) Conversely, it may be said that one of the main functions of the Senate was to be the guard-ian of "pluralism."[27] But recall that pluralism is a mixed blessing. While it may forestall the egalitarianism of a mass society, it may engender another evil, the evil of faction. Or while pluralism may hinder men from becoming united by some interest opposed to the common good, it may also hinder men from becoming united in behalf of the common good. Necessary for civilized society, pluralism is not suffi-cient for the achievement of a good society. Necessary for republican government, pluralism is not sufficient for achieving the ends of good government. Hence it is that the Senate must not only safeguard pluralism, but over and above this, it must foster among the members of society a sense of common direction and purpose, or as Madison said, a "sense of national character."[28] Over and above the diversity of opinions, passions, and interests, the Senate must uphold the authority of reason, justice, and truth.

It was just said that the Senate is to foster in America a sense of national character. This it can only do by fostering a regime of *law*. And it is precisely in this light that we are to understand why the tenure of the Senate was so important in Madison's thoughts. For without a lengthy tenure the Senate would be incapable of maintaining continuity in the laws, would be incapable of formulating consistent, comprehensive, and long-range plans of national significance. Without a lengthy tenure, the membership of the Senate would be subject to frequent change, and so too the laws. Madison states the problem this way:

> The mutability in the public councils arising from a rapid succession of new members, however qualified they may be, points out, in the strongest manner, the necessity of some stable institution in the government. . . . From this change of men must proceed a change of opinions; and from a change of opinions, a change of measures. But a continual change even of good measures is inconsistent with every rule of prudence and every prospect of success.[29]

To the pragmatist who tends to look upon law simply as a means of solving the current and ever-changing problems of society, this last statement may appear rather strange. Yet when Madison goes on to say that "the most deplorable effect of [excessive mutability in the laws] is that diminution of attachment and reverence which steals into the hearts of the people," it is evident that we have here a conception of law more profound and comprehensive than the pragmatic one. Indeed, reflection will show that the role of the Senate, as described in this and in the preceding chapter, necessarily depends on its capacity to inculcate, in all citizens, an attachment and reverence for law itself.

Now what is there about law which may reasonably earn men's attachment and even evoke their reverence? Religious explanations aside, perhaps it is something like this. Law is a bond which unites the generations of mankind, a bond which endows the individual with depth and solidity, which facilitates the use of his faculties—this, by securing, on the one hand, public tranquility, and on the other, life, liberty, and the rewards of honest labor. The attachment and reverence we owe to law is reasonable inasmuch as law gives us a place in the community, defines or clarifies our rights and duties, fosters justice and the common good. Finally, the attachment and reverence we owe to law is reasonable insofar as the rule of law exemplifies the rule of reason as opposed to the passions. To be sure, reverence is itself a passion. But as it mingles love with *awe,* the passion of reverence is not to rule but to obey, nay more, to preserve unchanged the very object to which it subordinates itself. Indeed, reverence will not cling to that which is ephemeral or mutable. Thus, in *Federalist 49* it is said that frequent change in the laws will deprive them "of that veneration which time bestows on every thing."[30] May it not even be said that such mutability will eventually lead to disrespect for law itself? If the laws of society are continually changing, is it not obvious that there exists in that society no settled convictions? Will not the members of that society regard law merely as a means of solving current problems? Will it not be true, however, that these solutions are no solutions at all—just makeshift or temporary expediency? "What indeed," asked Madison in *Federalist 62,* "are all the repealing, explaining, and amending laws, which fill and disgrace our voluminous codes, but so many monuments of deficient wisdom?" And yet, will not such a state of affairs be itself the cause of new problems, problems calling for new laws—and this because the community has no abiding goals, no wise consistency of purpose? But what kind of government would tolerate such a state of affairs? It was said a moment ago that the rule of law exemplifies the rule of reason. (And it was also said that the Senate is to uphold the authority of reason over against the passions.) Now when laws are voluminous and constantly changing, we may be certain that the government is not under the authority of reason so much as under the control of the passions.

> But it is the reason, alone . . . that ought to control and reg-
> ulate the government. The passions ought to be controlled
> and regulated by the government. (*Federalist 49*)

But if the government is controlled by the passions under a dispensation of constantly changing laws, we may safely assume that the government has wholly succumbed to the *democracy*. This being so, the very mutability of the laws will reflect the mutable wants and wills of changing majorities, or the aimless interplay of diverse and self-seeking interest groups. "Who gets what, when, and how"—this, I have already suggested, will become the science of legislation. But this may be the political science of a community in process of disintegration. Thus may we understand why Madison regarded a continual change even of good laws as unwise and self-defeating. But let us approach the problem from another perspective.

One of the principal purposes of law is to establish what is called "consensus," a term whose significance may better be understood in light of the consensus established by our fundamental law, the Constitution. We see in the Preamble of the Constitution a statement of ideal ends or purposes. Then follows a set of institutions and procedures all of which are intended to foster these ideal ends or purposes, and not only for the sake of the living, but for posterity as well. The whole document represents a consensus, an agreement entered into by diverse men, by diverse men seeking "to form a more perfect Union." Now whether a law be fundamental or not, the consensus it establishes will somehow reflect or embody the goals or values of the community as well as the manner in which the community has agreed to pursue these goals or values. More particularly, the law will prescribe and make known certain rules of action or standards of judgment without which diverse men could hardly unite in the pursuit of common objectives. Thus, to say that law establishes consensus is to say that law makes possible the enjoyment of a common way of life and hence the very existence of community. But can this be true where the laws are "so voluminous that they cannot be read, or so incoherent that they cannot be understood; . . . or undergo such incessant changes that no man, who knows what the law is to-day, can guess what it will be tomorrow."[31] Indeed, if the law is continually changing, does it not follow that the consensus—the very way of life of the community—is continually changing. But in what sense can we then speak of the community as a community? If, amidst change, nothing endures, the community can hardly be more than a willy-nilly aggregation of individuals. But this only means that a community given to such legislative mutability or to excessive law-making is preparing for its own ultimate disintegration—whatever be the quality of each law.

Through its power to initiate legislation and to restrain and modify the law-making propensities of the democratic House of Representatives, the Senate is to endow the laws with "system" and "wisdom" and the nation itself with consistency of purpose. The laws are to exemplify the authority of reason, and, by the justice of their ends, to gain the people's attachment and reverence. While the Senate will have a regard for, and partly reflect, different opinions as well as a diversity of interests, its members will have a higher regard for truth and for those interests which are conducive to the "collective and permanent welfare" of the nation. Length of tenure will give them a "permanent motive to devote the intervals of public occupation to the study of the laws, the affairs, and the comprehensive interests of their country." It will afford them "sufficient permanency to provide for such objects as require a continued attention," objects whose achievement will depend "on a succession of well-chosen and well-connected measures, which have a gradual and perhaps unobserved operation." Clearly, Madison—and it is from *Federalist* 62 and 63 from which these thoughts are taken—envisioned a Senate similar in character to that envisioned by Hamilton.

I shall now conclude this chapter by drawing certain contrasts between these two authors of *The Federalist*. Though Madison's language is more democratic than Hamilton's, it is also more cautious, more disguised, more *rhetorical*. Indeed, the secret of Madison's rhetoric lies simply in this: it seeks to promote aristocratic ends under a facade of democratic arguments. This is not to say that Madison's aristocratic sentiments are as deep and pervasive as Hamilton's. Still, the reader should bear in mind—and the remarkable unity of *The Federalist* bears witness to this—that the major differences between these two statesmen did not emerge until *after* the formation of the new government. Nevertheless, some lines of divergence were visible at the time of the Constitutional Convention.

If there is a single point from which these lines may be said to diverge, it is "pluralism." It is from pluralism that I derive the distinction between the Madisonian and Hamiltonian conceptions of American society. Not that Hamilton opposed, while Madison favored, a rich diversity. Quite the contrary, as may be seen in Hamilton's brilliant and comprehensive "Report on Manufactures," a report urging Congress to encourage and subsidize industries in various sections of the country.[32] But whereas Madison would foster diversity primarily as a means of avoiding an evil, namely, the evil of majority faction, Hamilton—who in this respect was less optimistic than Madison—would foster diversity primarily as a means of attaining a good, namely, a more perfect, *union!*[33] How diversity is to contribute to unity is explained elsewhere.* Here, suffice to say that Hamilton does not wish to foster mere diversity, but the diversity essential to *self-sufficiency*. Mere diversity, so far as he was concerned, is frequently petty, while its effects are apt to be pernicious.[34] In a country as vast as America, a country whose most urgent need is unity of will and purpose, diversity is not to be encouraged save under the guidance of a wise and energetic government—and then only with a view to strengthening the bonds of union. But it should not be supposed that Madison was unaware of the tension between diversity on the one hand, and unity of will and purpose on the other. Madison's Senate would certainly safeguard "pluralism." But it is not generally known that Madison would have given to the Senate the power to veto *all* laws passed by the state legislatures![35] The mere fact that he would invest such a power in the Senate, and not in Congress as a whole, indicates that he was well aware of the pernicious and divisive effects of an unguided pluralism. But here emerges another difference between Madison and Hamilton. For here the question arises: How are the diverse and competitive elements of American society to be guided?

---

* As I was about to point out, Hamilton did not wish to foster mere diversity, but the diversity essential to *self-sufficiency*. In the process of making a nation self-sufficient, the economic interests of the nation become more and more *interdependent*. Thus, one reason why he wished to encourage the growth of new industries was to make agriculture dependent on domestic as opposed to foreign manufactures. As the prosperity of the one would come to depend on the prosperity of the other, sectional rivalries would tend to diminish (especially if industries were introduced in the South and the various parts of the nation were linked by a system of roads and canals).

Both Madison and Hamilton were committed to the principle of checks and balances. Both recognized that this principle involves a relationship between two more fundamental principles, one democratic, the other aristocratic. They differed, however, as to the character of this relationship. For Madison, the aristocratic principle is to modify the operation of the democratic principle. Nevertheless, in respect to the exercise of political power, the Senate, though aristocratic, would be little more than a *coequal* branch of the legislature. Hamilton would have gone further. He wanted the Senate to be the principal law-making body. He wanted the aristocratic principle to chart the course of political life. He knew this posed dangers to the body politic. Power might be abused, the more so when concentrated. But no *great* good is to be expected from a mere division of power. Somewhere there must be leadership. That leadership might not come from the Senate. But the Senate, as a permanent law-making body, would facilitate the exercise of leadership. Restraints there must be; hence a system of checks and balances. But now, and as Hamilton intended, the democratic principle would check the operation of the aristocratic principle, and not vice versa!

I have put off to the last the problem of designating the Madisonian and Hamiltonian conceptions of American society. As for Hamilton, it would be all too easy to say that his vision of America is aristocratic. I prefer to think of it, however, as *political*. What does this mean? Hamilton wanted *the political to be the ruling principle of the whole.* The government would not be one entity amidst congeries of others. It would not exist merely to regulate, impartially, the diverse interests of society. It would not be a mere policeman maintaining law and order. No, Hamilton wanted more than this. He wanted the government to govern. He wanted a *constructive* government, a government of *creative* power, the power to shape the course of American society, to endow American society with a heightened sense of unity and national character. Hamilton loved liberty, but liberty with grandeur of purpose.

Turning to the problem of designating Madison's conception of American society, here I am somewhat at a loss. To make Madison the father of pluralism is to do him an injustice, or to endow his wayward and less thoughtful descendants with unwarranted respectability. For Madison, pluralism was yet an unsettled problem. For his descendants, pluralism is an unquestioned dogma. Still the mind lusts for a univocal concept to characterize a world of thought, a single unambiguous word which, like the word-magic of primitives, is to give us control over forces the mind cannot otherwise behold. I have no such word or concept to designate Madison's vision of America. He advances, and to an approximately equal extent, two principles which are not reducible to one: the democratic principle and the aristocratic principle. With great skill he helped to implant these two principles in the Constitution of American government. But these two principles would also coexist in the constitution of American society. They would enter the constitution of the human soul, the soul of the American citizen. That soul will be in tension. It will seek unity while it praises diversity. It will desire change and yet a sense of permanence. It will be acquisitive on the one hand, yet public spirited on the other. It will love equality, yet aspire to excellence.

9

The Presidency and its Intended Role In American Political Life

> You nor I, my friend, may not live to see the day, but most assuredly it will come, when every vital interest of the state will be merged in the all-absorbing question of *who shall be the next PRESIDENT.*
>
> ALEXANDER HAMILTON[1]

THUS FAR our inquiry into the political philosophy of the American Constitution has been concerned with the intended character of the Senate and the House of Representatives. We have examined the different ways in which the two law-making bodies were to be constituted, the different kinds of men intended to be legislators, and the different principles and purposes by which they were to be governed.[2] Hence, we may now turn to the Presidency.

[166]

§

Introduction

The Constitution was established "in Order to form a more perfect Union." The Presidency is the symbol of that Union. Indeed, it marks the decisive point of departure from the Articles of Confederation. The Articles did not provide for an *independent* executive; nor did they provide for a *unitary* executive. It was precisely here that opposition to the Presidency first arose. It was the fact that independent executive power was to be placed in the hands of a single man that occasioned fear of monarchy. It is with this fact, however, that the *nation* was born, was to take its place among the sovereign powers of the earth. But how are we to understand the Presidency in the light of political philosophy? How was it intended to function within the system of checks and balances? What is the significance of the so-called "electoral college"? Was it a mere compromise dictated by expedience? Or does it embody some architectonic principle? What did the Founders mean by *energy* in the executive? What did they mean by executive *responsibility*? What kind of man was expected to occupy the office of the Presidency? What motives were to influence his conduct? What kind of relationship was meant to exist between the Presidency and public opinion—between the President and the people? These and other questions will be elucidated during the course of this inquiry into the intended role of the Presidency in American political life.

We have seen that the system of checks and balances requires a division of the legislature between two bodies each exemplifying different political principles. Given such

a division, however, a tendency exists for one body to encroach upon the other. The reason is this: Each body has
different notions as to *who* should rule, different notions
corresponding to the different classes which the two bodies
represent. Because the question of who should rule is a
matter of justice, and because each of the two bodies wishes
to see its own conception of justice prevail, there is a constant tendency toward mutual encroachment.[3] To check
this tendency, or to preserve the balance of what would
otherwise be an unstable system, a third body is necessary.
This third body, it should be obvious, must be so constituted
as to be independent of the other two. What is less obvious
is that it must partake of the character of the other two and
yet have an identity of its own. It must partake of the
character of the two for a number of reasons, among which
are these: (1) to facilitate its alignment with one should
the one be encroached upon by the other; (2) to facilitate
its cooperation with both in the common enterprises of the
regime. It must have an identity of its own for a number of
reasons, among which are these: (1) to regulate or subor-
dinate, within itself, the jarring principles which it shares
with the other two; (2) to reinforce the desire for its own
preservation. In other words, that which is to balance two
opposing principles must somehow embody yet transcend
the mean between these two principles.[4] The House of Representatives exemplifies the democratic principle. Its members are elected by the people. Its tenure is of rather short duration. Its general purpose is to represent the interests of the
many. The Senate exemplifies the "oligarchic" principle.[5]
Its members are appointed by the state legislatures. Its tenure is of rather lengthy duration. Its general purpose is to
represent the interests of the *few*. Consider the mode of
choosing the President. On the surface, it lies roughly in a
mean between the modes of choosing Senators and Representatives. Consider the term of the President. It too lies in

a mean between the terms of Senators and Representatives. Consider the general function of the President as stated in *Federalist 70*, namely, to secure "liberty against the enterprises and assaults of ambition, of faction, and of anarchy." From this it may be inferred that the President is to guard the republic against the extremes of oligarchy and democracy. But here the question arises: What was to prevent the Presidency from succumbing to one or the other of these extremes? The answer to this question lies hidden in what I regard as the most brilliantly conceived aspect of the Constitution, namely, the presidential electoral system.* To elucidate the underlying purposes and philosophical implications of that system, I propose the following order of inquiry. I shall first reconstruct the debates out of which the electoral system emerged. With this as a foundation, I shall then proceed to analyze the system itself. This analysis will yield the architectonic principle of the Presidency, and it will then remain to consider how this principle was to shape the character of American political life.

I

Of the countless issues debated during the proceedings of the Convention, the mode of electing the President was the most difficult and perplexing. Not before September 6 was the issue finally resolved, and this, despite the fact that, as early as June 2, and twice again during the month of July, the Convention voted overwhelmingly in favor of an executive chosen by the national legislature. Why was this mode of election eventually rejected? Why, indeed, were a host of others?

* Fully aware of the failure of that system, I present the following as a refutation of the prevailing view represented by John Roche who describes the electoral college as a "Rube Goldberg mechanism" (*op. cit.*, p. 811).

On June 1, the Convention took up the seventh resolution of the Virginia Plan which provided, in part,

> that a National Executive . . . be chosen by the National Legislature for the term of (   ) years . . . and to be ineligible a second time . . .

Two considerations recommended this method of election to many of the delegates. First, it was thought to be the most simple and convenient: by having the President elected by Congress, the problem of instituting and convening a special body of Electors would be precluded. Second, it was thought that congressmen would be the best qualified to choose for the Presidency a person of distinguished character and of *national* reputation. Nevertheless, some delegates saw in this method certain dangers and disadvantages. Wilson warned that a President elected by Congress would be dependent upon that body. Mason disagreed. Referring to the ineligibility clause, he pointed out that the independence of the Presidency could be secured by limiting its incumbent to a single term, thus removing any temptation on his part to court members of Congress for reelection. It could be argued, however, that presidential elections would in any event be preceded by political intrigue and corruption; that members of Congress and candidates for the Presidency would exchange votes for the promise of favors; hence, that the successful candidate would later show partiality to those who had promoted him. This, in effect, was Gerry's reply to Mason.[7] But Mason did not rest his defense solely on the ineligibility clause. For he thought that the independence of the President would also be sustained by investing him with a tenure of seven years (a term much longer than that of Representatives, to whom he would largely owe his election). Whatever the force of this argument, it could have no effect on Wilson who was opposed to the ineligibility clause in the first place.

When the issue was resumed on June 2, Wilson proposed that the President be elected in the following manner:

> That the States be divided into ( ) districts; and that the persons qualified to vote in each district for members of the first branch of the National Legislature elect ( ) members for their respective districts to be Electors of the Executive magistracy; that the said Electors . . . meet at ( ) and . . . proceed to elect by ballot [the] person in whom the Executive authority of the National Government shall be vested.

Notice that Wilson's proposal embodies the idea of a *single* college of Electors: all the Electors would convene in one place, like our national party conventions. Now when Hugh Williamson opposed the idea on grounds that it would entail great inconvenience—presumably to Electors from the distant parts of the Union—no one suggested the expedient of having the Electors meet in their respective states. Nor did anyone reject the idea on grounds that a single college of Electors would be susceptible to cabal and corruption. But leaving these considerations aside for the moment, notice too that the Electors of the President would be chosen by the people, as a consequence of which the state governments would be utterly excluded from the electoral process. The immediate effect of this, Gerry warned, would be to rouse the state politicians against the Constitution. To avoid such an eventuality, Gerry suggested that candidates for the Presidency be nominated by the state legislatures, the final choice devolving upon Electors chosen, perhaps, by the people. On June 9, however, he formally proposed that the President be elected by the state governors. This method, he said, would result in a wiser choice of a President and, at the same time, secure the independence and integrity of the executive office. Randolph thought otherwise. Indeed, he saw in this proposal as many defects as Gerry had seen in the previous ones. Just as candidates for the Presidency might court members of the national legislature, so might they court the governors of the several states. In any event, each governor would very likely choose a local favorite, a candidate partial to the interests of his own state. Finally, the candidate ultimately chosen by the governors would probably be of mediocre caliber; or as Governor Randolph said with charming simplicity: "Can you suppose they will ever raise the great oak, when they must sit as shrubs under its shade?" Apparently, few delegates could envision so idyllic a scene, for Gerry was unable to win a single state in support of his proposal. But Wilson was hardly more successful. For returning to the debates of June 2, the Convention rejected his electoral scheme, voting in favor of election of the President by the national legislature—by a margin of eight states to two. By a similar margin, the President was invested with a seven-year term and made ineligible for reelection. Thus matters stood until July 17.

Now before turning to the debates of this date, let us summarize the major considerations which thus far entered into the debates over the mode of electing the President. First, the electoral system should permit the electors, whomever they be, to accomplish their task in the shortest possible time and with the least inconvenience to themselves. Second, the system should secure the independence and integrity of the President by making it extremely difficult for presidential candidates to court their electors. Third, the system should hold the promise of advancing to the office of the Presidency a person of preeminent character. Fourth and finally, the electoral system should be designed in such a way as to gain the widest possible support for the Constitution itself. Clearly the mode of election adopted on June 2 was not free from at least one serious defect. But the same may be said of the proposed alternatives. The problem here (as elsewhere) was to reconcile immediate and long-range considerations—considerations of expediency and considerations of principle. Let us see how the delegates dealt with this problem.

On July 17, Gouverneur Morris proposed that the President be elected directly by the people, more precisely, "by the freeholders of the country." He cautioned the delegates that a President elected by Congress was more apt to be obsequious than meritorious; whereas if elected by the people he would "always" be a person of "distinguished character" and of "continental reputation." Sherman disagreed. The people, he declared, would seldom be sufficiently informed of such persons. Even if they were, their natural tendency would be to vote for a citizen of their own state, as a consequence of which, no candidate was likely to receive a majority of the popular vote. Coming to Morris' aid, Wilson suggested the expedient used in Massachusetts where, in the event a majority of the people did not concur in favor of any candidate, the election was thrown into the legislature. But here Pinckney objected that popular election of the President would favor the interests of the large states, that the most populous states would combine and elect whomsoever they pleased. To this Morris replied that it was not the people of the large states who would (or could) form such combinations, but rather their representatives in Congress. Other delegates, however, thought it unwise and dangerous to have the President elected by the people, for which reason, no doubt, Morris' proposal was defeated by a vote of nine states to one (the exception being his own state of Pennsylvania). Following this, the Convention reaffirmed its earlier decision in favor of congressional election of the President. And so might matters have stood were it not for the fact that on this same day of July 17, the Convention also decided—though by the narrowest margin—to strike out the *ineligibility clause!* The implications were profound.

We have seen that the ineligibility clause would not preclude intrigue and corruption between congressmen and candidates for the Presidency. It cannot be denied, however, that the removal of the clause would enormously increase the power of Congress over any President who wished to succeed himself in office. Indeed, Madison warned the Convention that the removal of the clause would not only subvert the executive, but that it would lead to legislative tyranny.° So firmly was Madison convinced of this that he preferred to invest the President with a permanent tenure rather than have him eligible for reelection. And when James McClurg introduced a motion to this effect, four out of ten states (including Virginia and Pennsylvania) voted in the affirmative! Perhaps the closeness of the vote, together with Madison's warning, persuaded the delegates to reconsider the ineligibility clause—and this they did on July 19.

On that day, motion to reinstitute the clause was made by Luther Martin. Again Morris rose, now to object not only to the motion but to the entire constitution of the executive. In a powerful speech profound in meaning, Morris discoursed at length on the characteristics required of the Presidency, as well as on the various purposes which he thought this institution ought to serve. It is the Presidency, he said, upon which the blessings of the union will ultimately depend. To secure these blessings, the Presidency will require sufficient "vigor" to pervade every part of this union. The power of the President to appoint "officers for the administration of public affairs" as well as "officers for the dispensation of Justice"—this will make possible the uniform execution and interpretation of the laws. The power of the President to veto acts of the legislature—this will discourage or prevent the enactment of unjust laws, or of laws which are unconstitutional. But neither of these powers will be availing if the President is elected by the legislature. The

---

° In other words, at stake on this issue was one of the fundamental principles of constitutional government, namely, that the legislative and executive powers must be exercised by separate *and* independent bodies. Where these two powers are combined, said Madison, quoting Montesquieu, there can be no liberty.

power of appointment will become an instrument of corruption. The veto power—especially if the President is eligible for reelection—will not be used. The legislature, thus unrestrained, will encroach upon the other departments and will thus endanger the rights and liberties of the people. But the President, said Morris,

> should be the guardian of the people, even of the lower classes, against Legislative tyranny, against the Great and the Wealthy who, in the course of things, will necessarily compose the Legislative body.*

Notice that in referring to the President as "the guardian of the people," Morris significantly adds, "*even* of the lower classes." Does this mean, in view of what he says of the "Great and the Wealthy," that the President should be especially concerned to protect the *middle class?* However this may be, if the President, said Morris, is to be the guardian of the people, he ought to be elected by the people, in which case he need not be restricted to a single term. Indeed, such a restriction (and here Morris anticipated *Federalist 72*)

> will destroy the great incitement to merit public esteem by taking away the hope of being rewarded with a reappointment. [This] may give a dangerous turn to one of the strongest passions in the human breast. The love of fame is the great spring to noble and illustrious actions. Shut the Civil road to Glory and [an ambitious President] may be compelled to seek it by the Sword.

On the other hand, said Morris, if the President is made ineligible for reelection, he may be tempted "to make the most of the short space of time allotted him, to accumulate wealth and provide for his friends." Finally, the ineligibility will produce violations of the very Constitution it is meant to secure. "[For] in moments of pressing danger, the

---

* It is evident from the sequel that Morris has primarily in view the danger of an oligarchic tyranny originating in the *Senate*.

tried abilities and established character of a favorite [President] will prevail over respect for the forms of the Constitution."

There can be little doubt of the influence of Morris' speech on the Convention. King agreed that the President should be reeligible, but that he should be appointed by Electors chosen by the people. Paterson also favored reeligibility, but suggested that the Electors be chosen by the states in a ratio that would allow to the smallest state one Elector and three to the largest. And when Ellsworth moved to have the President appointed by Electors chosen by the state legislatures, the motion was adopted, and by a wide margin![8] The ineligibility clause was then overwhelmingly rejected and, by an almost unanimous vote, the President's tenure was reduced to six years—this, perhaps to have his term correspond with that of the Senate. Clearly Morris had carried the day. His victory, however, was short-lived; for on July 24, the Convention, much to his dismay, reverted to congressional election of the President!*

Although it is not evident from the records of July 24 why the Convention reversed itself, the main reason may be adduced in light of principles already established. Thus, consider a remark of William Houston, who thought it unlikely "that capable men would undertake the service of Electors *from the more distant States.*" From the words I have italicized it may be inferred that, as of July 24, it was still assumed that *all* the Electors would meet at *one* place. And to anticipate the debates of July 25, it was almost certainly assumed that the Electors would meet *at the nation's capitol.* But with this proximity of Electors to congressmen and to possible candidates for the Presidency, there would again arise the problem of intrigue and corruption. Hence it could be argued, and apparently it was, that reverting to

---

* It should be noted that the New Hampshire delegation, which voted for reversal, did not take its seat at the Convention until July 23. New Hampshire's vote, however, was not decisive on this issue.

congressional election of the President had the advantage, not of greater purity, so to speak, but of greater simplicity and convenience. What this means, however, is that the Convention had yet to transcend the idea of a *single* college of Electors.

Now here let us pause a moment to reflect upon the significance of the preceding discussion for a contemporary prejudice that parades as "political realism." It should be apparent, to all but dogmatic skeptics, that the decision of July 24 cannot be adequately explained by the "interest group" theory of politics referred to in an earlier chapter. No doubt the Founders were influenced by a variety of "interests," as are all sophisticated men who pursue the vocation of politics. But *one* of their *interests* was simply to secure the integrity of presidential elections. This is strikingly evident in Wilson's reaction to the decision in question. For although he was still opposed to congressional election of the President, Wilson attempted to mitigate its acknowledged defects by proposing: (1) that not more than fifteen congressmen be drawn by *lot;* (2) that they proceed *immediately* to choose the President; and (3) that they *not separate until the choice is made.* Can there by any doubt of Wilson's *interest* or intention: to eliminate, so far as possible, the opportunity for intrigue between presidential electors and presidential candidates?* But the Founders had yet another interest, an interest in solving the following political problem. Thus, given the decision reverting to election of the President by Congress, how could the President be made eligible for reelection without undermining his independence? Here, Ellsworth made a clever but unsuccessful attempt to solve this problem. On July 25 he proposed:

---

* It should be noted that one objection raised against Wilson's really brilliant idea was that it left too much to chance. It could be argued, however, that chance would be no more decisive here than in any of the other methods thus far proposed. After all, the fifteen presidential Electors would be congressmen who, presumably, would be as well qualified as any other group of elected officials.

> That the Executive be appointed by the [National] Legislature, except when the magistrate last chosen shall . . . be[come] reeligible, in which case the choice shall be by Electors appointed by the Legislatures of the States for that purpose.

Notice that with this arrangement, Congress would elect the President only if the incumbent died or declined to remain in office! I need hardly pause to comment, save to say here is another example of a proposed compromise governed by long-range interests or considerations—a matter unexplored by the "interest group" theory of politics. But we shall see other examples of this as we probe further into the debates.

Although the problem of preserving the integrity of presidential elections and of securing the independence of the Presidency was not resolved on July 25, Madison's speech of this date helped to place the problem in a clearer perspective. At the very outset, Madison acknowledged that

> there are objections against every mode [of election] that has been or can be proposed. The election must be made either by some existing authority under the National or State Constitutions, or by some special authority derived from the people, or by the people themselves.

For reasons similar to those already discussed, Madison opposed any method of election that would place the *nomination* of the President in the hands of any *permanent institution* or branch of government established under the state or national constitutions.* But there was one reason why he was especially opposed to election by the national legislature (a reason which may later have been of decisive

---

* Is it not remarkable that Roche (*op. cit.*, p. 810) should disparage the "electoral college" saying "it had little in its favor as an institution"—this, when the system was deliberately designed to avoid election of the President by any *permanent or pre-established institution* whatsoever? That he should fail to see this can be attributed to the dogmatic skepticism which dominates adherents of the "interest group" theory of politics.

significance). Thus, noting that a President elected by Congress would actually be elected, not by Congress as a whole, but by its *majority party*, he warned the Convention that the views of that party would dominate the entire administration of government.[9] (This further explains why Madison saw in the ineligibility clause the only safeguard against legislative tyranny—really, the tyranny of a majority party.) Hence there remained but two alternatives: either the President should be chosen by a special body of Electors, or he should be chosen by the people. As for the first of these alternatives, Madison thought it was "free from many of the objections which had been urged against it" (presumably, the previous day).

> As the Electors would be chosen for the occasion, would meet at once, and proceed immediately to an appointment, there would be very little opportunity for cabal or corruption. As a further precaution, it might be required that they should meet at some place, distinct from the seat of Government, and even that no person within a certain distance of the place at the time should be eligible.

Notice how concerned Madison is to insulate the Electors of the President from political influence, be it from members of Congress or from presidential candidates. (Notice, too, that Madison, and perhaps the Convention as a whole, had not yet transcended the idea of a *single* electoral college.) Nevertheless, since this mode of election had been rejected the previous day, Madison was reluctant to propose it anew. Accordingly, the only remaining alternative was election by the people.

We have seen that popular election of the President involved certain difficulties. Recall Sherman's objection that the people would usually vote for a citizen of their own state. The consequence of this, said Pinckney, would be to enable the large or most populous states to determine the outcome of the election. (Translated onto the present scene:

A President elected by the people will usually come from a state having large urban populations, thus placing the small or rural states at a disadvantage.) Madison acknowledged this difficulty and hoped there was some way of overcoming it. And so there was; for Gouverneur Morris advanced the ingenious idea of having "each man . . . vote for two persons one of whom at least should not be of his own state." It should be noted, however, that this idea would be feasible only if candidates were *first nominated* by a special body of Electors. Nevertheless, what is remarkable about Morris' proposal is that it would theoretically reconcile immediate and long-range interests. On the one hand, by placing the large and small states on a more equitable level, it would broaden the basis of support for the Constitution. On the other hand, by compelling an "elector" to vote for two persons at least one of whom could not be a citizen of his own state, it would increase the likelihood that a President, thus elected, would be a man of "distinguished character" and of "continental reputation."*

Despite the eventual significance of Morris' proposal, the debates of July 25 utterly failed to alter the decision reached the day before. But one of the consequences of that decision was taken up on July 26 when the Convention, after voting a third time in favor of congressional election of the President, and a second time in favor of a seven-year term, reinstituted that barrier to legislative tyranny—the ineligibility clause. Thus matters stood until August 24.

On that day a new issue arose, namely, whether, in the process of electing the President, the two branches of Congress should vote *separately or jointly*.[10] Here, Nathaniel Gorham pointed out that if the House and the Senate were to vote separately, and if each branch were firmly attached to its own candidate, great delay, contention and confusion would ensue. Indeed, an election for the Presidency might

* Consider, in this connection, the Twelfth Amendment.

lead to a paralysis of government. To this Jonathan Dayton replied that if the two branches were to ballot jointly, the votes of the Senate would be swamped by the votes of the House, as a consequence of which the large states would control the Presidency. Now it so happens that whereas Gorham was a delegate from Massachusetts, a rather large state, Dayton was a delegate from New Jersey, a relatively small state; so it may seem that the diverse "interests" of their respective states had biased their respective positions. However this may be, it can hardly be denied that the method of joint balloting has obvious technical advantages. And here the Convention could be guided by experience as well as by logic. For John Langdon informed the delegates that in his own state, separate balloting was used to elect the governor, and with results comparable to those predicted by Gorham. Accordingly, on a motion to institute joint balloting for the Presidency, Langdon voted with the majority in its favor. New Jersey, however, had chosen a most resourceful delegate. For Dayton saw a simple way of reconciling the "interests" of the small states with the technical advantages of joint balloting: he merely proposed that each state be entitled to only one vote! Significantly enough, the motion was just barely defeated, and would not have been were it not for Langdon who, by the way, was a delegate from *New Hampshire.*

Although Dayton's motion was to prove more significant than its defeat, it was shortly followed by another motion whose defeat was even more significant. For after again attacking—no, excoriating—that hotbed of corruption and tyranny, congressional election of the President, the indefatigable Gouverneur Morris proposed *that the President be appointed by Electors* chosen by the people; and what is remarkable is that the first part of this proposition, which I have italicized, was rejected by a *split* Convention: four states voting yea, four nay, and two divided! Clearly the decision of July 24 reverting to congressional election of the President had only the most precarious foundation. Clearly this method of election could not be the foundation upon which to establish so vital an office as the Presidency.

On Friday, August 31, a "Committee of Eleven" was formed consisting of one member from each state delegation. Its object: to consider those parts of the Constitution which had not been acted upon or which had yet to be resolved by the Convention. One member of the committee, the reader will guess, was Gouverneur Morris.

On September 4, the committee submitted a report of its deliberations on the constitution of the Presidency. The President, it proposed, "shall hold his office during the term of four years," and shall be elected in the following manner:

> Each State shall appoint in such manner as its Legislature may direct, a number of Electors equal to the whole number of Senators and members of the House of Representatives, to which the State may be entitled in the [National] Legislature. The Electors shall meet *in their respective States,* and vote by ballot for two persons, one of whom at least shall not be an inhabitant of the same State with themselves; and they shall make a list of all the persons voted for, and of the number of votes for each, which list they shall sign and certify and transmit sealed to the Seat of the General Government, directed to the President of the Senate. The President of the Senate shall in that House open all the certificates; and the votes shall then and there be counted. The Person having the greatest number of votes shall be the President, if such number be a majority of that of the Electors; and if there be more than one who have such a majority, and have an equal number of votes, then the *Senate* shall immediately choose by ballot one of them for President; but if no person have a majority, then from the five highest on the list, the *Senate* shall choose by ballot the President. (Italics added)

To the reader who has come this far, the report of the Committee of Eleven will not appear very surprising. Its recommendations on the mode of electing the President will not be regarded as a mere "improvization" or as "a patch-work sewn together under the pressure of both time and events." Quite the contrary, he will see in these recommendations the logical conclusion of a long and thoughtful process of deliberation. He will see that the Founders had at last transcended the idea of a single college of Electors; that by having the Electors meet in their respective states, not only was the problem of convenience resolved, but more important, the danger of cabal and corruption was virtually eliminated. Furthermore, he will see that the report of the committee is well calculated to win the widest possible support for the Constitution. On the one hand, the large states will find advantage in the *nominating stage* of the Presidency—this, in virtue of the greater number of Electors to which they will be entitled. On the other hand, should the nominating stage be inconclusive, the small states will find advantage in the *contingency election stage* of the Presidency—this, in virtue of the election devolving upon the Senate, where all the states are equally represented. Finally, the reader will see that the Committee of Eleven had made possible what almost all the delegates had sought and had deemed essential to the blessings of union: it had made possible the reeligibility *and* independence of the Presidency. Here, then, is a superb example of political sagacity— say of a compromise governed by principles or by long-range considerations.

So well-principled and persuasive was the committee's report on the Presidency that, within two days, it was adopted and with only one change of any significance. For on September 6, the Convention almost unanimously agreed that it would be safer, if only in view of the Senate's power over the executive patronage, to have the contingency election devolve upon the House of Representatives.* Thus

---

* It will be understood, of course, that each state was still to retain but one vote.

ended the deliberations of the Founding Fathers on the mode of electing the President of the United States.

Having reconstructed the debates on the presidential electoral system, I shall now proceed to analyze the system itself, and with a view to elucidating its underlying purposes as well as its philosophical implications for the character of the American Presidency. My point of departure is Hamilton's commentary in *Federalist 68*.

"It was desirable," wrote Hamilton, "that the sense of the people should operate in the choice of the person to whom so important a trust [as the Presidency] was to be confided." The discussion begins on democratic grounds. The sense of the people is to operate in the choice of a President. Hamilton continues: "This end will be answered by committing the right of making it, not to any pre-established body, but to men chosen by the people for the special purpose, and at the particular conjuncture." The *right* of choosing a President is not to reside in the people, but with men chosen by the people for this particular purpose. (The Constitution is established by the people and the people divest themselves of the right to choose the chief executive!) But this is not all. For as Hamilton well knew, the Constitution does not even grant the people a right to choose Electors! Article II, Section 1, provides that "each State shall appoint [the Electors] in such Manner as the Legislature thereof may direct . . ." The manner of appointing Electors is absolutely under the control of the state legislatures, at whose discretion the people may exercise the privilege which is now accorded them.[11] That privilege may be withheld. The legislatures have the constitutional power of themselves choosing Electors as indeed was the practice of most of the states during the early presidential elections. But even if the state legislatures were to accord to the people, as some did, the privilege of choosing Electors, for example, by a general ticket or by electoral districts, the *nomination* of

Electors would not be made by the people. The people would still be at least twice removed from the election of the President. But however the sense of the people is to operate in the choice of the President, the immediate choice is to be made, as Hamilton pointed out, "by men most capable of analyzing the qualities adapted to the station." Who would these men be? Again employing democratic language, Hamilton professed to believe they would "be selected by their fellow-citizens from the general mass." But as Hamilton must have known, and as the early elections bore out, the Electors of the President would generally be drawn from the more distinguished and influential members of the community.[12] It was precisely such men whom Hamilton had in mind when he said that the persons selected "will be most likely to possess the information and discernment requisite to such complicated investigations" as the choosing of a President.

The President was to be chosen by men who possess information and discernment, and they were to act, said Hamilton, "under circumstances favorable to deliberation." The circumstances favorable to deliberation are these: First, each college of Electors should consist of a small number of persons. Hence they would be relatively free from faction. Second, the Electors in each state would assemble in the state in which they were chosen and would vote on the same day. "This detached and divided situation," said Hamilton, "will expose them much less to heats and ferments, which might be communicated from them to the people, than if they were all to be convened at one time, in one place." Furthermore, because the electoral colleges were not to assemble in a general convention, the Electors would be less subject to "cabal, intrigue, and corruption." In other words, the electoral college of one state would not be in communication with the electoral college of another; no college would know how the others were voting; there would be no "negotiations," no "deals," no prostitution of votes. Third, each college of Electors was to deliberate in secrecy.[13] They not only would be insulated from each other, but from the public at large. Fourth, no Senator or Representative, or any person holding office under the federal government, could be appointed an Elector. Removed from the influence of congressmen, and insulated from the general public, the Electors could ballot for the person of their own choice. They would not be automatons registering the will of congressional parties or of popular majorities. They would not be pledged to some presidential candidate, or as Hamilton remarked, they would be "free from any sinister bias." In short, Hamilton, and the Founders generally, anticipated and sought to avoid all the evils of the national party conventions! They clearly understood that the independence and integrity of the Presidency would depend very much on the independence and integrity of his Electors.

Although the electoral colleges were intended to have absolute control over the nomination of persons for the Presidency, we have seen that the final choice from among those nominated might, under certain contingencies, devolve upon the House of Representatives. Thus, either the Electors might fail to give a majority of their votes to a single candidate, or they might bestow equal electoral majorities on two, and possibly even three, candidates.[14] However, neither of these contingencies was likely to occur often: the first, for obvious reasons; the second, if only because the Electors would frequently favor an *incumbent* President. This being so, the House of Representatives would usually be spared the task of electing the President of the United States.

Now the point I wish to elicit from the above paragraph is this: In deliberating upon possible candidates for the Presidency, the Electors would almost certainly nominate persons of *national* reputation. In this respect, Electors would not differ from the delegates at the national party conventions. But unlike these delegates, the Electors would choose presidential candidates *without thought that the candidates chosen would have to engage in a popular election.* Now this has profound implications for the intended character of the Presidency, indeed, for the government as a whole.

The first implication is this. Because a President, under the *constitutional* or *de jure* electoral system, would not have to engage in a popular election, presidential candidates would be chosen more on the basis of ability, less on the basis of popularity. Second, because a President would not campaign for his election, he could enter upon his office virtually unencumbered by "political debts." Since *relatively few men will have contributed to his election, relatively few men could claim his favor.** As a consequence, executive patronage would conform more to the principle of *merit,* less to the principle of *spoils.* This being so, the election of a new President would not result in a wholesale change of public office-holders. The administration of government would be more stable, and the very tone of political life more elevated. Third, because a President would not have to campaign for his election, he would assume the duties of his office unencumbered by party platforms. Unburdened by such commitments, he could then promote public policies truer to his own principles and with the energy of his own convictions. But to appreciate what is involved here, let us pause to reflect upon the two major purposes of party platforms.

* When asked why the Committee of Eleven had decided to have the contingency election devolve upon the Senate rather than on Congress as a whole, Morris replied that fewer men could then approach the President and say: "You owe your appointment to us." Here the reader might inquire into the appointments made by Jefferson when the election of 1800 was thrown into the House of Representatives; cf. *Annals of Congress,* 7th Cong., Feb. 20, 1801, pp. 640-641.

The first is to inform the public of the principles and policies which may be expected to guide the administration of government should a party's candidate for the Presidency be elected. The principles indicate what the party conceives to be the function of government in relation to the permanent ends of the community. The policies indicate what, in the party's opinion, are the major problems confronting the community and what government should do to solve them. It may be said, therefore, that the first purpose of party platforms is to inform the public of alternative philosophies of government (thus enabling the electorate to make a more intelligent choice between candidates for the Presidency). The second major purpose of party platforms is to gain or secure the broadest possible basis of electoral support—more simply, to win as many votes as possible. Accordingly, the platform is designed to accommodate a wide variety of interests, not only within society, but within the party itself. Now it will be obvious that the two major purposes of party platforms are in tension with one another. The first is *educative:* It addresses our reason and sense of rightness; it invites us to think about the public good, about the kind of community we want to live in. The second is *manipulative:* It addresses the passions of self-interest, the interests of multifarious individuals and groups striving for place and profit and adjusting their differences for the sake of winning an election. Viewed in this light, the principles and policies of party platforms will not reflect a philosophy of government so much as a medley of compromises dictated by expediency. Yet these are the very principles and policies to which a President will be committed upon assuming office. True, he may or will himself have contributed to their formulation—but not with a free hand, and not under circumstances favorable to deliberation. True, their generality of statement may leave him scope for maneuver and initiative—but his independence will be somewhat impaired, the integrity of his office somewhat compromised. This, let it be clearly understood, is the inevitable result of the *de facto* electoral system, a system which compels a President to campaign for his election by making his election dependent upon the mass of the people.

A fourth implication of the intended electoral system is that its operation, considered by itself, would contribute little to the political education of the public.[15] For since there would be no campaign for the Presidency, candidates for that office would not engage in public debate or discussion of national issues. However, that such debate or discussion, save, perhaps, in few instances,[16] has really served to elevate the public mind, or that it has not been attended with effects more harmful than good, is questionable. Certainly the Founders regarded the prospect with skepticism, to say the very least. If the people, as Hamilton intimated in *Federalist 68*, are incapable of analyzing the qualities required of a President, they are surely incapable of analyzing the complex issues confronting a nation. Hence, a system which makes the choice of a President dependent upon public debate or discussion of national issues would be regarded by Hamilton as an absurdity. No doubt this will sound strange to the modern ear. Perhaps it will be explained away by referring to Hamilton's aristocratic "bias." But it was George Mason, a man of supposedly democratic inclinations, who said: ". . . it would be as unnatural to refer the choice of a proper character for Chief Magistrate to the people, as it would to refer a trial of colors to a blind man."[17] Now I do not mean to suggest that the Founders were unmindful of the need to educate the people. They simply felt that an election, upon whose outcome hangs the personal ambitions and material interests of so many individuals and groups, is a most dangerous means of providing public education. For the Presidency is so replete with the power to dispense goods and favors that, were an election for this office predicated upon public debate and discussion of national issues, not reason so much as passion, not candor so much as deception, not statesmanship so much as demagoguery, would too often prevail over the public mind. Far from educating the people, such elections would lead to their corruption.

Now let me sum up the principal intentions underlying the constitutional mode of electing the President of the United States. We have seen that the President was never intended to appeal to the suffrages of the people. The people might or might not choose his Electors. But however chosen, the Electors were to nominate for the Presidency the person whom they themselves deemed best qualified for the office. Deliberating in secrecy, the electoral colleges were to insulate the future President from the democratic and oligarchic influences to which he would be exposed were he nominated by the likes of the national party conventions. Indeed, let it be said here and now: "It was the design of the Constitution, though it is not expressed, that the President should not know the characters to whom he is indebted for his election."* Clearly this electoral system was intended to favor neither the interests of the many nor the interests of the few. It held another promise. It held the promise of insuring wisdom in the choice of a President. It held the promise of securing the President's independence and integrity. It held the promise, so far as institutions can, of compensating for the frailties of human nature, those frailties which so often emerge when men actively seek or campaign for public office. *The President,* I repeat, *was not to appeal to the suffrages of the people or of any electoral body whatsoever.* The dignity and powers of his office were to be conferred upon him by a select body of men unknown, as it were, to himself. He was to assume office without any

* Jonathan Dayton, in *Annals of Congress,* 2nd Cong., Dec. 22, 1791, p. 279.

obligation on his part other than to uphold and defend the Constitution. This is not simply an idealized picture. It is simply the ideal which guided the architects of the Presidency. This ideal, I contend, is *monarchic* in principle.*
And it is precisely this principle which, by its effect upon the choice of a President, was to guard the republic against the extremes of oligarchy on the one hand, and of democracy on the other. This said, it remains to inquire into the intended operation of this principle in American political life.

II

In Plato's *Republic,* the key problem is to unite *wisdom* and *power.* This is precisely the problem of the Presidency.†
According to Hamilton, the electoral system was well designed to advance to the Presidency a person "preeminent for ability and virtue"—which is almost to say, a person preeminent for wisdom. But having advanced such a person to the Presidency, the next problem was to entrust him with great power.

---

* I do not mean to suggest, though it might well be argued, that the Founders regarded the Presidency as comparable to the office of a monarch. It is not the word, but the *thought,* that is crucial, and the thought is best conveyed by the last italicized sentence.

† And this is precisely what Richard Neustadt fails to see in his book, *Presidential Power* (New York: John Wiley & Sons, Inc., 1962). For Neustadt, the problem of the Presidency is to be understood in terms of *personal power,* by which he means the capacity to exert influence on others. What is remarkable, however, is that Neustadt, in speaking of personal power, does not relate *power* to the *wisdom* or intellectual and moral qualities of the *person,* that is, of the person who is to exercise presidential power. I attribute this failure to his ethically neutral approach to the problem of the Presidency (pref., pp. vii–viii). This approach may also explain one of the underlying (and unwarranted) assumptions of his book, namely, that there is an identity between the *personal* power of the President and the public interest, or that whatever the President does or tries to do is consistent with the public interest.

Near the outset of *Federalist 70*, Hamilton writes: "Energy in the Executive is a leading character in the definition of good government." Notice that Hamilton does not say that energy in the executive is *the* leading character, but only *a* leading character, in the definition of good government. Nor does he even refer to energy as *the* leading character of a *good* executive. But here a distinction must be made between the *man* and the *office*. Hamilton did in fact regard energy as "the most necessary qualification" of the *Presidency*. But to judge only from his commentary on the electoral system, it can hardly be doubted that he regarded *wisdom* as the most necessary qualification of the *President*. What is remarkable, however, is that in his notes of June 1, Hamilton referred to "wisdom" (along with self-confidence) as creative of energy.[18] This suggests that energy in the executive involves or requires a synthesis of certain *personal* and *institutional* qualities or elements. Let us call this synthesis "presidential power."

The institutional elements of presidential power were boldly yet subtly outlined by Hamilton in *Federalist 72*. There the President is spoken of as the head of the *administration*. But what is "administration"? Here is Hamilton's answer:

> The administration of government, in its larger sense, comprehends all the operations of the body politic, whether legislative, executive, or judiciary; but in its most precise signification, it is limited to executive *details*, and falls peculiarly within the province of the executive department. The actual conduct of foreign negotiations, the preparatory plans of finance, and the application and disbursement of the public moneys in conformity with the appropriations of the legislature, the arrangement of the army and navy, the direction of the operations of war,—these, and *other matters* of a like nature, constitute what *seems* to be most properly understood by the administration of government. (Italics added)

Is it not remarkable that Hamilton should refer to these matters as the mere "details" of administration? Is is not equally remarkable that he should allude to "other matters" which fall within the sphere of the executive department? Perhaps he had in mind the *implied powers* of the Presidency —powers which are essentially legislative and which emerge most dramatically during times of crisis. Whatever the case, the very breadth of Hamilton's conception of "administration" suggests that, in his view, the executive and legislative (and even judicial) functions of government blend into each other; that while they may be distinct in theory, they are inseparable in practice.* Certainly he was fully aware of the decisive influence a President could exert on the character of legislation (1) by the threat or actual use of his veto; (2) by his power to recommend public measures; and (3) by the manner in which he administers the laws. It is to be borne in mind, however, that these institutional elements of presidential power, as well as those previously mentioned, would be utterly ineffective were it not for the *unity* of the executive office. Only an executive consisting of a single person can exercise the powers of this office with "decision" and "dispatch." But consider Hamilton's explanation in *Federalist 70:*

> Wherever two or more persons are engaged in any common enterprise or pursuit, there is always danger of difference of opinion. If it be a public trust or office, in which they are clothed with equal dignity and authority, there is a peculiar danger of personal emulation and even animosity. From either, and especially from all these causes, the most bitter dissensions are apt to spring. Whenever these happen, they lessen the respectability, weaken the authority, and distract the plans and operations of those whom they divide.[19]

* As Madison cautioned in *Federalist 37:* "Experience has instructed us that no skill in the science of government has yet been able to discriminate and define, with sufficient certainty, its three great provinces—the legislative, executive, and judiciary . . ."

But while unity in the executive fosters decision and dispatch, the development of any great plans, or the pursuit of any great purposes, requires a tenure of considerable duration as well as *reeligibility*. Now all these institutional aspects of presidential power constitute what may be termed the "lure" of the Presidency. Together they excite and attract what Hamilton called "the ruling passion of the noblest minds," namely, "the love of fame"—the very same passion that Morris called "the great spring to noble and illustrious actions."

Now to appreciate the significance of this monarchic passion for Morris and Hamilton, we must bear in mind their ultimate objective: the building of a *new* nation, a nation which was to be an exemplar of greatness. To achieve greatness America had to have unity—meaning a sense of national character and purpose. To achieve such unity there must be *leadership*. That leadership can only come from the Presidency. But leadership requires two things: greatness of soul on the one hand, political power on the other. Both Hamilton and Morris presupposed that men "preeminent for ability and virtue" would generally be elected to the Presidency. However, for the task of building a *new* nation, ability and virtue are not enough. To undertake such a task the President must also have passion, the passion for fame. To attract a person of these qualities to the Presidency the office must be invested with great power. However, before that person would assume the burden of this office, one further inducement is necessary: he must be given a tenure of considerable duration with the hope of its indefinite renewal. Only then will he be prompted "to plan and undertake extensive and arduous enterprises for the public benefit," enterprises "requiring considerable time to mature and perfect." Only then will he venture to overcome the petty rivalries and hostilities of those who must review and affirm his plans for molding a nation. Only then

will he be willing to endure the occasional displeasures of
his people. Perhaps this is why a great President will require,
in addition to ability and virtue, the passion for fame. Lacking this passion, perhaps he would have sought paths other
than that of political leadership.

Now let us assume that wisdom, energized by the passion for fame, has been united with power. These are the
key elements of presidential leadership, and it is precisely
such leadership that Hamilton had in mind when he spoke
of energy in the executive as a leading character in the
definition of good government.

The President is to initiate and devise comprehensive
and long-range plans of public policy. In so doing he is to
risk not only the ill-humors of Congress but even the ill-
humors of the people.[20] What does this signify for the character of presidential leadership? If the President is to exercise leadership he must inform public opinion rather than
follow it. This is the very purpose of endowing him with a
lengthy tenure: that he may have sufficient time "to make
the community sensible of the *propriety* of the measures he
might incline to pursue";[21] that he may have the additional
"confidence" and "firmness" with which to exert his powers
according to the dictates of his own judgment. True, and as
Hamilton remarks in *Federalist 70*, the President, in exercising his powers, is to be subject to "the restraints of public
opinion." But the function of public opinion, as Hamilton
suggests, is not to determine the *uses* of presidential power,
but rather to serve as a check against possible *abuses* of
presidential power. Let us be clear on this point.

When Hamilton refers to the restraints of public opinion
upon the conduct of the Presidency, he is contrasting the
advantages of a unitary as opposed to a plural executive.
One of the defects of a plural executive is that it destroys
"responsibility," that is, it makes it difficult for the public
to detect and censure abuses on the part of individual

executive officers, or to hold them individually accountable for their official conduct. As Hamilton says, it tends to vitiate "the restraints of public opinion." In other words, political responsibility, for Hamilton, is virtually synonymous with *accountability*.

Now the fact that the President is to inform and yet be restrained by public opinion suggests that public opinion is to be understood on at least two levels. On the highest level it may be regarded as that set of beliefs or convictions which give the public its particular and *abiding* identity.[22] (It is that which distinguishes an ever-changing aggregation of individuals and groups pursuing their private interests from a community of men sharing a common destiny.) Presumably, it is public opinion on this level which is to impose limits on the exercise of presidential power. On a lower level, public opinion may be regarded as the opinions which men have on public issues. I do not mean the "opinions" conveyed by a "yes" or a "no" to the questions of so-called opinion polls, but rather the opinions of public spokesmen or of men whose views claim public attention. (It is the opinions of such men which both Hamilton and Madison had in mind when speaking of the "deliberate sense of the community.") The opinions of these men would no doubt have great weight with the President. But they too may be enlightened, given the superior information of the presidential office. And while their opinions would impose some restraint on the President's conduct, these would not take the place of his own judgment. As for that which is commonly regarded as public opinion, consider this passage from *Federalist 71*. The republican principle, Hamilton declares,

> does not require an unqualified complaisance to every sudden breeze of passion, or to every transient impulse which the people may receive from the arts of men, who flatter

their prejudices to betray their interests. It is just observation, that the people commonly *intend* the PUBLIC GOOD. This often applies to their very errors. But their good sense would despise the adulator who should pretend that they always *reason right* about the *means* of promoting it. They know from experience that they sometimes err; and the wonder is that they so seldom err as they do, beset, as they continually are, by the wiles of parasites and sycophants, by the snares of the ambitious, the avaricious, the desperate, by the artifices of men who possess their confidence more than they deserve it, and of those who seek to possess rather than to deserve it. When occasions present themselves, in which the interests of the people are at variance with their inclinations, it is the duty of the persons whom they have appointed to be the guardians of those interests, to withstand the temporary delusion, in order to give them time and opportunity for more cool and sedate reflection.

Notice Hamilton's caution. The people "commonly"—which is to say, the people do not *always*—intend the public good. And when they do intend the public good, they do not always reason right about the means of promoting the public good. Hence the people must be enlightened. It may be objected, however, that the people are to be enlightened, not by the President, but by themselves. The President is only to resist their passions and prejudices so as to afford them time for "cool and sedate reflection." Leaving this objection aside for the moment, notice that in resisting popular passions and prejudices, the President would not only afford the people time for cool and sedate reflection; he would also afford the enlightened and respectable members of the community time to exert their influence on society at large. This in itself would facilitate the rule of reason in public life. It would contribute to the people's education. But what are some of the specific aspects of this education?

We have seen that the President is to resist popular passions and prejudices. To do this is to teach the people that their government is not simply their creature. Not that the President would publicly deny one of the principles upon which the government rests, viz., the will of the people. Rather, he would point out that what the people presently will is not consistent with their true interests, that they have been deceived by demagogues, that it would be a betrayal of their trust and of the very purposes for which their government was founded were he to flatter their wishes for the sake of their praise. On the other hand, to resist popular passions and prejudices is to foster among the people moderation and thoughtfulness. The President is himself to exhibit moderation and thoughtfulness by informing the people, not simply of the policies he may wish to pursue, but of the *propriety* of these policies. In so doing he would show that these policies are not only expedient, but that they are consistent with right and lawful ends. The effect of this would be to teach the people that public policies, or proposed legislation, must be justified not only in terms of what is convenient or pragmatic, but also in terms of what is constitutional. But this is to teach the people that what is pragmatic is not necessarily constitutional. The importance of this teaching can hardly be exaggerated. For whenever the pragmatic gains ascendancy over the constitutional, it is a sure sign of mutability in the laws, indeed, of the ascendancy of democratic passions. The pragmatic, too often, looks only to the satisfaction of temporary wants and interests. Its method involves efficiency and compromise. Preoccupation with efficiency leads to constant innovation. Preoccupation with changing wants and interests eventuates in mere compromise. The constitutional, on the other hand, takes a more comprehensive view of things. Efficiency and compromise must be governed by enduring principles, by long-range considerations. The satisfaction of present wants and interests must be adjusted to the permanent ends of the community. It would hardly be sufficient for the President to resist popular passions and prejudices if he failed to teach the people about these ends. For it is only by the understanding and lawful pursuance of these ends that the people can become a people, a diverse nation a more perfect Union.[23]

III

I shall conclude this chapter by setting forth what may be termed the *dialectical* principle of presidential leadership, evidence of which is only vaguely suggested in *The Federalist* and not at all in the *Records of the Federal Convention.* A clue to this principle, however, may be found in the reports of Washington's Secretary of the Treasury: again I refer to Hamilton's "Report on Manufactures," but equally revealing are his reports on the public credit and on the establishment of a national bank.[24] In referring to these reports, it should be borne in mind that my concern is not with their substance, but with their dialectical significance for presidential leadership.

It will be evident to any candid reader that the reports in question are not the writings of a political pragmatist merely coping with the economic problems of the day. It would be closer to the truth to regard them as treatises on *political economy.* In the first place, the proposals contained in these reports are defended on political and even on moral grounds. They present *opposed* arguments. They are addressed to men capable of weighing these arguments, capable of drawing fine distinctions. They have in view not only the solution of immediate problems, but of distant ones as well. Envisioned is the development of a great and powerful nation, a nation no longer divided and enervated by conflicting interests and loyalties. But what is the ultimate significance of these reports in relation to the problem of presidential leadership? What they suggest is that the achievement of national unity and greatness requires *public* elucidation of the principles and objectives which are to govern the policies of the administration. The President, we have seen, is to make the community sensible of the *propriety* of the measures he may wish to pursue. It is not enough for the President to outline his policies. He must *justify* them in the light of political and moral principles—and not by an appeal to platitudinous generalities, but by drawing distinctions between what is prudent and what is *not* prudent, between what is permissible and what is *not* permissible. He must not only articulate his own position, he must *refute* opposing ones as well. The point is that political education requires a *joining* of issues. Unless issues are publicly joined, unless there is a genuine attempt on the part of the President to *anticipate* and publicly refute the arguments of his opponents, there can be no intelligent understanding of what his administration stands for—indeed, there can be no deepened sense of a public. It is not the President's function to encourage a diversity of opinions on public issues: Congress and society will provide for that, and in great abundance. At stake is not the diversity of opinions but the capacity of men to take opinions *seriously*. Let us be clear on this point. Mere opinions may be exchanged, like commodities on the market. But the mere exchange of opinions does not result in the forming of *right* opinions. The product of that exchange is not truth, but a babbling confusion. What is remarkable, however, is that a babbling confusion of opinions must ultimately lead to a deadening conformity: a conformity to those who speak with the force of mere numbers. If the President is to exercise leadership he must speak with the force of wisdom. He must infuse sanity and seriousness into the marketplace of undisciplined and irresponsible opinions. He must expose error and vice. But can a people be enlightened without gently reproving their baser passions and prejudices? Can a President really serve the public good if he is loath to reveal the source of public evils, evils which involve not merely the external conditions of men but the very character of their souls? Here, compassion will not serve the President well. For compassion tends to level the demands made upon men. It tends to obscure and obliterate the distinctions between the higher and the lower. It tends to foster the complaisancy of those who rule toward those who are ruled.[25] No, the President will require not compassion but *magnanimity*.[26] Greatness of soul: the capacity to endure without resentment the resentment of others, to pursue noble ends though they be unpopular—this is an aristocratic, one might even say, a monarchic virtue.

10

The Supreme Court and Its Intended Role in American Political Life

THE PHILOSOPHY OF JUDICIAL REVIEW

> . . . in so far as our judicial institutions may accelerate the performance of duties, promote the cause of virtue, and prevent the perpetration of crimes, in that same degree they ought to be estimated and cherished.
> GOUVERNEUR MORRIS,
> *in the Senate of the United States*[1]

To INQUIRE into the intended role of the Supreme Court is to inquire into the doctrine of "judicial review." The initial problem confronting such an inquiry is this: Was it the intention of the Founding Fathers to invest the Supreme Court with the power to nullify acts of Congress which, in the opinion of the Court, are repugnant to the Constitution? This question has been the subject of much learned controversy. A study of this controversy reveals four basic schools of thought. Some scholars have confirmed, while some have unqualifiedly denied, the Court's authority to exercise judicial review.[2] Others have maintained that the historical evidence is inconclusive.[3] Still others have so interpreted the doctrine of judicial review as to severely restrict the scope of its application.[4] Illuminating as this controversy has been, it has shed little light on the philosophy of judicial review and on the political consequences of its denial. We look in vain for any sustained attempt to examine the doctrine as a *philosophical* problem and to elucidate its significance for the political philosophy of the American Constitution. (The typical approach is legalistic and historical.) It is not my purpose, however, to belabor this much belabored controversy. I shall confirm the legitimacy of judicial review, but primarily for the sake of developing its philosophical principles, and with this, the intended role of the Supreme Court in American political life.

The judiciary, no less than the Senate and the executive, was instituted, in part, to limit the operation of the democratic principle embodied in the House of Representatives, but especially should that principle come to dominate the legislature as a whole. It is in this light that we are to understand the idea of *limited government* and with it the doctrine of judicial review. Briefly stated, limited government is that which restricts the legislative (but not only the legislative) power by fixed or permanent laws.[5] These fixed or permanent laws are contained in what is called the "fundamental law," namely, the Constitution. The fundamental law is paramount over ordinary or statutory law. Ordinary law, to be ultimately valid, must be consistent with the Constitution. Under a limited government, it cannot be the prerogative of those who make (or execute) the laws to be the ultimate judge of their constitutionality. Under the limited government established by the Founding Fathers, the final authority on questions affecting the constitutionality of the laws rests with the Supreme Court. Now what we want to know is this: (1) Why is the Constitution a *fundamental* law? (2) Why should this fundamental law be regarded as *permanent*? (3) Why must there be a *final* authority to resolve all questions affecting the constitutionality of the laws? (4) Why should that final authority be the Supreme Court? The answers to these questions constitute the philosophy of judicial review. To prepare the stage for the exposition of that philosophy, let us turn to the debates of the Constitutional Convention, there to reexamine the various proposals and ideas from which the institution of the Supreme Court emerged.

I

The original proposal for a national judiciary is contained in the ninth resolution of the Virginia Plan. This resolution provided, in part:

> that a National Judiciary be established to consist of one or more supreme tribunals, and of inferior tribunals to be chosen by the National Legislature, to hold their offices during good behaviour; . . . that the jurisdiction of the inferior tribunals shall be to hear and determine in the first instance, and of the supreme tribunal to hear and determine in the *dernier* resort . . . cases in which . . . citizens of other States applying to such jurisdictions may be interested . . . and questions which may involve the national peace and harmony.

The broad scope of judicial review implied here cannot be said to include the power to set aside acts of Congress; for that power is qualifiedly contained in the eighth resolution which provided, in part:

> that the Executive and a convenient number of the National Judiciary, ought to compose a council of revision with authority to examine every act of the National Legislature before it shall operate . . . and that the dissent of the said

council shall amount to a rejection, unless the Act of the National Legislature be passed again . . . by ( ) of the members of each branch.[6]

This proposal for a council of revision may be said to posit a doctrine of "prior" judicial review. In rejecting a council of revision, the majority of the Convention opted for a doctrine of "subsequent" judicial review. Their reasons will now be examined.

On June 4, immediately after the Convention adopted Wilson's proposal for a *unitary* executive, the motion for a council of revision was introduced. Elbridge Gerry questioned the wisdom of such a council. He expressed

> doubts whether the Judiciary ought to form a part of it, as they will have a sufficient check against encroachment on their own department by their exposition of the laws, which involved a power of deciding on their Constitutionality. In some States the Judges had actually set aside laws as being against the Constitution. This was done too with general approbation. *It was quite foreign from the nature of the office to make them judges of the policy of public measures.*
> (Italics added)

For Gerry, the function of the judiciary is not to judge of the "policy," which is to say, the *wisdom,* of the laws, but of their constitutionality. In objecting to the participation of judges in a council of revision, Gerry was saying, in effect, that such a council would blend two functions which ought to be kept distinct and separate: (1) the revision of laws which are unwise, and (2) the rejection of laws which are unconstitutional. "The right of revision," said Gerry, "should be in the executive only"—from which it may be inferred that the right of rejection should be lodged solely in the Supreme Court, and then only after the laws become operative. Much the same position was taken by Rufus King. The judges, he declared, "will no doubt stop the operation of such [laws] as shall appear repugnant to the Constitution."

But they ought to expound the law *"free from the bias of having participated in its formation."*[7] In other words, judicial impartiality requires the separation of the Supreme Court from the legislative process. Other delegates expressed the same view.[8] In so doing they confirmed the proposition that those who participate in the making of the laws— the executive not excluded—ought not be the final judge of their constitutionality. But there was yet a more subtle reason advanced in opposition to the council of revision. Thus, when the subject was reintroduced on July 21, Luther Martin had this to say:

> A knowledge of mankind, and of Legislative affairs cannot be presumed to belong to a higher degree to the Judges than to the Legislature. And as to the Constitutionality of the laws, that point will come before the judges in their proper official character. In this character they have a negative on the laws. Join them with the Executive in the Revision and they will have a double negative. *It is necessary that the Supreme Judiciary should have the confidence of the people.* This will soon be lost, if they are employed in the task of remonstrating against popular measures of the Legislature. (Italics added)

It is one thing for the judiciary to reject popular measures on grounds of their being unconstitutional; it is quite another thing for the judiciary to reject popular measures on grounds of their being unwise. Acting in their judicial capacity as the expounders of the laws, it will be presumed that the judges are personally detached and disinterested, that their sole concern is to determine whether the laws are constitutional. Should they act in a legislative capacity, however, it may be presumed that they are governed by partial motives and interests not unlike those which govern legislators.[9] What Martin was saying, in effect, is that the moral force of Supreme Court decisions would be lost if members of the Court participated in the legislative process or engage in a function other than that of subsequent judicial review.

It can be seen that the reasons advanced by King and Martin against a council of revision are elaborations of Gerry's position, a position which may be reformulated as follows.[10] If members of the judiciary participate in the revisionary council, they will be the judges as to the wisdom of proposed legislation. This they ought not be for two reasons. In the first place, it would bias their judgment as the expounders of the laws. In the second place, it would undermine public confidence in their role as the expounders of the Constitution. But what purpose is the revisionary council intended to serve? It is to review the acts of Congress, rejecting those which are unwise as well as those which are unconstitutional. This being so, to avoid the disadvantages mentioned, let the executive exercise "political" review prior to the operation of the laws, and let the Court exercise judicial review subsequent to the operation of the laws. By separating these two functions and placing them in the hands of distinct bodies, the twofold purpose of the revisionary council would be preserved.

Reasonable as this argument may appear, it failed to persuade the proponents of the revisionary council to relinquish the idea. It failed because they had a different estimate of the dangers to be avoided as well as of the benefits to be obtained by the institution of such a council. First of all, men like Wilson and Madison feared that the executive, acting alone—exercising his veto without the concurrent support of the judiciary—would be no match for a legislature bent on encroachment. They felt that a *constitutional alliance* between the executive and the judiciary was essential if either branch was to preserve its independence. This is all the more remarkable when we recall that the principal cause of their fears did not stem from the legislature as a whole, but from the House of Representatives.[11] After all, was not the Senate intended to perform functions comparable to those of a revisionary council?[12] Was it not intended to check encroachments by the popular branch? Was it not intended to infuse the laws with "system" and "wisdom"? Nor is this all. Consider the fact that the Senate is joined with the executive in the appointment of Supreme Court justices. Indeed, when Madison proposed, contrary to the Virginia Plan, to have judges appointed by the Senate alone rather than by the entire legislature—and note well his reasons°—the proposal was adopted without a dissenting voice. Now all this must be borne in mind if we are to grasp, comprehensively, the true design of the American Constitution. It is hardly an exaggeration to say that the Constitution represents a grand alliance between the Senate, the executive, and the judiciary vis-à-vis the democratic principle.[13] This is not to suggest, however, that the Founders were anti-democratic, or that the Constitution is primarily an aristocratic or an oligarchic instrument. What I mean to convey is that while the Founders were committed to the inclusion of the democratic principle in American government, such was their estimate of the power and dangerous tendencies of this principle, that they wished to check its operation by all means possible. It is in this light that we are

° The following is taken from Madison's notes of June 13:

Mr. Madison objected to an appointment by the whole Legislature. Many of them were incompetent judges of the requisite qualifications. They were too much influenced by their partialities. The candidate who was present, who had displayed a talent for business in the legislative field, who had perhaps assisted ignorant members in the business of their own, or of their Constituents, or used other winning means, would without any of the essential qualifications for an expositor of the laws prevail over a competitor not having these recommendations but possessed of every necessary accomplishment. He proposed that the appointment should be made by the Senate, which as a less numerous and more select body, would be more competent judges, and which was sufficiently numerous to justify such a confidence in them.

On July 21, however, Madison proposed an appointment of the Court by the Executive with confirmation by the Senate—perhaps as a consequence of which, some objection was then raised against the mode of appointment agreed to on June 13.

to understand why men like Madison persisted in their advocacy of a council of revision. What they feared most was that the national legislature might repeat the experience of those state legislatures which, despite their senatorial bodies, had succumbed to "the democracy"—legislatures which had then proceeded to enact laws encroaching upon the executive and judicial prerogatives, or laws impairing the rights of the propertied classes.[14] Here, according to Madison, a council of revision would be of considerable value.

> It would be useful to the Judiciary department by giving it an *additional* opportunity of defending itself against Legislative encroachments. It would be useful to the Executive, by inspiring additional confidence and firmness in exerting the revisionary power. . . . It would moreover be useful to the Community at large as an *additional* check against a pursuit of those unwise and unjust measures which constituted so great a portion of our calamities.[15]

In addition to these purposes, a council of revision would have a profound effect on the character of the laws. For as it would have the talents and wisdom of a permanent judiciary, it would promote continuity in the laws while ensuring their clarity, conciseness, and propriety.[16] Much the same argument was advanced by Mason (though with significant additions to be treated later). Because the legislature, said Mason, "must be expected to frequently pass unjust and pernicious laws," the restraining power of a council of revision was essential. Such a council, he continued,

> would have the effect not only of hindering the final passage of such laws; *but would discourage demogogues from attempting to get them passed.* It had been said . . . that if the Judges were joined in the check on the laws, they would have a double negative, since in their expository capacity of Judges they would have one negative. [I] would reply that in this capacity they could impede in one case only, the

operation of the laws. They could declare an unconstitutional law void. *But with regard to every law however
unjust, oppressive or pernicious, they would be under the
necessity as Judges to give it free course.*[17]

Mason concluded by saying that the assistance of the judges
in a council of revision "will be the more valuable as they
are in the habit and practice of considering laws in their
true principles, and in all their consequences."

Now let us collect and reformulate the major advantages
ascribed to the council of revision. First, such a council
would unite the executive and the judiciary against legislative, especially, democratic, encroachment. Second, it would
increase the weight of the executive veto. Third, it would
insure the exercise of the veto over laws whose impropriety
might otherwise escape the President's attention (were he
acting without the wisdom and legal knowledge of a permanent judiciary). Fourth, it would discourage the legislature
from enacting improper laws in the first place. Finally, the
proposed council would preserve continuity in the laws by
bringing them into conformity with the fundamental principles and purposes of the Constitution.

It will be seen that the advantages ascribed to the revisionary council are predicated upon the opportunity of the
judges to review the laws before the laws are given effect.
They are predicated upon the resulting power of the judges
to annul not only laws which are unconstitutional, but
laws which are unwise or unjust. Now the question arises:
Disregarding the council of revision, would it lie within the
authority of the Supreme Court, in cases coming before it,
to nullify laws of the latter description as unconstitutional?
(This question, be it noted, does not fundamentally affect
the doctrine, but only the *scope,* of judicial review.) Recall
Mason's statement to the effect that the Supreme Court is
under the necessity of giving free course to every law which,
"however unjust, oppressive or pernicious," is not "plainly"

unconstitutional. Now Mason's statement (leaving its rhetoric aside) cannot reasonably be regarded as a practical principle of judicial review. And if the principle, as stated, is impractical, it ought not be imputed to the Convention as a whole unless "plainly" confirmed by the evidence of that Convention. Consider the principle only as it affects a law recognized by the Court as *plainly* unjust.[18] The question which would confront the Court is whether this plainly unjust law is "plainly" unconstitutional. It will not be denied that the Court wishes to do justice. It will not be denied that the Court is not insensitive to its own reputation as the highest tribunal of justice. Admitting this, it could seldom happen that the judges of that tribunal, recognizing the obvious injustice of the law, would give to it the positive or negative sanction of the Constitution.[19] No man of character, of courage and integrity, would readily submit to such violence, would abet the perpetration of injustice upon a particular citizen, save, perhaps, under public necessity. Would the justices of the Supreme Court do less? This would be a strange way of enhancing the Court's reputation. It would be a strange way of fostering reverence for the Constitution. No, rather than allow the Constitution to sanction a law which, though plainly unjust, may not be plainly unconstitutional, the judges would comb the document and, more often than not, discover, in its broad principles, the reasons in virtue of which the law must be invalidated. Besides, who is best qualified to say what is and what is not "plainly" unconstitutional? Certainly not the legislature, which, according to Mason, "must be expected frequently to pass unjust and pernicious laws." Presumably, it must be the Supreme Court, for again, according to Mason, the members of the Court "are in the habit and practice of considering laws in their true principles, and in all their consequences." Only admit the basic doctrine of judicial review, as Mason does, and the question as to what may or may not be declared unconstitutional—that is, the scope of judicial review—must be left, as a matter of logic, to the Supreme Court.

It should not be thought, however, that Mason's statement touching the scope of judicial review is without relevance to the problem. (Of this, more in a moment.) But we ought to bear in mind that that statement serves a rhetorical function, which is to win acceptance of a revisionary council composed partly of Supreme Court justices. Failure to take account of the rhetoric of the debates will inevitably lead to the uncritical acceptance of statements which, on their face, attest neither to constitutional principles nor to the true intentions of their authors. Instead, we must examine the debates dialectically and with a view to their implications for action. If dialectical analysis reveals inconsistencies, or absurdities, or clearly impractical principles, we ought to suspect ulterior motives. Consider, for example, Wilson's statement of July 21 concerning the issue in question: "Laws may be unjust, may be unwise, may be dangerous, may be destructive; yet not be *so* unconstitutional as to justify Judges in refusing to give them effect" (italics added). One implication of this statement is that laws may be a *little* unconstitutional but not *enough* so for judges to invalidate them! Are we to believe that Wilson would uphold such a doctrine as a *practical* principle of judicial review[20]—the same Wilson who, on June 4, declared: "In Courts of Justice there are two sides only to a question."* Probably not. On the other hand, it would be unwise to dismiss Wilson's statement as a mere rhetorical effusion. For viewed within the context of the debates, that statement is significant for

---

* In the Pennsylvania ratifying convention Wilson declared: "If a law should be made inconsistent with those powers vested by [the Constitution] in Congress, the judges . . . will declare such a law to be null and void. For the power of the Constitution predominates. *Anything* therefore that shall be enacted by Congress contrary thereto will not have the force of law." Cited in Robert G. McCloskey, *Essays in Constitutional Law* (New York: Vintage Books, 1957), p. 49 (italics added).

our understanding of the delicate role of the Supreme Court in American political life. What Wilson may have had in mind—and this applies to Mason as well—could be stated as follows: If the judiciary is not joined with the executive in a council of revision, it will be *more difficult* for judges (and even for the executive) to stop the operation of improper laws, even if there exist some grounds for declaring such laws unconstitutional. After all, the judges could hardly claim the support of the President; and since they do not comprise an elected body, they could hardly claim the support of the people. Or consider: Congress may pass a law which is unwise in the sense of being inexpedient or untimely. Or the law may be unjust in that it places certain classes of citizens at a disadvantage, but not in any inordinate way. Or again, a law may be dangerous or even destructive, but only *in the long run.* Such laws may not be unconstitutional, or *clearly* unconstitutional; the question may be open to debate. But the Supreme Court, more than any other department of government, and certainly more than the public at large, is "in the habit and practice of considering laws in their true principles, and in all their consequences." Despite this, the Court may be restrained from invalidating many of such laws as Wilson describes, and for the reasons mentioned above. Prudence may dictate self-restraint. Prudence may dictate that the Court refuse jurisdiction over certain politically controversial cases, especially those which no decision of the Court can effectively resolve. But that the judges of the Court would or should regard it as their *duty* to uphold laws which, though unjust or destructive, are not clearly unconstitutional, is a doctrine closer to judicial self-denial than to one of judicial self-restraint. The paucity of the evidence notwithstanding, it is doubtful that either Wilson or Mason would have adhered to such a doctrine.

Finally, in reflecting upon the kinds of laws which the Supreme Court (the council of revision notwithstand-

ing) may or may not invalidate, consider Madison's proposal of August 27 to the effect that the Court's jurisdiction
be limited to "judicial" as opposed to "political" questions.[21]
In view of Madison's position with respect to the revisionary
council, it may be inferred that under judicial questions he
included those involving the constitutionality of the laws,
as opposed to questions involving their wisdom or expediency. Notice, I do not exclude from the category of judicial
questions those involving the justice of the laws. I do not
because the line between what is unjust and what is unconstitutional cannot be clearly defined, and this if only because
the Constitution embodies rather comprehensive principles
of justice. Admittedly, it will be often difficult to distinguish
between unwise laws and laws which are either unjust or
unconstitutional. (But when laws are challenged before the
courts, they are not challenged for their unwisdom.) The
implication here is that "political" questions cannot always
be distinguished from "judicial" questions. *Who*, then, is to
draw the line between the two? This is not to argue a doctrine of unlimited judicial review. Rather, it is to suggest
that the intended scope of judicial review cannot be clearly
ascertained—indeed, does not admit of being clearly ascertained. For apart from the meagerness and ambiguity of
the evidence, when we raise the question of *scope* we enter
the realm of infinite shades and nuances, where the complexity of human affairs cannot be neatly categorized, where
formulas may provide points of departure for thinking about
a particular case in controversy, but which formulas can
seldom lead us, by a chain of logical deduction, to the solution of that controversy.

It should be evident from the preceding analysis that
the arguments for *and* against the council of revision *equally*
confirm the Court's authority to exercise "subsequent" judicial review. *The rejection of the council in no way affects
this question.*[22] Nevertheless, its rejection has profound con-

sequences and implications for the Court's character. Separated from the executive, and precluded from exercising "prior" judicial review, the Court was now the weakest branch of government. And being the weakest branch, it could not safely exercise subsequent judicial review without self-restraint, indeed, without caution and circumspection. However, if, by the rejection of the council, the scope of the Court's authority was considerably limited, it was limited without being clearly defined. If the Court's role was thus made ambiguous, this ambiguity could be a source of great power. For only admit its authority to exercise judicial review, and sooner or later the Court might largely determine the scope of that authority. To be sure, the Court would still have to be cautious and circumspect. For having been separated from the executive, it would be more dependent upon the executive. And having been removed from the legislative process, it could only indirectly affect that process. Thus separated and thus removed, the Court's orientation—say its *modus operandi*—was shifted from the exercise of "will" toward the exercise of "judgment." And yet, it may well be that the Court would now give voice to a higher will, a will more consonant with judgment. With this, I turn from the debates of the Convention to the philosophy of judicial review.

II

In developing the philosophy of judicial review, I shall rely less on the method of historical exposition and more on the method of philosophical construction. This means that I shall set forth a rationale of judicial review which, in some respects, may not have been consciously intended by the Founders, but which nonetheless will be fully *consistent* with their intentions. Such an approach is made necessary in view of the paucity of evidence available in the *Records of the Federal Convention,* but also in view of the fact that the fundamental principles of judicial review are barely elaborated by the great architects of the Supreme Court, Alexander Hamilton and Chief Justice John Marshall. I begin on the surface.

The philosophy of judicial review is rooted in the principle that the Constitution is a *fundamental* law. This principle is clearly implied, if not enunciated, in Article VI, Section 2, where it is written: "This Constitution, and the Laws of the United States which shall be made in Pursuance thereof . . . shall be the supreme Law of the Land . . ." We have here two kinds of laws. The first mentioned is the Constitution itself. This law is unqualifiedly supreme. The second mentioned are the laws of the United States, that is, the laws enacted by the national legislature. These laws are *not* unqualifiedly supreme. To be supreme they must be made in *pursuance* of the Constitution, meaning, they must carry out, or be consistant with, the plan or principles of the Constitution. It follows that the law of the Constitution is paramount over the laws of the legislature: the first is *original,* the second are *derivitive.* But this is precisely what is implied in distinguishing the Constitution as a fundamental law.

Now the status of the Constitution as a fundamental law is determined by two factors: its *efficient* cause and its *formal* cause. The efficient cause of the Constitution, juridically considered, is none other than the *original* will of the American people.° Precisely because the original will of the

° Compare the Preamble of the Constitution with its counterpart in the Articles of Confederation. Note carefully that the efficient cause of the Constitution is not, of itself, determinative of the *genus* of the Constitution. The genus of the Constitution is determined by its *formal* cause, that is, by its formative principles. It is precisely here that the democratic interpretation of the Constitution flounders. That interpretation posits the principle of popular sovereignty as determinative of the *genus* of the Constitution. But that principle is the *efficient* cause of the Constitution,

American people is prior and superior to the will of any representatives of the people, the Constitution, as the expression of that original will, is binding upon all subsequent legislatures, executives, and judicial bodies.[23]

Considered under the aspect of its *formal* cause, the Constitution is a fundamental law in that it prescribes the decisive principles of political rule. By "decisive" I mean (1) that which is not ordinarily subject to question; and (2) that which fixes the general course and character of things. By "principles of political rule" I mean (1) those powers and procedures which determine the ruler-ruled relationship; and (2) the political and moral ends for which these powers and procedures were established. Now the principles of the fundamental law enunciate the basic rights and duties of every citizen. They empower institutions and provide standards for the conduct of public affairs. They facilitate rational inquiry and cooperative effort for the solution of public problems and for the satisfaction of public needs. They enable men to rise above necessity and expediency, to anticipate future problems, to introduce ordered change, and ultimately, to enhance and elevate the quality of individual and community life. In short, the principles of

not its *formal* cause. Thus, if the people had established a monarchy, we should have to say, in virtue of its efficient cause, that that monarchy was really a democracy! Furthermore, although the principle of popular sovereignty is *one* of the formative principles of the Constitution, the principle is misconstrued by proponents of the democratic thesis. They identify that principle with the rule of the majority (or of the "many"); whereas the principle posits the rule of the people *qua* people. This means that the source of political power does not reside in any part or class of society, but in society *as a whole*—in the *common*wealth. Hence, to grasp the generic form of the Constitution, one would have to consider the actual character of the various classes composing American society at the time of the founding, the factual distribution of power among those classes, and how this factual distribution of power is reflected in the Constitution itself. Finally, the democratic interpretation overlooks the notion of "divested sovereignty" involved in the *compact theories* of earlier philosophies insofar as these affected the founding of the Constitution. (Cf. *infra,* p. 317, *n.* 36.)

which I am speaking are fundamental in that they establish the generic character of the regime.

Now if these principles are considered under the aspect of their efficient cause, it would seem that they derive their decisive or binding character from the original will of the American people, and from that alone. But let us consider this more closely. The principles of government originally established by the American people are of three kinds: (1) those which they deemed best suited for the needs and circumstances of their own society—for example, the principle of federalism; (2) those which they deemed best suited for any civilized society—for example, the principle of checks and balances or the constitutional division of powers or functions; and (3) those which they deemed intrinsic to the very nature of society. The first kind of principles would be binding upon them simply as Americans; the second, say, as Americans sharing a common heritage with nations of the West, especially with the English-speaking peoples. The third kind of principles—and these may be placed under the category of *natural justice*—would be binding upon them as men, as men *sub specie eterni*.[24] Now it should be noted that of this third category of principles (but of the second as well), the original will of the American people is a *mediative* cause, not a *creative* one. Such principles are binding not in virtue of having been willed, but in virtue of their universal (or general) validity.[25] But let us consider some of these principles, for they enhance the status of the Constitution as a fundamental law.

Although the Constitution does not distinguish between the three kinds of principles mentioned above, there can be little doubt that the prohibition against *ex post facto* laws and bills of attainder, as well as the prohibition against laws impairing the obligation of contracts, were generally regarded as exemplifying principles rooted in natural justice. These are by no means the only constitutional provisions exemplifying such principles, the most obvious of which, though not necessarily the most important, are embodied in parts of the First, Fourth, and Fifth Amendments. But I single out the above prohibitions because of their conspicuous place in the rationale of judicial review developed by John Marshall. Indeed, in the case of *Fletcher* v. *Peck*, Marshall suggests that these prohibitions are prescribed by the very "nature of society and of government," suggesting, thereby, that they are based on natural justice. Apropos of the issue in that case, consider the constitutional prohibition against laws impairing the obligation of contracts. This prohibition is usually taken to reflect the concern of the Founding Fathers to protect the interests of wealth. While there is truth in this contention, it obscures a more fundamental truth. For the prohibition against laws impairing the obligation of contracts is also the reflection of an ethical principle coterminous with civilized society, the principle that men should honor their promises. This principle is the basis of mutual trust and confidence. It is the basis of friendship and community. Above all, it is the affirmation of man as that earthly being who alone regards the *word* as the external sign of a commitment to truth, a commitment which transcends the here and now and so unites the generations of mankind. Such, then, is the principle embodied in the contract clause, a principle which, together with others rooted in natural justice, determines and enhances the status of the Constitution as a fundamental law.[26]

From the second factor which determines the Constitution as a fundamental law, that is, from its formal cause, may be deduced the second principle of judicial review, namely, that the Constitution is a *permanent law*. That the Constitution is a permanent law is in no way contradicted by the amending article, for that article does not contemplate any change in the *generic* form of the regime.[27] Again, the principle of federalism—that the Union shall consist of equal states having independent spheres of authority; the principle of checks and balances—that the powers or functions of government shall be divided among separate and independent branches; and finally, those principles which are rooted in natural justice and which have their general statement in the Preamble—all these principles comprise, in their subtle interdependence, the *genus* of the Constitution, its permanent form. Of course, the *operation* of these principles is subject to change, and not only *de jure* but *de facto* as well. A good example of a change *de jure* is the Twelfth Amendment altering the mode of electing the President but not the form of the Constitution. As for *de facto* changes, these bear two aspects. On the one hand, changes in society at large may increase or diminish the force of certain constitutional principles.[28] On the other hand, *judicial interpretations* of the Constitution may produce the same result.[29] From these considerations the conclusion may be drawn that while the Constitution is absolutely permanent *in essence*, it is only relatively permanent *in fact*. This conclusion, however, would be challenged by skeptics of the judicial process. Looking primarily to the multitudinous opinions which comprise the body of constitutional law, these skeptics contend that the Constitution is continually changing. It is continually changing, they say, because the opinions of the Court are continually changing; and what is the Constitution but what the Supreme Court says it is? Now while it is not my purpose to engage in polemics, a critique of this rather charming idea may help us to further elucidate wherein the Constitution is a permanent law.

Those who contend that the Constitution is what the Supreme Court says it is belong to the school of "legal realism." This school emerged as a reaction to a formalistic view of the judicial process (which may be called "legal formalism"). What the realist rejected, and quite rightly, is the naive notion that judges, in deciding whether a law is consistent with the Constitution, are merely involved in a problem of legal or formal logic. Looking more closely at the judges' pronouncements, the realists saw, and continue to see, not logic but *rhetoric*. And here they seem to have made some startling discoveries. For example: beneath the pronouncements of the Court they see the personality or personal preferences of individual judges; they see considerations of expediency or of public policy; they see accommodations to the dominant morality or sentiments of the times; and all this judiciously couched in language conveying to the unsophisticated a paramount and dutiful regard for the meaning of the Constitution and for the intentions of the Founders.[30] Apparently, these skeptics of the judicial process do not disapprove of what they see. Otherwise, having penetrated this judicial facade, they would have informed us that the Constitution is *not* what the Supreme Court says it is! Suppose they had done so. Since this would be a most serious charge against the Court, we would want to see the evidence. We would want to determine for ourselves whether, or to what extent, the Constitution is or is not what the Supreme Court says it is. For instance, we would want to know whether the Court has ever said that the states may be consolidated by the national government. We would want to know whether the Court has ever said that Congress may execute the laws or nominate who shall be President; or whether the President may decree the laws or nominate who shall be congressmen. Finally, we would want to know whether any Court has ever said that Americans may be deprived of life, liberty, and property without due process of law, in other words, that freedom means slavery. No doubt we would discover erroneous pronouncements of the Court, some which are more like commentaries on the passing scene than on the Constitution. But without minimizing these errors, we would not want to mistake the forest for the trees.[31] Furthermore, granting that judicial pronouncements are influenced, and even *ought* to be influenced, by considerations of public policy and public opinion —is this necessarily inconsistent with the Constitution or with the intentions of the Founders? (To anyone who has studied the political context of Marshall's greatest decisions, the idea is preposterous.)[32] Besides, the real question in every case is whether the pronouncement of the Court conforms to the "great outlines" and "objects" of the Constitution. And as for the personality of individual judges affecting Supreme Court decisions—what is meant by "personality"? Surely the personality of judges includes their intellectual and moral qualities, and these qualities may partake of excellence or of mediocrity; may be disciplined or undisciplined; may be manly or obsequious; may yield constructive thought or issue in rigid prejudice. Such qualities color the Court's decisions: How could they fail to?* But here again the question arises: However much the personal preferences of the judges may affect their decisions, are those decisions in continuity with the intentions of the Founders? But here the skeptics of the judicial process have made another profound discovery. To bolster their argument they maintain that judges do not really inquire into what the Founders willed centuries ago, but what they would have willed had they known what our conditions would be

---

* A study of judicial decisions would reveal the influence of the following factors: (1) the meaning of words both in the original and in the present context; (2) the will and general purposes of the Founders; (3) the will and general purposes of legislators; (4) precedent; (5) the wisdom of a particular law or act, including its immediate as well as its long-range consequences; (6) related to (5), consideration of public policy; (7) considerations of public opinion; (8) considerations of justice or of fairness; (9) related to (8), the rights of individuals as opposed to the requirements of public order; (10) the reaction of Congress or of the executive; (11) related to (10), the efficacy of the decision, that is, whether the decision will be enforced; (12) the personality—including the values—of the individual judges, which factor will influence the judges' understanding or estimate of all the preceding factors.

today.[33] Strange that the skeptics should not have seen that this admission, far from bolstering their argument, largely destroys it. For the only way in which the judges can determine what the Founders would have willed here and now is to inquire into their *general* principles and purposes. But insofar as the judges are guided by such an inquiry they cannot but preserve the general principles and purposes of the Constitution—in which case, however, it might be said that the Constitution *is* what the Supreme Court says it is![34]

Now the point to be elicited from the above critique is this: Let "extra-constitutional" considerations influence the Court's decisions, still the judges must justify their decisions on constitutional grounds, ultimately, by appealing to the intentions of the Founders.[35] This is of profound significance for the philosophy of judicial review, indeed, for the philosophy of the Constitution. For to inquire into the intentions of the Founders is to consider the present, not simply in the light of the past, but in the light of the enduring principles and purposes of American government. To expound these principles and purposes is to develop their relevant implications for the particular and the concrete. I say "relevant" because the implications of a general principle (or purpose) are multitudinous. Selection from among them must be made on the basis of their capacity to control and integrate present and forseeable occasions. Thus, while certain implications of a general principle may recede into the background, others may emerge into the foreground. Or one principle might be judiciously enlarged or contracted for the purpose of adjusting or correcting present occasions or for vitalizing potential ones. This is not "judicial activism": it is judicial activism *under* judicial self-restraint. It is not a surrender to expediency: it is expediency governed by a *comprehensive and long-range view of the whole.* It is a government of law as opposed to a government of men. But this requires some elaboration.

A government of men is preoccupied with the exigencies of the moment. Its rule is the rule of temporary interests and passions. It presents a scene of ceaseless innovation, improvization, and change. It is man's bondage to the present. In contrast, a government of law is one which is guided by long-established principles and long-range objectives. With such a government, the body of wisdom inherited from the past is preserved, enriched by the present, and transmitted to the future. A common venture unites one generation with the next, each responsive to those which have gone by, each responsible for those which are to come. There is no bondage to the past. Rather, it is the act of the new deepened by the old. It is the wisdom of present decision guided by philosophy mediated by law. It is an exacting discipline, the discipline of free, of civilized, men. But this is the discipline required of the Supreme Court *par excellence.* For to expound the Constitution is to bring philosophy to bear on action, again through the medium of law. To expound the Constitution is to elaborate its "great outlines" and "objects" that they may embrace the welter of human happenings and strivings and endow those happenings and strivings with order and purpose. It is to reconcile permanence and change.

Each time the Supreme Court expounds the Constitution it confirms an absolutely permanent aspect of that Constitution, namely, the compelling obligation to consider the intentions of the Founders. This permanent aspect of the Constitution may be attributed to its efficient cause (although, as an ingredient of the rule of law, it may be attributed to its formal cause). For whereas the Constitution is the expression of the original will of the people, and whereas the original will of the people is superior to all subsequent legislative, executive, and judicial bodies, the judges must inquire into the intentions or purposes of that will in the process of performing their duties. But the decisive question affecting the Constitution as a permanent law arises precisely at this point. That question is: Why should the will of the people who established the Constitution be binding upon the people now living?

To begin with, consider these familiar but hallowed words:

WE THE PEOPLE of the United States, in Order to form a more perfect Union, establish Justice, insure domestic Tranquility, provide for the common defence, promote the general Welfare, and secure the Blessings of Liberty to ourselves and our Posterity, do ordain and establish this CONSTITUTION for the United States of America.

Let us call this Constitution the *covenant* of the American people, for this term denotes its juridical basis as a permanent law.[36] Hence Hamilton could say in *Federalist 78:* "Until the people have, by some solemn and authoritative act, annulled or changed the established form, it is binding upon themselves collectively, as well as individually . . ." By "some solemn and authoritative act" Hamilton must have meant either the act of a constitutional convention or an act of revolution.[37] But since such acts are of rare occurrence, the status of the Constitution as a relatively permanent law is not affected. Therefore, when Hamilton says that the Constitution is binding upon the American people "collectively, as well as individually," we may be fairly certain that he deems it binding upon their descendants as well. For, unlike Jefferson, he did not regard each generation of men as comprising a new and distinct nation. He did not believe, as did the sage of Monticello, that no constitution, no law, no contract, is binding beyond the span of *nineteen* years.[38] (Indeed, we have seen that Hamilton was deeply concerned to establish in American government a *permanent will,* that he wished to develop among the American people a sense of *national character*—neither of which could be achieved if the Constitution of government, the covenant of the people, were to change with each succeeding generation.) Nevertheless, while rejecting a formula for chaos, Hamilton was not content to base the permanence of the Constitution on the juridically binding character of covenants. He was well aware of the need to answer, on other grounds, the question raised earlier, namely: Why should the will of those who established the Constitution be binding upon posterity? Even if Hamilton had thought, along with Burke, that a people constitutes an organic unity joining, in a common enterprise, the dead with the living and the living with the unborn, he could hardly have meant to apply this vision to a people which had so recently severed itself from much of its past, a people, moreover, which was now in the very process of adopting a new Constitution of government. That Constitution might eventually become the one enduring bond of this people. Its unifying influence might, in time, become truly profound—perhaps in ways unnoticed even by otherwise discerning men. But now it was necessary to prepare the rational foundations upon which this hope and promise might be realized. A future statesman might look to *Federalist* 78 to establish the principle that the Constitution is a fundamental and paramount law. There he would find the juridical basis of the Constitution as a permanent law. But if he wished to justify the permanence of the Constitution on other grounds—say on grounds of *prudence*—he could hardly do better than turn to *Federalist* 49.

Although it is not material to this discussion, I shall assume that *Federalist* 49 is the joint effort of Madison and Hamilton—Madison first because I believe he was the principal author.[39] Now the general problem presented by *Federalist* 49 may be stated as follows: Why is it unwise to subject the Constitution to frequent change? This question is especially relevant in virtue of its efficient cause. For inasmuch as the Constitution is supposed to express the will of the people, why should there not be frequent references to the people, the more accurately to ascertain their will? Suppose, therefore, that it was the practice to refer *all* constitutional questions to a decision of the people acting through conventions. What would be the consequences of such a practice? In answering this question, it should first be noted that such a practice would preclude judicial review. But then, *it is the only genuine alternative to judicial review.* I say this despite the idea fostered by scholars and statesmen alike that yet another alternative exists, namely, that which would allow each department of government to be the constitutional judge of its own powers—but therefore of the Constitution as a whole.[40] For inasmuch as such a system would inevitably lead to disputes among the departments over the boundaries of their respective powers, hence over the meaning of the Constitution, some method would be required for resolving these disputes. But can there be any doubt that such disputes would be "resolved"—*one way or another*—by an appeal to the people? Indeed, this is precisely the method proposed by Jefferson in his draft of a constitution for the state of Virginia, a method which *Federalist 49* explicitly takes to task. So, in discussing the consequences of referring all constitutional questions to a decision of the people, I am discussing, in effect, the consequences of affirming the notion of "departmental" review on the one hand, and of denying judicial review on the other.

Bearing these considerations in mind, suppose conventions were called to resolve all constitutional questions. These conventions, of course, would have the authority to alter and even remodel the Constitution should they deem it necessary. Now it should be obvious that the most frequent cause leading to such conventions would be none other than those disputes arising among the various branches of government over their respective powers, hence, over the meaning of the Constitution. It should also be obvious that the legislature would almost always be a party to such disputes; for its powers are not only the most extensive, but for that very reason the most difficult to define. Besides, and as so often noted in *The Federalist*, there is a constant tendency of the legislature to encroach upon its coordinate branches; and in any contest with these other branches, it would usually enjoy a distinct advantage. For unlike the executive and the judiciary, the legislature is a numerous body. It is drawn from all parts of the community; and since it is chosen by the people, its members may be presumed to have "a personal influence among the people."[41] But the "same influence which had gained them an election into the legislature, would gain them a seat in [a constitutional] convention." Hence, in the event of jurisdictional disputes between the various departments of government, the legislature, or a dominant party in the legislature, could control the convention and thus impose its will, or its interpretation of the Constitution, on the government as a whole. Suppose, however, that the executive were in the hands of "a peculiar favorite of the people," and suppose he were to undertake certain measures whose constitutionality was challenged. Were a convention called to resolve the issue, he might readily determine the outcome by the mere force of his popularity.

> In such a posture of things, the public decision might be less swayed by prepossessions in favor of the legislative party. But still it could never be expected to turn on the true merits of the question. It would inevitably be connected with the spirit of preexisting parties, or of parties springing out of the question itself. It would be connected with persons of distinguished character and extensive influence in the community. It would be pronounced by the very men who had been agents in, or opponents of, the measures to

which the decision would relate. The *passions*, therefore, not the *reason*, would sit in judgment. But it is the reason, alone, of the public, that ought to control and regulate the government. The passions ought to be controlled and regulated by the government. (*Federalist 49*)

Thus, to subject the Constitution to frequent change by referring constitutional questions to a decision of the people is to invite the rule of the passions. It is to enable one part of the people to impose its will or its interpretation of the Constitution on the remainder. More precisely, it is to enable either a powerful executive or a dominant party in the legislature to foist its designs on the uninformed multitude. But let us consider more deeply the consequences of referring constitutional questions to a decision of the people, bearing in mind that this is the only real alternative to judicial review.

In a passage of *Federalist 49* worthy of the most serious consideration, its author declares:

. . . as every appeal to the people would carry an implication of some defect in the government, frequent appeals would, in a great measure, deprive the government of that veneration which time bestows on everything, and without which perhaps the wisest and freest governments would not possess the requisite stability. If it be true that all governments rest on opinion, it is no less true that the strength of opinion in each individual, and its practical influence on his conduct, depend very much on the number which he supposes to have entertained the same opinion. The reason of man, like man himself, is timid and cautious when left alone, and acquires firmness and confidence in proportion to the number with which it is associated. When the examples which fortify opinions are *ancient* as well as *numerous*, they are known to have a double effect. In a nation of philosophers, this consideration ought to be disregarded. A reverence for the laws would be sufficiently inculcated by the voice of an enlightened reason. But a nation of philosophers is as little to be expected as the philosophical race of kings wished for by Plato. And in every other nation, the most rational government will not find it superfluous advantage to have the prejudices of the community on its side.

This is one of the boldest statements to be found in *The Federalist*. More than this, it is a profound and almost Platonic commentary on the inherent limitations of the political life. It reflects the pathos of a statesman who, untouched by the naiveté of the Enlightenment, knows well that the "noble lie" is the original and the enduring bond of even the best of human societies. Of course, a noble lie, to be noble, must somehow reflect a truth, a truth which is not ignoble. And it must have as its object a good, a good which would not be attained were it not for the lie. Now it may seem that to enlist the prejudices of the people on the side of the laws is to deepen their very prejudices. But insofar as the laws are reflections of reason and justice, these very prejudices, in the process of being assimilated to the laws, become reasonable and right opinions. In this way does the welter of individual opinions become modified and ordered according to their relevance. In time, but through the persuasion of the laws, they are transformed into public opinion or into a *public philosophy*. Hence, to inculcate among the people a reverence for the laws is to imbue them with a noble prejudice—noble in that it partakes of reason and justice, but a prejudice nonetheless insofar as it is *identified* with reason and justice. Yet this is the highest to which most people can possibly attain: Not a love of reason, but a reverence for the laws; not the knowledge of truth, but the acquisition of right opinion—more than this is beyond the capacity of political life. But suppose, now, that the laws in general, and the fundamental law in particular, are subject to frequent change. Can such laws inspire reverence? Can we respect a man who is constantly changing his opinions? Can we trust him or have confidence in his judgment? Indeed, must we not regard him as either a fool or a knave? How more serious the consequences of an ever-changing Constitution. That law embodies or reflects fundamental notions of what is right and reasonable. Subject that law to frequent change and the very notions of what is right and reasonable will change as frequently. So undermine respect for that law and respect for *all* forms of authority will crumble beside it, above all, "the authority of reason, justice, and truth."[42] What will take their place? What will be the new order of things? As the laws will be in a constant state of flux, so too will public opinion. But this means there will be no public philosophy, no unifying sense of tradition, no venture in a common destiny, but rather a restless pursuit of private interests, a general state of anomie or alienation. Hence, with the mutability of public opinion, the very notion of a "public" will become questionable. No one, of course, will deny the existence of opinions. But many will no longer distinguish between opinion and *right* opinion. All opinions will come to enjoy an equal status, except the opinion which renders everything equal. This being so, public standards or the rule of law will have been replaced by subjective feelings or the rule of numbers. The passions of ever-changing majorities, or of a dominant majority, will gain ascendancy. Temporary interests, expediency, unqualified pragmatism will dominate political life. As a consequence, the powers of government (no longer restrained by the principles of a permanent law) will vastly increase, although its purposes will be as obscure as "public opinion" or as variable as the passions of popular majorities. The government, having almost a complete license to do as it pleases, will engender or reinforce that notion of freedom in society at large. Crime and violence, a contempt for all forms of authority, will increase; and the government, ironically enough, will be virtually powerless to stem the tide. The end is all too obvious: anarchy is but a prelude to tyranny. That end had its beginning when government lost its firmest support, a reverence for the laws; and this was lost when the Constitution was made a mutable thing, when it was no longer regarded—*or faithfully adhered to*—as a permanent law, a law binding for all who are born, or who come to live, under its dispensation.*

I remind the reader of the topic under discussion, namely: Why should the Constitution be regarded as a permanent law?

> Prudence, indeed, will dictate, that Governments long established should not be changed for light and transient causes; and accordingly, all experience hath shown, that mankind are more disposed to suffer, while evils are sufferable, than to right themselves by abolishing the forms to which they are accustomed.

In other words, it is unwise to permit or encourage a people continually to upset and remodel their basic institutions, whatever the intrinsic merit of these institutions.[43] But there is yet another reason why, as a matter of prudence, the Constitution, *in particular*, should be regarded as a permanent law. Indeed, with this reason emerges the fundamental presupposition of the present argument. That presupposition is simply this: The Constitution was formed under political circumstances highly favorable to the establishment of good government, political circumstances whose equivalent will not likely occur in the future. Here is the way this presupposition is elaborated in *Fedaralist 49:*

---

* Here, recall Lincoln's "Lyceum Address": "Let reverence for the laws be breathed by every American mother to the lisping babe that prattles on her lap; let it be taught in schools, in seminaries, and in *colleges;* let it be written in primers, spellingbooks, and in almanacs; let it be preached from the pulpit, proclaimed in legislative halls, and enforced in courts of justice. And, in short, let it become the political religion of the nation; and let the old and the young, the rich and the poor, the grave and the gay of all sexes and tongues and colors and conditions, sacrifice unceasingly upon its altars." (Italics added) Consider, in this connection, the *economic*, the *historicist*, and the *realist* interpretations of the Constitution discussed in Chapter One.

Notwithstanding the success which has attended the revisions of our established forms of government, and which does so much honor to the virtue and intelligence of the people of America, it must be confessed that the experiments are of too *ticklish* a nature to be unnecessarily multiplied. We are to recollect that all the existing constitutions were formed in the midst of a danger which *repressed the passions most unfriendly to order and concord;* of an enthusiastic confidence of the people in their patriotic leaders, which stifled the ordinary diversity of opinions on great national questions; . . . and whilst *no spirit of party* connected with the changes to be made, or the abuses to be reformed, could mingle its leaven in the operation. The future situations in which we must expect to be usually placed, do not present any equivalent security against the danger which is apprehended. (Italics added)

The Constitution was formed in a period free from organized political parties, parties as we now know them. Repeat that experiment now and a dominant party will shape the very foundations of government. Or, if there be two or more parties of equal power, the new constitution will be nothing more than a medley of compromises *ungoverned by principles.* Temporary passions, temporary interests—those of a multiplicity of individuals and groups—will predominate rather than reason and the common good. But let us go back, back to the Constitution of 1787. That Constitution was formed by an extraordinary body of men, a body of men whose combined virtues and talents have seldom if ever been equaled. These men were not philosophers; they were politicians. But they were politicians well-versed in the philosophic tradition of Western civilization. They were keen students of history, of English and Roman law. They possessed that rare quality of mind which unites theory and practice, which seeks to guide action by reference to principles, and principles by their relevance to facts. They were not doctrinaire, they were not mere pragmatists. They adapted their principles to the character of the American people while seeking to elevate that people by the persuasion of those principles. They well understood America's *unique* conditions and potentialities, the *enduring* needs and aspirations of its people. And they possessed the confidence of the people. Their great prestige enabled them to overcome the diversity of interests and opinions which hitherto had made the American experiment in self-government a questionable endeavor. Finally, they were not the spokesmen of parties. They enjoyed that spirit of detachment which parties cannot suffer to exist. Hence they were the more capable of exercising dispassionate reason in the founding of the American Constitution. It would be imprudent to remodel that Constitution; it would be highly dangerous to do so.

Having considered, both on grounds of principle and of prudence, why the Constitution must be regarded as a fundamental and permanent law, it remains to consider why that law requires a *final* authority to ascertain its meaning or to resolve all constitutional issues, and why that final authority should be the Supreme Court. But surely these two remaining questions have essentially been answered in the previous discussion. For when I examined the factors which determine the Constitution as a fundamental law, and when I drew the consequences of subjecting that law to frequent change—consequences which would obtain if each department of government, in the last resort, were to determine for itself the meaning of the Constitution—I was then anticipating the argument for judicial review. Nevertheless, the problem must be considered in its own light.

It should be obvious that if there were no final authority to resolve all constitutional questions, the Constitution would be a subject of ceaseless controversy. Despite this, and as I have already noted, scholars as well as statesmen have maintained that each department of government was intended to be the ultimate judge of its own powers—as if each department were an utterly separate and independent entity, as if each could perform its function without ever coming into conflict with that of another! But let us adopt their "system" for the moment and see where it leads us. Under such a "system" the construction which the legislature (or which the executive or the judiciary) puts upon its own powers would be conclusive upon the government as a whole. That being the case, every legislative act would be "constitutional." This means that every legislative act would be determinative of the meaning of the Constitution; for to determine the meaning of a part is to imply the meaning of the whole.[44] But as the act of one legislature may be diametrically opposed to the act of a previous legislature—and not merely as to policy—the meaning of the Constitution might change with each succeeding election. We have seen the consequences of a mutable constitution. Behold now the spectacle of statesmen—of all legislative, executive, and judicial officers, both of the United States and of the several states—solemnly taking an oath to support a constitution that means one thing today and another tomorrow, that means anything and everything and therefore nothing! But this is not the only absurdity of presuming that each branch of government was intended to determine for itself, in the last resort, the extent of its constitutional powers. Thus, suppose the legislature were to pass an *ex post facto* law or perhaps a law impairing the obligation of contracts. The law deprives a citizen of his liberty or perhaps of his property. To whom shall he appeal against the enforcement of the law? Shall he appeal to the courts? Shall he there contend that the legislature, by the enactment of that law, has exceeded its constitutional powers and has thereby violated his constitutional rights? But the legislature is the ultimate judge of its own powers, and be his rights what they may, the constitutionality of the law is beyond question; its mere enactment is conclusive upon the courts and they have no alternative but to give it effect. *But not quite!* For having supposed that *each* branch of government is the ultimate judge of its own powers, what is to prevent the courts from *claiming* the right to nullify the law in question as being unconstitutional? Indeed, what is to prevent the executive from refusing to enforce the law on the very same grounds? Clearly such a "system" is a political monstrosity.[45] Clearly the Constitution requires a single and final authority to resolve all constitutional issues. The question remains: Which department of government should exercise that authority?

That legislatures are ill-suited to exercise such an authority should be apparent. In the first place, their membership is too large and too mutable.[46] If this were not enough to disqualify them, there is also the fact that legislatures are prone to faction, to party divisions and loyalties. Furthermore, as elective bodies, legislatures are too closely bound up with their own immediate interests and passions; and as representative bodies, they are too closely bound up with the immediate interests and passions of their constituents. But this means they lack the detachment required for a just and wise interpretation of the fundamental law.[47] Much the same may be said of the executive. Not only is his office too mutable, but he is too preoccupied with the details of administration to acquire a thorough understanding of constitutional law, or to resolve, with steady and considered judgment, controversies involving that law. On the other hand, as his office is elective, his judgment may be swayed by his passion for power or by the immediate interests of his party. Nor is this all. For if the executive were invested with final authority on constitutional issues, he would have, in effect, an *absolute* veto, and not only over the laws, but over the entire operation of government. When we consider the enormous political power already invested in the executive—and this applies to the legislature as well—clearly it would be dangerous to augment that power with the power of "judicial review." In short, prudence, to say nothing of justice, would dictate that neither those who make nor those who execute the laws should be the final judge as to their constitutionality.

Contrast now the Supreme Court. Unlike the legislature and the executive, the Court is not only devoid of immediate interests, but is without material power. Here, consider how Hamilton compares the three branches in *Federalist 78*:

> The Executive not only dispenses the honors, but holds the sword of the community. The legislature not only commands the purse, but prescribes the rules by which the duties and rights of every citizen are to be regulated. The judiciary, on the contrary, has no influence over either the sword or the purse; no direction either of the strength or of the wealth of the society; and can take no active resolution whatever. It may truly be said to have neither FORCE nor WILL, but merely judgment; and must ultimately depend on the aid of the executive arm even for the efficacy of its judgments.

Now it is precisely because the Supreme Court is without material power that it is safe to entrust it with the function of judicial review. Lacking such power, the members of the Court cannot hope to gain control over the material interests of the community, or to advance themselves by their judicial decisions. This being so, they can hardly be tempted to deviate from their sworn duty, especially in view of their permanent tenure. But to rest the case for judicial review solely on the basis of prudence is hardly sufficient. Indeed, to appreciate fully the intentions of its authors, it will be necessary to show how judicial review is also based on justice.

Again recall the three kinds of principles embodied in the Constitution, namely, those prescribed by the very nature of society, those required by any civilized society, and those which are peculiar to our own society. In different degrees these principles partake of justice, some of universal, some of general, and some of particular validity. Together these principles endow American political life with order and purpose. Together they give us a place, not only in our own society, but in the society of mankind. Hence they ought not be disturbed, not even by an overwhelming popular will. Now the Supreme Court alone is well designed to interpret and preserve these principles. On the one hand, only the Court is removed from the temporary passions of the people, from the pressures and importunities of interest groups, and from that bane of disinterested judgment, political parties. On the other hand—and as already noted—only the Court is without immediate interests and personal amibtions to be advanced by its public function. Finally, only the Court can devote itself wholly to the study of the laws and to the wise and just interpretation of the fundamental law.[48] But there is yet another reason why justice makes the Court's function of judicial review mandatory.

In *Marbury* v. *Madison,* Marshall advanced an argument which even friendly skeptics of judicial review have rejected, but which a little attention to the meaning of words will vindicate. Near the end of his opinion Marshall wrote:

> From these, and many other selections which might be made [and Marshall's selections from the Constitution should be more carefully studied by critics of what soon follows], it is apparent, that the framers of the constitution contemplated that instrument as a rule for the government of *courts,* as well as of the legislature.
>
> Why otherwise does it direct the judges to take an oath to support it? This oath certainly applies in an especial manner, to their conduct in their official character. How immoral to impose it on them, if they were to be used as the instruments, and the knowing instruments, for violating what they swear to support![49]

Skeptics have countered by saying that legislators and executives are also bound by oath to support the Constitution. But Marshall has anticipated and answered this objection by saying that the oath applies *in an especial manner* to judges acting *in their official character*. The oath applies in an especial manner to judges because, when the judges are acting in their official character, they are acting as *jurisprudents,* as men versed in the science of the laws, including the law of the Constitution. Hence the immorality of imposing the oath upon them if they were to be used as the *knowing* instruments for violating what they swear to support. But let us consider Marshall's argument in another light. Critics of that argument seldom if ever attend to or even mention the sequel of the passage cited above. Again, here are Marshall's words:

> The oath of office, too, imposed by the legislature, is completely demonstrative of the legislative opinion on this subject. It is in these words, "I do solemnly swear that I will administer *justice* without respect to persons, and do equal right to the poor and to the rich; and that I will faithfully and impartially discharge all the duties incumbent upon me . . . according to the best of my abilities and understanding, agreeably to *the constitution,* and laws of the United States.
>
> Why does a judge swear to discharge his duties agreeably to the constitution of the United States, if that constitution forms no rule for his government? If it is closed upon him and cannot be inspected by him?
>
> If such be the real state of things, this is worse than a solemn mockery. To prescribe, or to take this oath, becomes equally a crime.[50]

Notwithstanding the well-known subtlety of *Marbury* v. *Madison,* there is nothing subtle here: the pathos is unmistakably genuine. It is the pathos of a statesman who understands the sacrament of his word. The oath of office imposed by the legislature confirms wherein the oath required by the Constitution applies especially to the judges of the Supreme Court. For when the judges are acting in their official capacity they constitute *the highest tribunal of justice*. They bring justice to the individual citizen. On their decisions may depend his life, his liberty, his property. Shall they knowingly deprive a citizen of his life, or of his liberty, or of his property by affirming a law which they know, *as jurists,* to be in conflict with the Constitution, the Constitution which they themselves have solemnly sworn to uphold? Surely the idea is monstrous. It would make this Constitution—this written and limited constitution—an exercise in futility. It would render every law just—as if the Constitution were the work of *legal positivists!* It would turn courts of justice into the mere creatures of the legislature—courts which were deliberately designed as a distinct and separate department of government; courts which were invested with a permanent tenure to secure their independence.[51] It would reduce the oath of judges to mere sound signifying nothing —nay, much worse. For that oath is the ultimate promise that the laws shall be consistent with the principles of justice embodied in the Constitution. This is the promise of judicial review. Only betray that promise—*even under the color of judicial review*—and respect for both law and justice must ultimately wane.

With judicial review established on the basis of justice it only remains to relate this function of the Court to the Court's intended role in American political life. That done, the rationale of judicial review will have been essentially completed.[52]

As with any living thing, the Constitution may undergo change without having its generic character affected. This is one reason why the Constitution may be regarded as absolutely permanent in essence and relatively permanent in fact. Now to preserve the Constitution as a permanent law is to render what is permanent in essence permanent in fact, and this is the function of the Supreme Court. Indeed, to preserve the Constitution as a permanent law is the only theoretical justification for investing judges with a permanent tenure and with the power of judicial review. Otherwise the judiciary, far from being the least, would be the most dangerous branch of American government.[53] A President may err; a Congress may be partial; but the error and the partiality may be corrected by the turn of the electorate. Not so with the judges of the Court. Their errors and partialities are permanently engrafted upon the Constitution, become part of the body of constitutional law. Should they read what is merely their own personal preferences into the Constitution, or should they simply ratify, by their interpretation of the Constitution, the dominant opinions of the day, that Constitution will have been permanently damaged. Its fabric will not be repaired, even by a future Court composed of wise and judicious men. For to upset frequently the decisions of a previous Court is to undermine the durability and respectability of one's own. Prudential considerations aside, if judges were to regard the Constitution simply as a "developing law"—and advocates of this notion have in mind a law without fixed or permanent standards[54]—or if the judicial interpretation of the Constitution were simply to reflect the changing opinions of popular majorities, the Supreme Court might as well be a temporary body chosen by the people or by the people's representatives.[55] But then there would be no theoretical justification for the Court to review, with the power to annul, the acts of a popularly elected legislature.* Basically, such a court would be nothing more than an instrument of democratic justice.

Imagine such a court. It would be governed by two not always harmonious values: unmitigated equality and unre-

---

* For the moment, I am *not* referring to the legislature as intended by the Founding Fathers, for as the reader knows, only the House was popularly elected.

strained freedom. Both values are opposed to any meaningful and enduring standards of public life. Such standards inform us of what differences among men are to be tolerated or protected, and what differences are not to be tolerated or protected. Furthermore, these standards make possible intellectual discrimination between what is proper and improper, between what is lawful and unlawful. Now many of the standards of public life are embodied in the Constitution and are elaborated in Supreme Court decisions. By elaborating constitutional standards, the Court establishes standards at a lower level of generality. But insofar as a court has succumbed to the democratic principle, that is, insofar as it fosters unmitigated equality and unrestrained freedom, it establishes no standards. It may ratify the "standards" of the day, but by so doing, it leaves things to the flux of tomorrow. Far from being "activist," such a court should be called "passive" or "self-restrained." But such a court would be the degradation of the Court established by the Founders.

Now it is the duty of the Supreme Court to give to each principle of the Constitution its due. But since the Constitution embodies both aristocratic and democratic principles, the Court must do justice to the first as well as to the second. Strange were this not the case, for the Court is the most aristocratic branch of American government. To admit this, however, is to admit that the Court's *primary* duty is to uphold the very principle which it exemplifies. Indeed, were it not for the operation of that principle the Constitution could not be a permanent law. For as we have seen in previous chapters, were it not for the aristocratic principle embodied in the Senate, there would be no stability or continuity in the laws; that is, the laws would conform, not to the fundamental law, but to the changing sentiments and opinions of popular majorities as these happen to affect the membership of the House of Representatives. But whatever its primary duty, the very fact that the Court must do justice to *both* the democratic and aristocratic principles is precisely what makes its role in American political life so ambiguous. To clarify this and related ambiguities, I shall reformulate Hamilton's discussion of the problem in *Federalist 78.*[56]

The role of the Court may be divided into two distinct but inseparable functions. Its first function—and this may be termed "juridical"—is to hinder or thwart *unconstitutional* change, or changes which are contrary to the generic character of the regime. We have seen that the republic established by the Founders is susceptible to two forms of degradation, one oligarchic, the other democratic. Now the Supreme Court, according to Hamilton, was "designed to be an intermediate body between the people and the legislature, in order, among other things, to keep the latter within the limits assigned to their authority." This means ("among other things") that the Court is to protect the people against oligarchic legislation, or against laws which violate the people's rights and liberties. As we might suspect, however, there is another juridical function of the Court, and that function, said Hamilton, is "to guard the Constitution and the rights of individuals from the effects of those ill humors, which the arts of designing men . . . sometimes disseminate among the people themselves, and which . . . occasion dangerous innovations in the government, and serious oppressions of the minor party in the community." Here Hamilton had in mind the danger of democratic tyranny. The *many,* aroused by demagogues, may pressure their representatives in Congress to enact laws which would not only oppress the *few,* but which would also be destructive of those principles and institutions of government which were designed to protect the interests of the few. Should the representatives of the people enact such laws, they will have radically altered, *de facto,* the established form of government. It was in this connection, by the way, that Hamilton declared: "Until the people have, by some solemn and authoritative act, annulled or changed the established form, it is binding upon themselves collectively, as well as individually;" to which he then added: "and no presumption, or even knowledge, of their sentiments, can warrant their representatives in a departure from it, prior to such an act." How much the more so does this apply to an aristocratic body such as the Supreme Court. For that Court was designed, not to represent the changing wants and wishes of the people, but to be the permanent guardian of those ends and institutions of government without which that people would be nothing more than a mere aggregation of individuals. Hence, should the legislature, in subservience to the will of the people, enact laws repugnant to the Constitution, it would be incumbent upon the Supreme Court to resist the will of the people by declaring those laws null and void. "But it is easy to see," Hamilton continued, "that it would require an uncommon portion of fortitude in the judges to do their duty as faithful guardians of the Constitution, where legislative invasions of it had been instigated by the major voice of the community." As Hamilton well knew, more than fortitude would be required of judges if they were to preserve the Constitution as a permanent law. But of this, more in a moment.

Having discussed the juridical function of the Court, I turn now to examine what may be termed its "political" function—say its function of "creative interpretation." Again *Federalist 78* will be my point of departure.

To begin with, Hamilton notes that the Supreme Court is in the position of "mitigating and confining the operation" of laws which injure "the private rights of particular classes of citizens," laws which, though "unjust and partial," cannot readily be declared unconstitutional. Now the fact that the

Court is in the position to mitigate and confine the operation
of unjust laws is of profound significance. Said Hamilton:

> It not only serves to moderate the immediate mischiefs of
> those which may have been passed, but it operates as a
> check upon the legislative body in passing them; who, per-
> ceiving that obstacles to the success of iniquitous intention
> are to be expected from the scruples of the courts, are in a
> manner compelled, by the very motives of the injustice they
> meditate, to qualify their attempts.

This "circumstance" of the Court, Hamilton continued, is
"calculated to have more influence upon the character of
our governments than but few are aware of." Certainly
John Marshall was one of these few. For if the Court can
confine the operation of some laws, it can *enlarge* the operation of others—and both by creative interpretation. And if
it can enlarge the operation of ordinary law, it can enlarge
the meaning of certain terms or principles of the *fundamental law*—and again by creative interpretation. It can
enlarge the meaning of the *contract clause* and thereby
restrict the powers of the state legislatures (*Fletcher* v.
Peck). Or it can enlarge the meaning of the *necessary and
proper clause* and thereby enlarge the powers of the national legislature (*McCulloch* v. *Maryland*). In other words,
the Supreme Court can foster political change which is
constitutional as well as hinder change which is unconstitutional. But all this suggests how subtle and profound is the
role of the Court in American political life. Without material
power, without popular and party mandates—nevertheless
the Court is to adjust and modify the operation of the laws
according to the rule of that higher law, the Constitution.
Without material power, but through creative interpretation
of the "great outlines" and "objects" of that Constitution,
the Court is to influence, so far as prudence will allow, the
very course and character of American life. It is to do this,

however, not by judicial activism, but by judicial activism *under* judicial self-restraint. Clearly the judges of the Court will require not only fortitude, but judgment, judgment of a most wise and subtle kind. They will have to understand the various currents of American society—not to bend to these currents, so much as to direct them toward the mainstream of the Constitution. They will have to know how to mollify their more powerful "equals" while preserving the essential principles of that Constitution. They will have to know how to disarm their adversaries by making them appear as the enemies of the people. But they will also have to know how to temper and divert those "ill humors" of the people while appearing as the guardians of the people. And so they must be. For they must teach the people. They must teach them about the rule of law. They must teach them about the meaning of justice. They must teach them about liberty, the liberty which virtue renders a sacred blessing. Finally they must teach them about the Constitution, the covenant of this people. Therein is the supreme task of men who would *rule* by our fundamental law.

11

The Work of the Founding Fathers:

CRITIQUE AND CONCLUSION

I HAVE attempted to set forth the *heights* of the Founding Fathers, the *reach* of their intentions and aspirations. At that level it is tempting to draw an analogy between their work, the Constitution, and Plato's conception of the soul. Consider Congress the *desiring* part of the soul. It represents the many changing wants and wishes of society. Consider the Presidency the *spirited* part of the soul. It represents the passion for greatness: to transcend the petty interests and rivalries of men, to undertake arduous enterprises, to inspire a people with lofty goals, to imbue them with a sense of unity—this is its object. Consider the Supreme Court the *philosophic* part of the soul. To preserve and interpret the permanent principles of the Constitution, to uphold the rule of reason in public life, to restrain and limit the operation of the desiring and spirited elements—this is its function. The analogy, of course, is a rather loose one. The Constitution divides the powers of government between three coequal branches. For Plato, the three parts of the soul are not coequal. They constitute a hierarchical order, and the ruling element is philosophic reason. True, the President may suspend the acts of Congress; the Court may nullify the acts of both. But philosophy does not rule in its own right. Indeed, its closest friend, the Court, is the weakest part of the system. Furthermore, the Constitution does not provide for the education of the rulers. And therein is the paramount failure of the Founding Fathers.*

Philosophically, the Founders stand between the classics and the neo-moderns. For the classics, the primary purpose

---

* I say this in full cognizance of my critique of Diamond (*supra*, pp. 27-28). Where I differ from Diamond on this point may be explained as follows. From the fact that the Founders did not provide for education, Diamond concludes (1) that they were politically indifferent to this end; and (2) that they sought to establish a Constitution conformable to a democratic regime. I have shown that both conclusions are fallacious. Now it is my contention that the Founders' failure to provide for the education of statesmen was based largely on an error of judgment. For as we have seen, the Convention came very close to investing Congress with the power of establishing a national university, the proposal having been voted down apparently because some delegates thought that Congress could establish such a university in any event. Had the Convention invested Congress with that power, perhaps Congress would have enacted President Washington's proposal for a national university, a university which would have trained men in the science of government. But when I say that the Founders' failure here was based "largely" on an error of judgment, I also have in mind the apparent fact they did not give *due* weight to the importance of providing for the education of statesmen. This is far from saying that they did not regard education as a legitimate object of government, as Diamond contends. Nevertheless, in what follows, it is the *work* of the Founders, not their *intentions,* that I will subject to criticism—the distinction being that their work, the Constitution, is incommensurate with, and incapable of fulfilling, the reach of their intentions.

of laws and institutions is to make men good. For the Founders, the primary purpose of laws and institutions is to prevent evil. For the neo-moderns, the primary purpose of laws and institutions is to make men comfortable. Here the neo-moderns are caught in a dilemma, one aspect of which may be traced to the Founders. To make men comfortable, the neo-moderns seek to satisfy men's wants and to resolve their conflicts.[1] The laws, *qua* laws, serve no higher purpose: they are fundamentally unconcerned with habituating men in the ways of virtue, especially the virtue of moderation.[2] But to satisfy men's wants without fostering moderation is to feed the very causes of conflict. Men's wants are insatiable; they are constantly changing; they are constantly in competition with one another. The laws, while attempting to satisfy men's wants without fostering moderation, will be constantly required to *re*solve their conflicts. Far from contributing to men's comfort, the laws will contribute to their discomfort.[3] Now the Founders did not wish to establish a comfort-seeking society, a society of self-indulgent men. Nevertheless, they helped to "prepare" that society for its interminable conflicts. If we may take *Federalist 10* as representative of their views, it may be said that the Founders were aware of "two methods of curing the mischiefs of faction: the one, by removing its causes; the other, by controlling its effects." They chose to control the effects of faction, rather than to remove its causes, which causes they saw latent in human nature, in men's diverse and unequal faculties.[4] To remove the causes of faction would require, so they believed, the giving to every citizen the same opinions, the same passions, and the same interests. This, they readily concluded, would not only be impracticable, but destructive of liberty. Now what is remarkable is that this conclusion is based on a misconception.[5] For the practical problem—the political problem—is not one of *removing* the causes of faction, so much as one of *minimiz-*

ing these causes. Accordingly, it is not a question of giving to every citizen the same opinions, but of cultivating *right* opinions on the most important things, especially the things which make community, especially a good community, possible. Nor is it a question of giving to every citizen the same passions, but of tempering their passions, of fostering moderation, of discouraging envy and avarice and overweening ambition. Nor again is it a question of giving to every citizen the same interests, but of refining and harmonizing their interests. Finally, the political problem is not one of curing the mischiefs of faction so much as one of cultivating the blessings of friendship.[6] To strive for something less, that is, to control the effects of faction without minimizing its causes, is to control the symptoms of a disease while leaving the disease itself to fester beneath the surface: it is to sustain a "cold war" among men. But it is precisely because the Founders did not choose to "remove" the causes of faction that they made no constitutional provision for educating men in the ways of virtue. This decision, it is true, was influenced by certain *de facto* considerations involving the moral and political character of eighteenth-century American society. Before I touch upon this, however, allow me to reconsider how the Founders intended to control the effects of faction.

The reader will recall that the Founders sought to control the effects of faction in two ways. One involves the structure of government: dividing the powers of government among distinct and separate branches—the system of checks and balances. The other involves the structure of society: dividing society into a multiplicity of diverse interests—*pluralism*. Consider, first, the system of checks and balances.

Insofar as the system of checks and balances is intended to control the effects of faction within government itself, it is intended to guard against the various passions to which the elected branches of government are most susceptible: the House of Representatives, the passion of envy; the Senate, the passion of avarice; the Presidency, the passion of ambition. Here the Founders stand between the classics and the neo-moderns. For the classics the passions are to be refined. For the Founders the passions are to be restrained. For the neo-moderns the passions are to be liberated. The Founders appreciated the power of the passions. Often as they emphasize the need in government for men of virtue, they more frequently emphasize the necessity of guarding against the passions of self-interest, for therein lies the major cause of various evils, especially the evil of faction. (This twofold emphasis is no more. On the one hand, the neo-moderns emphasize the need in government, not for men of virtue, but for men who can get things done. Indeed, virtue is a term hardly used in contemporary political discourse.[7] On the other hand, the neo-moderns emphasize, not the necessity of guarding against the evils which spring from men's passions, but of alleviating the evils in men's conditions. Indeed, evil, as applied to man himself, is a term which contemporary dictionaries might yet classify as archaic.) But to return to the system of checks and balances: it may be said that the Founders sought to restrain men's passions by means of the passions themselves. But this is true only at one level of the Founders' intentions. Thus, consider the passions of envy and avarice. The Founders well realized that a popularly elected House of Representatives would introduce the danger of majority faction, a faction motivated by the passion of envy. But they also realized that a Senate elected by the state legislatures, and representing the interests of property, might introduce the danger of minority faction, a faction motivated by avarice. However, given the probable connection between wealth and merit, it was expected that the Senate, elected by the state legislatures and invested with a lengthy tenure, would constitute an aristocratic body, one composed of men of virtue and talent. Such a Senate would not only check the vice or passion peculiar to the popular body, it would elevate the character of the legislature as a whole. But suppose the Senate were to represent mere wealth or had succumbed to the vice of avarice. This would be preferable to a legislature wholly dominated by the vice of envy, that is, by a majority faction. Stated another way: If the refined mode of electing the Senate should succeed in advancing men of distinguished character, as was deemed likely, the tenure would insure their independence, would reinforce their virtues on the one hand, and enable them to exercise their talents on the other. However, should the electoral process sometimes result in the advancement of self-seeking men, the system of checks and balances would limit their vices or prevent the worst of political evils. Unfortunately, there is a flaw in this otherwise excellent arrangement—and now consider the government as a whole.

The Founders admit (and who would deny?) that enlightened statesmen will not always be at the helm. Nevertheless, they assume that enlightened statesmen will *generally* or *frequently* be at the helm. What is the basis of this assumption? The Founders presuppose that the system of checks and balances will preserve *the factual distribution of power* which then existed in American society between the few and the many.[8] That factual distribution of power, let us acknowledge, was highly favorable to the establishment of good government. It was favorable to the establishment of good government because the propertied classes, notwithstanding the vices from which no class is immune, were public-spirited, well educated, and by and large possessed the confidence of the people—and lest this be denied, when has a people raised up so remarkable a number of brilliant statesmen? The ascendancy of such statesmen speaks well of the moral and political character of American society at the time of the founding. But what was to insure the ascendancy of such statesmen in the future? Stated another way: What, in the Constitution, was to preserve the *de facto* status of the *few?* Three things: first, the indirect modes of electing the aristocratic branches of government; second, the duration of their tenure; third the constitutional protection of the rights of private property.[9] But suppose the moral character of the propertied classes were to decline? The Founders knew—and Hamilton as well as any—that the moneyed and commercial class is especially susceptible to corruption. But avarice begets envy: It is primarily the rich who set the standards of the poor. Yet there is no provision in the Constitution explicitly aimed at moderating the acquisitive instincts. Supposing, then, the corruption of the propertied classes, the indirect modes of election would generally result in the advancement of self-seeking and mediocre men. True, the system of checks and balances may prevent the worst of political evils. But meantime petty vices and the results of ineptitude will accumulate. Meantime the character of government will be degraded. Politics will become a term of contempt. The best men will avoid political office. What would be their prospect? To be associated with fools and knaves? To check the follies and vices of small-souled politicians? To restrain the passions of avarice, envy, and ambition? Consider. The Founders wished to secure the rule of reason, justice, and truth. They knew that the rule of reason, justice, and truth is ultimately dependent upon the rule of wise and virtuous men, but mediately upon the rule of law. Now given a society in which the factual distribution of power is favorable to the political advancement of good men, the problem is to establish laws which can at least preserve the moral standards implicit in that distribution of power, especially those standards which make the advancement of good men possible. This is but to enable the *de jure* to control the *de facto,* rather than to allow the reverse.[10] It is to institutionalize commonly accepted but auspicious standards the more readily to prevent their degradation. Foremost among these standards are those which involve the qualities required of statesmen, the qualities of statesmen admired by the general public. *These qualities must be explicitly recognized and fostered by the fundamental law.*[11] Notice, however, they are *not* explicitly recognized and fostered by the Constitution. Apart from *de facto* considerations, virtually any man may be elected to the Senate or to the Presidency of the United States.[12] These two branches wield enormous powers; they were intended to serve aristocratic ends. Yet the choice of those who are to wield these powers and serve these ends is left to depend upon indirect modes of election the aristocratic character of which is based upon probabilities in which the *de facto* is superior to the *de jure*.[13] Before a man may practice the art and science of medicine, he must go through a long and arduous school of training; he must meet certain standards of excellence; he must be licensed by recognized authorities. The rule of reason, justice, and truth requires no less of those who are to practice the art and science of government.

It will be evident from the foregoing that the institutions established by the Founders presuppose a fairly good society, though one not free from the danger of faction. To guard further against this danger, the Founders deemed it prudent to encourage the development of a pluralistic society. Yet they realized that pluralism, or diversity, is itself a cause of faction, a cause which cannot be removed, however, without destroying an essential characteristic of civilized society. As noted earlier, the Founders regarded pluralism as a mixed blessing. For the neo-moderns pluralism is an unqualified good. This suggests that the pluralism embraced by the neo-moderns may not be the same as the pluralism envisioned by the Founders. Recall that the pluralism of the Founders was primarily directed against the evil of majority faction, against the rule of the many. But this is to say that pluralism was primarily intended to secure the political status of the few without endangering the political status of the many. It follows that the pluralistic society envisioned by the Founders requires that both the few and the many be divided into a multiplicity of diverse interests without fundamentally altering the political status of each class taken as a whole. It requires that each class, again taken as a whole, be represented in different political institutions: the few in the Senate, the many in the House of Representatives. Now as we have seen, this division between the few and the many would involve no hereditary ranks or privileges—wealth and merit being the avenues of advancement. Accordingly, no citizen would be prevented by law from rising above the station of his birth or from pursuing any lawful interest or vocation. But notice that each citizen would have a fairly defined place in the political order: he would be represented in one of the two law-making branches of government. At the same time, however, he would have a President representing the nation as a whole, uniting yet transcending its diverse interests, exercising what may be termed architectonic leadership. This means that the pluralistic society envisioned by the Founders would be ordered or ruled by the *political*. In contrast, the neo-moderns have embraced the pluralism of the Founders abstracted from the political. Hence we now witness a phantasmagoria of cross-membered and conflicting interest groups and associations with no recognized political status, nevertheless represented in *every* elected branch of government, surreptitiously influencing and sometimes obstructing the course of legislation and administration—in short, we now witness a pluralism ruled by *society,* or by the *social*. In this pluralistic society government is primarily the instrument of the passions, and the passions, high and low, are

virtually equal. This is *democratic* pluralism. In the pluralistic society envisioned by the Founders, the government
would govern, would rule the passions, and the passions
would not be equal. This is *aristocratic* pluralism. And yet,
here again the Founders failed to provide adequately for
that pluralism. Again they made no *explicit* provision in the
Constitution for the political representation of wealth and
merit, none which could legitimate and long secure the
political status of the few. Thus, a pluralistic society, intended to be ruled by the *de jure,* and so ruled to a considerable extent in times past, is now ruled more and more
by the *de facto*—by the rule of *chance.*

This transformation is ironic. For let us never forget that
the Constitution does not prescribe pluralism as an end of
government. Quite the contrary: The Constitution was established "in Order to form a more perfect Union." But there
is a difficulty here: for the Preamble posits a multiplicity of
ends or purposes. Consider. The President is said to represent the unity of the nation. But a nation can hardly have
or achieve unity unless it has unity of purpose; and it cannot have unity of purpose unless it has one purpose which
is paramount above all others. What may that purpose be?
The Preamble does not say—at least not explicitly. Nevertheless, perhaps this purpose may be adduced by a process
of elimination. Surely that purpose is not *self-preservation,*
although "defence" is one of the ends for which the Constitution was established. Of course, I am thinking of self-
preservation in the narrow sense of the term, namely, as
the preservation of mere life. It is not certain, however,
whether the Founders thought of self-preservation in such
terms. But assuming they did, are we to believe that men
of their caliber would regard physical survival as the nation's
highest purpose? Would it not be more just and more
plausible to say that they regarded self-preservation as but
a precondition for the attainment of that purpose? On the
other hand, there is no need to reduce the *self* in self-pres-

ervation to animal existence. We could think of national self-preservation as the preservation of the nation's way of life, its political institutions, above all, its ends or purposes. But this only brings us back to the necessity of inquiring into which of these ends or purposes is the highest. Surely it is not *peace,* although "Tranquility" is one of the ends which the Constitution was meant to ensure. Of course, I am thinking of peace or tranquility in the narrow sense of the term, namely, as the absence of strife. But peace may also be understood as that state of society where men live in friendship or in harmony with one another. Still, harmony requires some ultimate purpose, one which endows other purposes with order. Surely that ultimate purpose is not the acquisition of *property.* The Preamble makes no mention of property, although it does speak of "Welfare." Of course, I am thinking of property in the narrow sense of the term, namely, as material wealth. In this sense, however, property was regarded as but a means of acquiring the advantages which wealth may afford—for example, *independence.* (Indeed, had the Founders regarded wealth as an end in itself, they would have praised avarice as a virtue rather than have condemned it as a vice.) But again I point out that property was also understood as encompassing whatever is proper to oneself, including the enjoyment of one's faculties, one's rights and privileges. So much for the meaning of property. But what of "Welfare"? Is it to be identified with mere wealth or material prosperity? Not according to Hamilton. For among the goods which government might foster under the general welfare clause, Hamilton included the advancement of education.[14] Indefinite (or comprehensive) as welfare would thus appear to be, let us look elsewhere for the nation's highest purpose. Is that purpose *freedom?*

The Preamble does not mention freedom. Instead, it speaks of liberty, or rather, of the *"Blessings* of Liberty."

What may these blessings be? Presumably, they include the right of citizens to participate in public elections as well as the right to hold public office. It is to be noted, however, that in almost all of the state constitutions, both of these rights were limited by property qualifications. Now this is particularly significant for our understanding of constitutional liberty. For it was generally thought (even by men like Jefferson and Paine) that persons without property are not, or are not likely to be, "freemen." They are not likely to have the *independence*, let alone the education, required for the proper exercise of the rights just mentioned. Their votes may more readily be "influenced" or corrupted, and, should they hold public office, they may more readily succumb to venal temptations. It would seem, therefore, that certain blessings of liberty must be earned, though all men have a right to earn them. Be this as it may, let us also include among these blessings the right to form political and other associations, the right to publicly criticise government policies, and let us add those rights affecting the enjoyment of privacy as well as of property. All these and other rights were not intended to be absolute. To argue the contrary is to make a mockery of constitutional liberty. For constitutional liberty is liberty under the urbane restraint of law, without which restraint no nation can achieve domestic tranquility, to mention nothing else. Nor should we think—and it would be absurd to do so—that the Constitution was intended to restrain government and not the governed. I have abundantly shown that this is not the case. But it might be well to recall the words of *Federalist 51:*

> In framing a government which is to be administered by men over men, the great difficulty lies in this: you must *first* enable the government to control the governed; and in the *next* place oblige it to control itself. (Italics added)

Notice that the government is to control itself, that it is *not* to be controlled by the governed. Bear in mind that the Constitution was founded partly with a view to curbing excesses of liberty, especially the excesses of democratic liberty. These excesses sometimes spring from the vulgar notion of freedom as "doing as one pleases." This is a notion of freedom which the Founders identified with license and which they wished to discourage by the discipline of law. There is not a scintilla of evidence to indicate that freedom was regarded by these highly self-disciplined men as an absolute, or that freedom occupies a "preferred position" in the Constitution. Indeed, of all the ends enumerated in the Preamble, liberty is mentioned not first, but last! What *is* mentioned first (excluding the unity clause) is *Justice.* Unlike the case with liberty, if not with all the other ends enumerated in the Preamble, there can be no excess of justice. Is this justice the nation's highest purpose?

In *Federalist 51,* wherein is to be found perhaps the most precise elaboration of the principle of checks and balances, recall that "justice" is said to be "the end of government"; it is said to be "the end of civil society." But we have seen that, underlying the system of checks and balances are two conceptions of justice, one aristocratic, the other democratic; the first exemplified by the Senate, the second by the House. Hence we must ask which of these two conceptions of justice was deemed the higher? The mere fact that we still speak of the Senate as the "upper" branch of the legislature is suggestive. But recall the terms which Madison and Hamilton used to describe this institution. They referred to it as the "select" member of the government; they said it was to be composed of the "enlightened and respectable" members of the community; they said it was to be composed of men noted for "wisdom and virtue." Did they apply such terms to the House of Representatives? Quite the contrary. It was precisely to check the follies and licentiousness of this branch that the Senate was instituted—instituted, let us remember, to uphold the authority of reason, *justice,* and truth. Are we to conclude from this that the Senate was instituted for the purpose of upholding democratic justice? The idea is absurd. Are we to conclude that the Senate was instituted to check the excesses of democratic justice? No doubt. But with a view to *what* was the Senate to perform this function if not with a view to aristocratic justice? And yet, granting that aristocratic justice was deemed superior to democratic or egalitarian justice, and granting further that aristocratic justice is the highest purpose of the Constitution, one thing is lacking, namely, *explicitness.* This would not have been the case had the Preamble included *virtue* among the ends of government, or had the Constitution made provision for the cultivation of *excellence.* But perhaps this is not to be expected from a *mixed regime,* a regime whose very foundations have been formed according to different ideas of justice (meaning different criteria as to who should rule). Such a regime, it would seem, would not only have different ideas of justice, but different notions of liberty, different notions of what constitutes the general welfare, and, to further complicate matters, different notions as to which of these ends, however understood, is to be cherished as the nation's highest purpose.

The Founders sought to establish a more perfect Union. With great skill they implanted two conflicting principles in the Constitution of that Union. This they did for the sake of the common good. Democracy is a powerful principle. It must ever have great weight in a large and civilized society. But democracy is a principle which can lead to the tyranny of the many. If only for its own sake, democracy requires restraints, the restraints of a contrary principle, the principle of aristocracy. What will be the effects of these principles on the American soul? Once again I say, that soul will be in tension. It will seek unity while praising diversity. It will desire change yet a sense of permanence. It will be acquisitive on the one hand, yet public-spirited on the other. It will love equality, yet aspire to excellence.

Appendix 1

Electoral Data from the State Constitutions In Force in 1787

The data included in this (and in the following) Appendix are important for evaluating the political character of the Constitution. A review of the data will reveal how superficial is the judgment that the Constitution represents a "conservative reaction" against the "democratic spirit" of 1776. Except for the tenure and modes of electing the various branches of government, most of the state constitutions were more "conservative" than the Federal Constitution. I say this in view of the property qualifications required of state office holders and their electors (of which, more in a moment), and in view of the provisions which many of the state constitutions made for education, religion, and the cultivation of virtue (Appendix 2). Nevertheless, the political character of the *state* constitutions, though distinct, are not separable from the political character of the *Federal* Constitution, as the latter presupposes the former. This fact is important for understanding *and* evaluating the intentions of the Founding Fathers.

Appendix 1

Table 1—The Tenure of the Various Branches of the State Governments

STATE	HOUSE	SENATE	EXECUTIVE	JUDICIARY
Conn.	1 year	none	1 year	Note[a]
Del.	1 year	3 years	3 years (not reeligible)	Good behavior
Ga.	1 year	Note[b]	1 year (but no more than 1 out of 3)	Note[b]
Md.	1 year	5 years	1 year (3 suc. and 4 yr. ineligibility)	Good behavior
Mass.	1 year	1 year	1 year	Good behavior
N.H.	1 year	1 year	1 year	Good behavior
N.J.	1 year	1 year	1 year	7 years
N.Y.	1 year	4 years	3 years	Good behavior
N.C.	1 year	1 year	1 year	Good behavior
Penn.	1 year	none	1 year	7 years
R.I.	6 months	none	Note[c]	Note[c]
S.C.	2 years	2 years	1 year	Good behavior[d]
Va.	1 year	4 years	1 year (same as Maryland)	Good behavior

a) Connecticut's Constitution of 1776 continued in force the colonial charter of 1662 which did not provide for a judiciary.

b) Under its Constitution of 1777, the Georgia legislature was unicameral, and the tenure of the judiciary is not specified. The Constitution of 1789 provides for a senate with a 3-year term and for a judiciary with a term of the same duration.

c) Rhode Island did not adopt a constitution until 1842, up to which time it continued in force the colonial charter of 1663.

d) The judiciary was appointed and could be removed by the legislature.

SOURCE: *The Federal and State Constitutions, Colonial Charter, and Other Organic Laws of the United States*, (2 vols.; Washington, D.C.: Government Printing Office. 1878).

Table 2—Property Qualifications for State Officers

STATE	HOUSE	SENATE	EXECUTIVE
Conn.	none	—	none
Del.	freehold	freehold	(chosen by legislature)
Ga.	250 acres or 250£ property	—	500 acres and 1000£ property
Md.	500£ real or personal property	1000£ real or personal property	500£ real or personal property, 1000£ in land
Mass.	100£ freehold or 200£ estate	300£ freehold or 600£ estate	1000£ freehold
N.H.	100£ estate, one-half in freehold	200£ freehold	500£ estate, one-half in freehold
N.J.	500£ real or personal property	1000£ real or personal property	(chosen by legislature)
N.Y.	20£ freehold	freehold	freehold
N.C.	100 acres	300 acres	1000£ freehold
Penn.	none	—	none
R.I.a			
S.C.	500 acres or 150£ sterlingb	200£ freehold	10,000£ freehold
Va.	freehold	freehold	(chosen by legislature)

a) None specified in the colonial charter of 1663 (Table 1, Note c).
b) Constitution of 1790.
SOURCE: *Ibid.*

Table 3—Property Qualifications for Suffrage

Conn.	40 shilling freehold or 40£ personal estatea
Del.	50 acres or 40£ personal estate
Ga.	10£ property
Md.	50 acres or 30£ in money
Mass.	3£ annual rental income or 60£ estate
N.H.	50£ in money
N.Y.	20£ freehold or 40 shilling annual rental value (House); 100£ freehold (Senate)
N.C.	taxpayer (House); 50 acres (Senate)
Penn.	taxpayer; and sons of freeholders who do not pay taxes
R.I.	40£ freehold or 40 shilling annual rental valueb
S.C.	50 acres of town lot; or tax equal to tax on 50 acres
Va.	50 acres or 25 acres with house; or town lot and house

a) Cf. Albert E. McKinley, *Suffrage Franchise in the Thirteen English Colonies in America* (Philadelphia: University of Pennsylvania, 1905), pp. 415-416.
b) Cf. Elisha R. Potter, *Considerations on the Rhode Island Question* (Boston: Thomas H. Webb & Co., 1842), p. 10.
SOURCE: *Ibid.* Cf. Chilton Williamson, *American Suffrage from Property to Democracy 1760-1860* (Princeton: Princeton University Press, 1960).

Appendix 2

Provisions in the State Constitutions

RESPECTING RELIGION, MORALITY, EDUCATION
AND THE QUALITIES REQUIRED OF STATESMEN

My object here is to inform the reader of facts relevant
to any evaluation of the general character of American society as reflected in the various state constitutions in force
at the time of adopting the federal Constitution.* These
facts are especially pertinent in evaluating the work of the
Founding Fathers, as well as my concluding critique. Thus,
contrary to my position, it might be argued that the Founders did not have to make provision, say, for education, in
view of the facts indicated in this Appendix. (It might also
be argued that they could not have done more than they
did, even had they so desired.) But consider well the
following.

CONNECTICUT

As already noted, the Connecticut Constitution of 1776
continued the colonial charter of 1662 in force as the organic law of the state. The Preamble declared:

* *The Federal and State Constitutions, op. cit.*

[264]

The People of this State . . . by the Providence of God . . . have the sole and exclusive Right of governing themselves as a free, sovereign, and independent State; . . . and forassuch as the free Fruition of such Liberties and Privileges as *Humanity, Civility* and *Christianity* call for, as is due to every Man in his Place and *Proportion* . . . hath ever been, and will be the Tranquility and Stability of Churches and Commonwealths; and the Denial thereof, the Disturbance, if not the Ruin of both. (Italics added)

Notice the aristocratic conception of justice implicit in these words. I might add, by the way, that Connecticut did not adopt a new constitution until 1818.

DELAWARE

Article 22 of the Constitution of 1776 (in force until 1792) required the following oath of office:

I, A B, do profess faith in God the Father, and in Jesus Christ His only Son, and in the Holy Ghost, one God, blessed for evermore; and I do acknowledge the holy scriptures of the Old and New Testaments to be given by divine inspiration.

Article 29 provided: "There shall be no establishment of any one religious sect in this State in preference to another . . ." Article 1, Section 1, of the Constitution of 1792 provided:

Although it is the duty of all men frequently to assemble together for the public worship of the Author of the Universe, and piety and morality, on which the prosperity of communities depend, are thereby promoted; yet no man ought to be compelled to attend any religious worship. . . and no power shall or ought to be vested or assumed by any magistrate that shall in any case interfere with, or in any manner control, the rights of conscience, in the free exercise of religious worship, nor a preference be given by law to any religio[n]. . . .

This same provision is contained in the Constitution of 1831.

GEORGIA

Article VI of the Constitution of 1777 required that "representatives . . . shall be of the Protestant religion . . ." Article LVI provided that: "All persons whatever shall have the free exercise of their religion; provided it be not repugnant to the peace and safety of the State; . . ." Article LIV provided that "schools shall be erected in each county, and supported at the general expense of the State . . ." These three provisions were not preserved in the Constitution of 1789.

MARYLAND

Article XXXIII in the Declaration of Rights of the Constitution of 1776 provided:

> That, as it is the duty of every man to worship God in such manner as he thinks most acceptable to him; all persons professing the Christian religion, are equally entitled to protection in their religious liberty; wherefore no person ought by any law to be molested . . . on account of his religious persuasion or profession, or for his religious practice; unless, under colour of religion, any man shall disturb the good order, peace or safety of the State, or shall infringe the laws of morality . . . yet the Legislature may, in their discretion, lay a general and equal tax, for the support of the Christian religion. . . .

Article XXXV required "a declaration of a belief in the Christian religion" for all state officers. (This was also required in the Constitution of 1864.) Article I of the Plan of Government stated that the electors of the House of Delegates were to choose "the most wise, sensible, and discreet of the people"; Article XV, that the electors of the Senate were to choose "men of the most wisdom, experience, and virtue, shall be chosen Governor." All the above articles were in force at least until 1851.

MASSACHUSETTS

Part I, Article II of the Constitution of 1780 provided:

It is the right as well as the duty of all men in society, publicly and at stated seasons, to worship the Supreme Being, the great Creator and Preserver of the universe. And no person shall be hurt, molested, or restrained . . . for worshiping God in the manner and season most agreeable to the dictates of his own conscience . . . provided he doth not disturb the public peace or obstruct others in their religious worship.

Article III provided:

As the happiness of a people and the good order and preservation of civil government essentially depend upon piety, religion, and morality, and as these cannot be generally diffused through a community but by the institution of the public worship of God and of public instructions in piety, religion, and morality: Therefore, to promote their happiness and to secure the good order and preservation of their government, the people of this commonwealth have a right to invest their Legislature with power to authorize and require, the several towns, parishes, precincts, and other bodies-politic or religious societies to make suitable provision, at their own expense, for the institution of the public worship of God and for the support and maintenance of public Protestant teachers of piety, religion, and morality in all cases where such provision shall not be made voluntarily. And the people of this commonwealth have also a right to, and do, invest their legislature with authority to enjoin upon all the subjects an attendance upon the instructions of the public teachers aforesaid, at stated times and seasons, if there be any on whQse instructions they can conscientiously and conveniently attend.

Article XVIII provided:

A frequent recurrence to the fundamental principles of the constitution, and a constant adherence to those of piety, justice, moderation, temperance, industry, and frugality, are absolutely necessary to preserve the advantages of liberty and to maintain free government. The people ought, con-

sequently, to have a particular attention to all these principles, in the choice of their officers and representatives . . .

Part II, Chapter V, Section 2 declared:

> Wisdom and knowledge, as well as virtue, diffused gen-
> erally among the people, being necessary for the preserva-
> tion of their rights and liberties; and as these depend on
> spreading the opportunities and advantages of education
> . . . among the different orders of the people, it shall be the
> duty of legislatures and magistrates, in all future periods of
> this commonwealth, to cherish the interests of literature and
> the sciences, and all seminaries of them; especially the uni-
> versity at Cambridge, public schools, and grammar-schools
> in the towns; to encourage private societies and public insti-
> tutions . . . for the promotion of agriculture, arts, sciences,
> commerce, trades, manufactures, and a natural history of
> the country; to countenance and inculcate the principles of
> humanity and general benevolence, public and private char-
> ity, industry and frugality, honesty and punctuality in their
> dealings; sincerity, and good humor, and all social affections
> and generous sentiments, among the people.

The provisions cited were in force as late as 1863.

NEW HAMPSHIRE

The New Hampshire Constitution of 1784 (as well as
of 1792) contained virtually the same provisions of the
Massachusetts Constitution cited above, as concerns religion, morality, and education. (The executive, by the way,
had to be of the Protestant religion.) The Constitution also
provided for a religious qualification for office (as did that
of Massachusetts), which qualification was not repealed
until 1877.

NEW YORK

Article XXXVIII established freedom of religion: *"Provided,* that the liberty of conscience, hereby granted, shall
not be so construed as to excuse acts of licentiousness, or

justify practices inconsistent with the peace or safety of this State."

NORTH CAROLINA

Article XXXII of the North Carolina Constitution of 1776 declared:

That no person, who shall deny the being of God or the truth of the Protestant religion, or the divine authority of the Old or New Testaments, or who shall hold religious principles incompatible with the freedom and safety of the State, shall be capable of holding any office or place of trust or profit in the civil department within this State.

Article XXXIV provided, however, "that there shall be no establishment of any one religious church or denomination in this State, in preference to any other . . ."; Article XLI, "that a school or schools shall be established by the Legislature, for the convenient instruction of youth, with such salaries to the masters, paid by the public . . . and all useful learning shall be duly encouraged and promoted, in one or more universities." The essence of these provisions were in force in 1876.

PENNSYLVANIA

As with the Massachusetts and New Hampshire constitutions, the Constitution of Pennsylvania of 1776 had a religious qualification for office. Like these other two constitutions, it referred to "justice, moderation, and temperance" as essential to liberty and free government. In virtually the same words as the Constitution of North Carolina, it provided for the establishment of schools in each county of the state as well as for one or more universities. Section 45 declared:

Laws for the encouragement of virtue, and prevention of vice and immorality, shall be made and constantly kept in force . . . : And all religious societies or bodies of men heretofore united or incorporated for the advancement of religion or learning . . . shall be encouraged and protected. . . .

Finally, Section 7 stated that "the house of representatives of the freemen of this commonwealth shall consist of persons most noted for wisdom and virtue. . . ."

RHODE ISLAND

As already noted, the colonial charter of 1663 was in force as the organic law in Rhode Island (save for the question of independence) until 1842. The charter provided for the public support of the Christian religion. (Article I, Section 3 of the Constitution of 1842, I might note in passing, established religious freedom. Article XII, Section 1 declared: "The diffusion of knowledge, as well as of virtue, among the people being essential to the preservation of their rights and liberties, it shall be the general assembly to promote public schools, and to adopt all means which they deem necessary and proper to secure to the people the advantages and opportunities of education.")

SOUTH CAROLINA

Article XXXVIII of the South Carolina Constitution of 1778 provided: "The Christian Protestant religion shall be deemed, and is hereby constituted and declared to be, the established religion of this State." The article goes on to enumerate various religious principles and moral precepts. As might be expected, the Constitution required that the governor of the state, as well as Representatives and Senators, be of the Protestant religion. All this was abolished by the Constitution of 1790.

VIRGINIA

Section 16 of the Virginia Bill of Rights of 1776 established freedom of religion, but at the same time acknowledged "the duty we owe to our Creator."

(The various decisions of the Supreme Court regarding the First Amendment and the "establishment of religion" clause should be reviewed in the light of the information contained in this Appendix.)

Appendix 3

The Constitution of the United States

WE THE PEOPLE of the United States, in Order to form a more perfect Union, establish Justice, insure domestic Tranquility, provide for the common defence, promote the general Welfare, and secure the Blessings of Liberty to ourselves and our posterity, do ordain and establish this CONSTITUTION for the United States of America.

ARTICLE I

SECTION 1. All legislative Powers herein granted shall be vested in a Congress of the United States, which shall consist of a Senate and House of Representatives.

SECTION 2. The House of Representatives shall be composed of Members chosen every second Year by the People of the several States, and the Electors in each State shall have the Qualifications requisite for Electors of the most numerous Branch of the State Legislature.

No Person shall be a Representative who shall not have attained to the Age of twenty five Years, and been seven Years a Citizen of the United States, and who shall not, when elected, be an Inhabitant of that State in which he shall be chosen.

[Representatives and direct Taxes[1] shall be apportioned among the several States which may be included within this Union, according to their respective Numbers, which shall be determined by adding to the whole Number of free Persons, including those bound to Service for a Term of Years, and excluding Indians not taxed, three fifths of all other Persons.][2] The actual Enumeration shall be made within three

---

[1] The income tax provision was modified by the Sixteenth Amendment.
[2] Replaced by the Fourteenth Amendment.

Years after the first Meeting of the Congress of the United States, and within every subsequent Term of ten Years, in such Manner as they shall by Law direct. The Number of Representatives shall not exceed one for every thirty Thousand, but each State shall have at Least one Representative; and until such enumeration shall be made, the State of New Hampshire shall be entitled to chuse three, Massachusetts eight, Rhode-Island and Providence Plantations one, Connecticut five, New York six, New Jersey four, Pennsylvania eight, Delaware one, Maryland six, Virginia ten, North Carolina five, South Carolina five, and Georgia three.

When vacancies happen in the Representation from any State, the Executive Authority thereof shall issue Writs of Election to fill such Vacancies.

The House of Representatives shall chuse their Speaker and other Officers; and shall have the sole Power of Impeachment.

SECTION 3. [The Senate of the United States shall be composed of two Senators from each State, chosen by the Legislature thereof, for six Years; and each Senator shall have one Vote.][3]

Immediately after they shall be assembled in Consequence of the first Election, they shall be divided as equally as may be into three Classes. The Seats of the Senators of the first Class shall be vacated at the Expiration of the second Year, of the second Class at the Expiration of the fourth Year, and of the third Class at the Expiration of the sixth Year, so that one-third may be chosen every second Year; [and if Vacancies happen by Resignation, or otherwise, during the Recess of the Legislature of any State, the Executive thereof may make temporary Appointments until the next Meeting of the Legislature, which shall then fill such Vacancies.][4]

No Person shall be a Senator who shall not have Attained to the Age of thirty Years, and been nine Years a Citizen of the United States, and who shall not, when elected, be an Inhabitant of that State for which he shall be chosen.

The Vice President of the United States shall be President of the Senate, but shall have no vote, unless they be equally divided.

The Senate shall chuse their other Officers, and also a President pro tempore, in the absence of the Vice President, or when he shall exercise the Office of President of the United States.

[3] Superseded by the Seventeenth Amendment.
[4] Modified by the Seventeenth Amendment.

The Senate shall have the sole Power to try all Impeachments. When sitting for that purpose, they shall be on Oath or Affirmation. When the President of the United States is tried, the Chief Justice shall preside: And no person shall be convicted without the Concurrence of two thirds of the Members present.

Judgment in Cases of Impeachment shall not extend further than to removal from Office, and disqualification to hold and enjoy any Office of Honor, Trust, or Profit under the United States: but the Party convicted shall nevertheless be liable and subject to Indictment, Trial, Judgment, and Punishment, according to Law.

Section 4. The Times, Places and Manner of holding Elections for Senators and Representatives, shall be prescribed in each State by the Legislature thereof; but the Congress may at any time by Law make or alter such Regulations, except as to the Places of chusing Senators.

[The Congress shall assemble at least once in every Year, and such Meeting shall be on the first Monday in December, unless they shall by Law appoint a different Day.][5]

Section 5. Each House shall be the Judge of the Elections, Returns and Qualifications of its Own Members, and a Majority of each shall constitute a Quorum to do Business; but a smaller Number may adjourn from day to day, and may be authorized to compel the Attendance of absent Members, in such Manner, and under such Penalties, as each House may provide.

Each House may determine the Rules of its Proceedings, punish its Members for disorderly Behavior, and, with the Concurrence of two thirds, expel a Member.

Each House shall keep a Journal of its Proceedings, and from time to time publish the same, excepting such Parts as may in their Judgment require Secrecy; and the Yeas and Nays of the Members of either House on any question shall, at the Desire of one fifth of those Present, be entered on the Journal.

Neither House, during the Session of Congress, shall, without the Consent of the other, adjourn for more than three days, nor to any other Place than that in which the two Houses shall be sitting.

Section 6. The Senators and Representatives shall receive a Compensation for their Services, to be ascertained by Law, and paid out of the Treasury of the United States. They shall in all Cases, except Treason, Felony, and Breach of the Peace, be privileged from Arrest during their Attendance at the Session of their respective Houses, and

[5] Superseded by the Twentieth Amendment.

in going to and returning from the same; and for any Speech or Debate in either House, they shall not be questioned in any other Place.

No Senator or Representative shall, during the Time for which he was elected, be appointed to any civil Office under the Authority of the United States, which shall have been created, or the Emoluments whereof shall have been increased, during such time; and no Person holding any Office under the United States shall be a Member of either House during his continuance in Office.

Section 7. All Bills for raising Revenue shall originate in the House of Representatives; but the Senate may propose or concur with Amendments as on other bills.

Every Bill which shall have passed the House of Representatives and the Senate, shall, before it become a Law, be presented to the President of the United States; If he approve he shall sign it, but if not he shall return it, with his Objections, to that House in which it shall have originated, who shall enter the Objections at large on their Journal, and proceed to reconsider it. If after such Reconsideration two thirds of that House shall agree to pass the bill, it shall be sent, together with the objections, to the other House, by which it shall likewise be reconsidered, and if approved by two thirds of that House, it shall become a Law. But in all such Cases the Votes of both Houses shall be determined by Yeas and Nays, and the Names of the Persons voting for and against the Bill shall be entered on the Journal of each House respectively. If any Bill shall not be returned by the President within ten Days (Sundays excepted) after it shall have been presented to him, the Same shall be a Law, in like Manner as if he had signed it, unless the Congress by their Adjournment prevent its Return, in which Case it shall not be a Law.

Every Order, Resolution, or Vote to which the Concurrence of the Senate and House of Representatives may be necessary (except on a question of Adjournment) shall be presented to the President of the United States; and before the Same shall take Effect, shall be approved by him or being disapproved by him, shall be repassed by two thirds of the Senate and House of Representatives, according to the Rules and Limitations prescribed in the Case of a Bill.

Section 8. The Congress shall have Power To lay and collect Taxes, Duties, Imposts and Excises, to pay the Debts and provide for the common Defence and general Welfare of the United States; but all Duties, Imposts and Excises shall be uniform throughout the United States;

To Borrow Money on the Credit of the United States;

To regulate Commerce with foreign Nations, and among the several States, and with the Indian Tribes;

To establish an uniform Rule of Naturalization, and uniform Laws on the subject of Bankruptcies throughout the United States;

To coin Money, regulate the Value thereof, and of foreign Coin, and fix the Standard of Weights and Measures;

To provide for the Punishment of counterfeiting the Securities and current Coin of the United States;

To establish Post Offices and post Roads;

To promote the Progress of Science and useful Arts, by securing for limited Times to Authors and Inventors the exclusive Right to their respective Writings and Discoveries;

To constitute Tribunals inferior to the supreme Court;

To define and punish Piracies and Felonies committed on the high Seas, and Offences against the Law of Nations;

To declare War, grant Letters of Marque and Reprisal, and make Rules concerning Captures on Land and Water;

To raise and support Armies, but no Appropriation of Money to that Use shall be for a longer Term than two Years;

To provide and maintain a Navy;

To make Rules for the Government and Regulation of the land and naval Forces;

To provide for organizing, arming, and disciplining, the Militia, and for governing such Part of them as may be employed in the Service of the United States, reserving to the States respectively, the Appointment of the Officers, and the Authority of training the Militia according to the discipline prescribed by Congress;

To exercise exclusive Legislation in all Cases whatsoever, over such District (not exceeding ten Miles square) as may, by Cession or particular States, and the Acceptance of Congress, become the Seat of the Government of the United States, and to exercise like Authority over all Places purchased by the Consent of the Legislature of the State in which the Same shall be for the Erection of Forts, Magazines, Arsenals, dock-Yards, and other needful Buildings;—And

To make all Laws which shall be necessary and proper for carrying into Execution the foregoing Powers, and all other Powers vested by this Constitution in the Government of the United States, or in any Department or Officer thereof.

Section 9. The Migration or Importation of such Persons as any of the States now existing shall think proper to admit, shall not be prohibited by the Congress prior to the Year one thousand eight hundred and eight, but a Tax or duty may be imposed on such Importation, not exceeding ten dollars for each Person.

The Privilege of the Writ of Habeas Corpus shall not be suspended, unless when in Cases of Rebellion or Invasion the public Safety may require it.

No Bill of Attainder or ex post facto Law shall be passed.

No capitation, or other direct, Tax shall be laid unless in Proportion to the Census or Enumeration herein before directed to be taken.

No Tax or Duty shall be laid on Articles exported from any State.

No Preference shall be given by any Regulation of Commerce or Revenue to the Ports of one State over those of another; nor shall Vessels bound to, or from, one State, be obliged to enter, clear, or pay Duties in another.

No Money shall be drawn from the Treasury, but in Consequence of Appropriations made by Law; and a regular Statement and Account of the Receipts and Expenditures of all public Money shall be published from time to time.

No Title of Nobility shall be granted by the United States: And no Person holding any Office of Profit or Trust under them, shall, without the Consent of the Congress, accept of any present, Emolument, Office, or Title, of any kind whatever, from any King, Prince, or foreign State.

SECTION 10. No State shall enter into any Treaty, Alliance, or Confederation; grant Letters of Marque and Reprisal; coin Money; emit Bills of Credit; make any Thing but gold and silver Coin a Tender in Payment of Debts; pass any Bill of Attainder, ex post facto Law, or Law impairing the Obligation of Contracts, or grant any Title of Nobility.

No State shall, without the Consent of the Congress, lay any Imposts or Duties on Imports or Exports, except what may be absolutely necessary for executing its inspection Laws: and the net Produce of all Duties and Imposts, laid by any State on Imports or Exports, shall be for the Use of the Treasury of The United States; and all such Laws shall be subject to the Revision and Control of the Congress.

No State shall, without the Consent of Congress, lay any duty of Tonnage, keep Troops, or Ships of War in time of Peace, enter into any Agreement or Compact with another State, or with a foreign Power, or engage in War, unless actually invaded, or in such imminent Danger as will not admit of delay.

ARTICLE II

SECTION 1. The executive Power shall be vested in a President of the United States of America. [He shall hold his Office during the Term of four years,]⁶ and, together with the Vice President, chosen for the same Term, be elected as follows:

Each State shall appoint, in such Manner as the Legislature thereof may direct, a Number of Electors, equal to the whole Number of Senators and Representatives to which the State may be entitled in the Congress: but no Senator or Representative, or Person holding an Office of Trust or Profit under the United States, shall be appointed an Elector.

[The Electors shall meet in their respective States, and vote by Ballot for two persons, of whom one at least shall not be an Inhabitant of the same State with themselves. And they shall make a List of all the Persons voted for, and of the Number of Votes for each; which List they shall sign and certify, and transmit sealed to the Seat of the Government of the United States, directed to the President of the Senate. The President of the Senate shall, in the Presence of the Senate and House of Representatives, open all the Certificates, and the Votes shall then be counted. The Person having the greatest Number of Votes shall be the President, if such Number be a Majority of the whole Number of Electors appointed; and if there be more than one who have such Majority, and have an equal Number of Votes, then the House of Representatives shall immediately chuse by Ballot one of them for President: and if no Person have a Majority, then from the five highest on the List the said House shall in like Manner chuse the President. But in chusing the President, the Votes shall be taken by States, the Representation from each State having one Vote; A quorum for this Purpose shall consist of a Member or Members from two thirds of the States, and a Majority of all the States shall be necessary to a Choice. In every Case, after the Choice of the President, the Person having the greatest Number of Votes of the Electors shall be the Vice President. But if there should remain two or more who have equal Votes, the Senate shall chuse from them by Ballot the Vice President.]⁷

The Congress may determine the Time of chusing the Electors, and the Day on which they shall give their Votes; which Day shall be the same throughout the United States.

No Person except a natural born Citizen, or a Citizen of the United States, at the time of the Adoption of this Constitution, shall be eligible to the Office of President; neither shall any Person be eligible to that

⁶ Number of terms limited to two by the Twenty-second Amendment.
⁷ Superseded by the Twelfth Amendment, which, in turn, is modified by the Twentieth Amendment.

Office who shall not have attained to the Age of thirty five Years, and been fourteen Years a Resident within the United States.

In Case of the Removal of the President from Office, or of his Death, Resignation, or Inability to discharge the Powers and Duties of the said Office, the Same shall devolve on the Vice President, and the Congress may by Law provide for the Case of Removal, Death, Resignation, or Inability, both of the President and Vice President, declaring what Officer shall then act as President, and such Officer shall act accordingly, until the Disability be removed, or a President shall be elected.

The President shall, at stated Times, receive for his Services, a Compensation, which shall neither be encreased nor diminished during the Period for which he shall have been elected, and he shall not receive within that Period any other Emolument from the United States, or any of them.

Before he enter on the Execution of his Office, he shall take the following Oath or Affirmation:—"I do solemnly swear (or affirm) that I will faithfully execute the Office of President of the United States, and will to the best of my Ability, preserve, protect and defend the Constitution of the United States."

SECTION 2. The President shall be Commander in Chief of the Army and Navy of the United States, and of the Militia of the several States, when called into the actual Service of the United States; he may require the Opinion, in writing, of the principal Officer in each of the executive Departments, upon any Subject relating to the Duties of their respective Offices, and he shall have Power to grant Reprieves and Pardons for Offences against the United States, except in Cases of Impeachment.

He shall have Power, by and with the Advice and Consent of the Senate, to make Treaties, provided two thirds of the Senators present concur; and he shall nominate, and by and with the Advice and Consent of the Senate, shall appoint Ambassadors, other public Ministers and Consuls, Judges of the supreme Court, and all other Officers of the United States, whose Appointments are not herein otherwise provided for, and which shall be established by Law: but the Congress may by Law vest the Appointment of such inferior Officers, as they think proper, in the President alone, in the Courts of Law, or in the Heads of Departments.

The President shall have Power to fill up all Vacancies that may happen during the Recess of the Senate, by granting Commissions which shall expire at the End of their next Session.

SECTION 3. He shall from time to time give to the Congress Information of the State of the Union, and recommend to their Consideration such Measures as he shall judge necessary and expedient; he may, on extraordinary occasions, convene both Houses, or either of them, and in Case of Disagreement between them, with respect to the Time of Adjournment, he may adjourn them to such Time as he shall think proper; he shall receive Ambassadors and other public Ministers; he shall take Care that the Laws be faithfully executed, and shall Commission all the Officers of the United States.

SECTION 4. The President, Vice President and all civil Officers of the United States, shall be removed from Office on Impeachment for, and Conviction of, Treason, Bribery, or other high Crimes and Misdemeanors.

ARTICLE III

SECTION 1. The judicial Power of the United States, shall be vested in one supreme Court, and in such inferior Courts as the Congress may from time to time ordain and establish. The Judges, both of the supreme and inferior Courts, shall hold their Offices during good Behaviour, and shall, at stated Times, receive for their Services, a Compensation, which shall not be diminished during their Continuance in Office.

SECTION 2. The judicial Power shall extend to all Cases, in Law and Equity, arising under this Constitution, the Laws of the United States, and Treaties made, or which shall be made, under their Authority;—to all Cases affecting ambassadors, other public ministers and consuls;—to all cases of admirality and maritime Jurisdiction;—to Controversies to which the United States shall be a Party;—to Controversies between two or more states;—between a State and Citizens of another State;[8]—between Citizens of different States,—between Citizens of the same State claiming Lands under Grants of different States, and between a State, or the Citizens thereof, and foreign States, Citizens or Subjects.

In all Cases affecting Ambassadors, other public Ministers and Consuls, and those in which a State shall be party, the supreme Court shall have original Jurisdiction. In all the other Cases before mentioned, the supreme Court shall have appellate Jurisdiction, both as to Law and Fact, with such Exceptions, and under such Regulations as the Congress shall make.

[8] Restricted by the Eleventh Amendment.

The trial of all Crimes, except in Cases of Impeachment, shall be by Jury; and such Trial shall be held in the State where the said Crimes shall have been committed; but when not committed within any State, the Trial shall be at such Place or Places as the Congress may by Law have directed.

SECTION 3. Treason against the United States, shall consist only in levying War against them, or in adhering to their Enemies, giving them Aid and Comfort. No Person shall be convicted of Treason unless on the Testimony of two Witnesses to the same overt Act, or on Confession in open Court.

The Congress shall have power to declare the Punishment of Treason, but no Attainder of Treason shall work Corruption of Blood, or Forfeiture except during the Life of the Person attained.

ARTICLE IV

SECTION 1. Full Faith and Credit shall be given in each State to the public Acts, Records, and judicial Proceedings of every other State. And the Congress may by general Laws prescribe the Manner in which such Acts, Records, and Proceedings shall be proved, and the Effect thereof.

SECTION 2. The Citizens of each State shall be entitled to all Privileges and Immunities of Citizens in the several States.

A Person charged in any State with Treason, Felony, or other Crime, who shall flee from Justice, and be found in another State, shall on Demand of the executive Authority of the State from which he fled, be delivered up, to be removed to the State having Jurisdiction of the Crime.

No Person held to Service or Labour in one State, under the Laws thereof, escaping into another, shall, in Consequence of any Law or Regulation therein, be discharged from such Service or Labour, but shall be delivered up on Claim of the Party to whom such Service or Labour may be due.

SECTION 3. New States may be admitted by the Congress into this Union; but no new State shall be formed or erected within the Jurisdiction of any other State; nor any State be formed by the Junction of two or more States, or Parts of States, without the Consent of the Legislatures of the States concerned as well as of the Congress.

The Congress shall have Power to dispose of and make all needful Rules and Regulations respecting the Territory or other Property belonging to the United States; and nothing in this Constitution shall be so construed as to Prejudice any Claims of the United States, or of any particular State.

SECTION 4. The United States shall guarantee to every State in this Union a Republican Form of Government, and shall protect each of them against Invasion; and on Application of the Legislature, or of the Executive (when the Legislature cannot be convened) against domestic Violence.

ARTICLE V

The Congress, whenever two thirds of both Houses shall deem it necessary, shall propose Amendments to this Constitution, or, on the Application of the Legislatures of two thirds of the several States, shall call a Convention for proposing Amendments, which, in either Case, shall be valid to all Intents and Purposes, as Part of this Constitution, when ratified by the Legislatures of three fourths of the several States, or by Conventions in three fourths thereof, as the one or the other Mode of Ratification may be proposed by the Congress; Provided that no Amendment which may be made prior to the Year One thousand eight hundred and eight shall in any Manner affect the first and fourth Clauses in the Ninth Section of the first Article; and that no State, without its Consent, shall be deprived of its equal Suffrage in the Senate.

ARTICLE VI

All Debts contracted and Engagements entered into, before the Adoption of this Constitution, shall be as valid against the United States under this Constitution, as under the Confederation.

This Constitution, and the Laws of the United States which shall be made in Pursuance thereof; and all Treaties made, or which shall be made, under the Authority of the United States, shall be the supreme Law of the Land; and the Judges in every State shall be bound thereby, any Thing in the Constitution or Laws of any State to the Contrary notwithstanding.

The Senators and Representatives before mentioned, and the Members of the several State Legislatures, and all executive and judicial Officers, both of the United States and of the several States, shall be bound by Oath or Affirmation, to support this Constitution; but no religious Test shall ever be required as a Qualification to any Office or public Trust under the United States.

ARTICLE VII

The Ratification of the Conventions of nine States shall be sufficient for the Establishment of this Constitution between the States so ratifying the same.

Done in Convention by the Unanimous Consent of the States present the Seventeenth Day of September in the Year of our Lord one thousand seven hundred and Eighty seven, and of the Independence of the United States of America the Twelfth. In Witness whereof We have hereunto subscribed our Names.

George Washington
President and deputy from Virginia

New Hampshire
John Langdon
Nicholas Gilman

Connecticut
William Samuel Johnson
Roger Sherman

New Jersey
William Livingston
David Brearley
William Paterson
Jonathan Dayton

Delaware
George Read
John Dickinson
Jacob Broom
Gunning Bedford, Jr.
Richard Bassett

Virginia
John Blair
James Madison, Jr.

South Carolina
John Rutledge
Charles Pinckney
Charles Cotesworth Pinckney
Pierce Butler

Massachusetts
Nathaniel Gorham
Rufus King

New York
Alexander Hamilton

Pennsylvania
Benjamin Franklin
Robert Morris
Thomas Fitzsimons
James Wilson
Thomas Mifflin
George Clymer
Jared Ingersoll
Gouverneur Morris

Maryland
James McHenry
Daniel Carroll
Daniel of St. Thomas Jenifer

North Carolina
William Blount
Hugh Williamson
Richard Dobbs Spaight

Georgia
William Few
Abraham Baldwin

Attest:
William Jackson, Secretary

AMENDMENTS

(The first ten amendments were adopted December 15, 1791, and form what is known as the "Bill of Rights.")

AMENDMENT I

Congress shall make no law respecting an establishment of religion, or prohibiting the free exercise thereof; or abridging the freedom of speech, or of the press; or the right of the people peaceably to assemble, and to petition the Government for a redress of grievances.

AMENDMENT II

A well regulated Militia, being necessary to the security of a free State, the right of the people to keep and bear Arms, shall not be infringed.

AMENDMENT III

No Soldier shall, in time of peace be quartered in any house, without the consent of the Owner, nor in time of war, but in a manner to be prescribed by law.

AMENDMENT IV

The right of the people to be secure in their persons, houses, papers, and effects, against unreasonable searches and seizures, shall not be violated, and no Warrants shall issue, but upon probable cause, supported by Oath or affirmation, and particularly describing the place to be searched, and the persons or things to be seized.

AMENDMENT V

No person shall be held to answer for a capital, or otherwise infamous crime, unless on a presentment or indictment of a Grand Jury, except in cases arising in the land or naval forces, or in the Militia, when in actual service in time of War or public danger; nor shall any person be subject for the same offence to be put in jeopardy of life or limb; nor shall be compelled in any criminal case to be a witness against himself, nor be deprived of life, liberty, or property, without due process of law; nor shall private property be taken for public use, without just compensation.

AMENDMENT VI

In all criminal prosecutions the accused shall enjoy the right to a speedy and public trial, by an impartial jury of the State and district wherein the crime shall have been committed, which district shall have been previously ascertained by law, and to be informed of the nature and cause of the accusation; to be confronted with the witnesses against him; to have compulsory process for obtaining witnesses in his favor, and to have the Assistance of Counsel for his defence.

AMENDMENT VII

In suits at common law, where the value in controversy shall exceed twenty dollars, the right of trial by jury shall be preserved, and no fact tried by a jury shall be otherwise reexamined in any Court of the United States, than according to the rules of the common law.

AMENDMENT VIII

Excessive bail shall not be required, nor excessive fines imposed, nor cruel and unusual punishments inflicted.

AMENDMENT IX

The enumeration in the Constitution, of certain rights, shall not be construed to deny or disparage others retained by the people.

AMENDMENT X

The powers not delegated to the United States by the Constitution, nor prohibited by it to the States, are reserved to the States respectively, or to the people.

AMENDMENT XI
(Adopted January 8, 1798)

The Judicial power of the United States shall not be construed to extend to any suit in law or equity, commenced or prosecuted against one of the United States by Citizens of another State, or by Citizens or Subjects of any Foreign State.

AMENDMENT XII
(Adopted September 25, 1804)

The Electors shall meet in their respective states and vote by ballot for President and Vice President, one of whom, at least, shall not be an inhabitant of the same state with themselves; they shall name in their ballots the person voted for as President, and in distinct ballots the person voted for as Vice President, and they shall make distinct lists of all persons voted for as President, and of all persons voted for as Vice President, and of the number of votes for each, which lists they shall sign and certify, and transmit sealed to the seat of the government of the United States, directed to the President of the Senate;—The President of the Senate shall, in the presence of the Senate and House of Representatives, open all the certificates and the votes shall then be counted;—The person having the greatest number of votes for President, shall be the President, if such number be a majority of the whole number of Electors appointed; and if no person have such majority, then from the persons having the highest numbers not exceeding three on the list of those voted for as President, the House of Representatives shall choose immediately, by ballot, the President. But in choosing the President, the votes shall be taken by states, the representation from each state having one vote; a quorum for this purpose shall consist of a member or members from two-thirds of the states, and a majority of all the states shall be necessary to a choice. And if the House of Representatives shall not choose a President whenever the right of choice shall devolve upon them, before the fourth day of March next following, then the Vice President shall act as President, as in the case of the death or other constitutional disability of the President.—The person having the greatest number of votes as Vice President, shall be the Vice President, if such number be a majority of the whole number of Electors appointed, and if no person have a majority, then from the two highest numbers on the list, the Senate shall choose the Vice President; a quorum for the purpose shall consist of two-thirds of the whole number of Senators, and a majority of the whole number shall be necessary to a choice. But no person constitutionally ineligible to the office of President shall be eligible to that of Vice President of the United States.

AMENDMENT XIII
(Adopted December 18, 1865)

SECTION 1. Neither slavery nor involuntary servitude, except as a punishment for crime whereof the party shall have been duly convicted, shall exist within the United States, or any place subject to their jurisdiction.

SECTION 2. Congress shall have power to enforce this article by appropriate legislation.

AMENDMENT XIV
(Adopted July 28, 1868)

SECTION 1. All persons born or naturalized in the United States, and subject to the jurisdiction thereof, are citizens of the United States and of the State wherein they reside. No State shall make or enforce any law which shall abridge the privileges or immunities of citizens of the United States; nor shall any State deprive any person of life, liberty, or property, without due process of law; nor deny to any person within its jurisdiction the equal protection of the laws.

SECTION 2. Representatives shall be apportioned among the several States according to their respective numbers, counting the whole number of persons in each State, excluding Indians not taxed. But when the right to vote at any election for the choice of electors for President and Vice President of the United States, Representatives in Congress, the Executive and Judicial officers of a State, or the members of the Legislature thereof, is denied to any of the male inhabitants of such State, being twenty-one years of age, and citizens of the United States, or in any way abridged, except for participation in rebellion, or other crime, the basis of representation therein shall be reduced in the proportion which the number of such male citizens shall bear to the whole number of male citizens twenty-one years of age in such State.

SECTION 3. No person shall be a Senator or Representative in Congress, or elector of President and Vice President, or hold any office, civil or military, under the United States, or under any State, who, having previously taken an oath, as a member of Congress, or as an officer of the United States, or as a member of any State legislature, or as an executive or judicial officer of any State, to support the Constitution of the United States, shall have engaged in insurrection or rebellion against the same, or given aid or comfort to the enemies thereof. But Congress may by a vote of two-thirds of each House, remove such disability.

SECTION 4. The validity of the public debt of the United States, authorized by law, including debts incurred for payment of pensions and bounties for services in suppressing insurrection or rebellion, shall not be questioned. But neither the United States nor any State shall assume or pay any debt or obligation incurred in aid of insurrection or rebellion against the United States, or any claim for the loss or emancipation of any slave; but all such debts, obligations and claims shall be held illegal and void.

SECTION 5. The Congress shall have power to enforce, by appropriate legislation, the provisions of this article.

AMENDMENT XV
(Adopted March 30, 1870)

SECTION 1. The right of citizens of the United States to vote shall not be denied or abridged by the United States or by any State on account of race, color, or previous condition of servitude.

SECTION 2. The Congress shall have power to enforce this article by appropriate legislation.

AMENDMENT XVI
(Adopted February 25, 1913)

The Congress shall have power to lay and collect taxes on incomes, from whatever source derived, without apportionment among the several States, and without regard to any census or enumeration.

AMENDMENT XVII
(Adopted May 31, 1913)

The Senate of the United States shall be composed of two Senators from each State, elected by the people thereof for six years; and each Senator shall have one vote. The electors in each State shall have the qualifications requisite for electors of the most numerous branch of the State legislatures.

When vacancies happen in the representation of any State in the Senate, the executive authority of such State shall issue writs of election to fill such vacancies: Provided, That the legislature of any State may empower the executive thereof to make temporary appointments until the people fill the vacancies by election as the legislature may direct.

This amendment shall not be so construed as to affect the election or term of any Senator chosen before it becomes valid as part of the Constitution.

AMENDMENT XVIII
(Adopted January 29, 1919)

SECTION 1. After one year from the ratification of this article the manufacture, sale, or transportation of intoxicating liquors within, the importation thereof into, or the exportation thereof from the United States and all territory subject to the jurisdiction thereof for beverage purposes is hereby prohibited.

SECTION 2. The Congress and the several States shall have concurrent power to enforce this article by appropriate legislation.

SECTION 3. This article shall be inoperative unless it shall have been ratified as an amendment to the Constitution by the legislatures of the several States, as provided in the Constitution, within seven years from the date of the submission hereof to the States by the Congress.[9]

AMENDMENT XIX
(Adopted August 26, 1920)

The right of citizens of the United States to vote shall not be denied or abridged by the United States or by any State on account of sex.

Congress shall have power to enforce this article by appropriate legislation.

AMENDMENT XX
(Adopted February 6, 1933)

SECTION 1. The terms of the President and Vice President shall end at noon on the 20th day of January, and the terms of Senators and Representatives at noon on the 3d day of January, of the years in which such terms would have ended if this article had not been ratified; and the terms of their successors shall then begin.

SECTION 2. The Congress shall assemble at least once in every year, and such meeting shall begin at noon on the 3d day of January, unless they shall by law appoint a different day.

[9]Repealed by the Twenty-first Amendment.

Section 3. If, at the time fixed for the beginning of the term of the President, the President elect shall have died, the Vice President elect shall become President. If a President shall not have been chosen before the time fixed for the beginning of his term, or if the President elect shall have failed to qualify, then the Vice President elect shall act as President until a President shall have qualified; and the Congress may by law provide for the case wherein neither a President elect nor a Vice President elect shall have qualified, declaring who shall then act as President, or the manner in which one who is to act shall be selected, and such person shall act accordingly until a President or Vice President shall have qualified.

Section 4. The Congress may by law provide for the case of the death of any of the persons from whom the House of Representatives may choose a President whenever the right of choice shall have devolved upon them, and for the case of death of any of the persons from whom the Senate may choose a Vice President whenever the right of choice shall have devolved upon them.

Section 5. Sections 1 and 2 shall take effect on the 15th day of October following the ratification of this article.

Section 6. This article shall be inoperative unless it shall have been ratified as an amendment to the Constitution by the legislatures of three-fourths of the several States within seven years from the date of its submission.

AMENDMENT XXI
(Adopted December 5, 1933)

Section 1. The eighteenth article of amendment to the Constitution of the United States is hereby repealed.

Section 2. The transportation or importation into any State, Territory, or possession of the United States for delivery or use therein of intoxicating liquors, in violation of the laws thereof, is hereby prohibited.

Section 3. This article shall be inoperative unless it shall have been ratified as an amendment to the Constitution by conventions in the several States, as provided in the Constitution, within seven years from the date of the submission hereof to the States by the Congress.

AMENDMENT XXII
(Adopted March 1, 1951)

Section 1. No person shall be elected to the office of the President more than twice, and no person who has held the office of President, or acted as President, for more than two years of a term to which some other person was elected President shall be elected to the office of the President more than once. But this Article shall not apply to any person holding the office of President when this Article was proposed by the Congress, and shall not prevent any persons who may be holding the office of President, or acting as President, during the term within which this Article become operative from holding the office of President or acting as President during the remainder of such term.

SECTION 2. This article shall be inoperative unless it shall have been ratified as an amendment of the Constitution by the legislatures of three-fourths of the several States within seven years from the date of its submission to the States by the Congress.

AMENDMENT XXIII
(Adopted March 29, 1961)

SECTION 1. The District constituting the seat of Government of the United States shall appoint in such manner as the Congress may direct;

A number of electors of President and Vice President equal to the whole number of Senators and Representatives in Congress to which the District would be entitled if it were a State, but in no event more than the least populous State; they shall be in addition to those appointed by the States, but they shall be considered, for the purposes of the election of President and Vice President, to be electors appointed by a State; and they shall meet in the District and perform such duties as provided by the twelfth article of amendment.

SECTION 2. The Congress shall have power to enforce this article by appropriate legislation.

AMENDMENT XXIV
(Adopted January 23, 1964)

SECTION 1. The right of citizens of the United States to vote in any primary or other election for President or Vice President, for electors for President or Vice President, or for Senator or Representative in Congress, shall not be denied or abridged by the United States or any State by reason of failure to pay any poll tax or other tax.

SECTION 2. The Congress shall have power to enforce this article by appropriate legislation.

Notes

Chapter 1

1. Cf. Stanley Pargelles, "The Theory of Balanced Government," in Conyers Read (ed.), *The Constitution Reconsidered* (New York: Columbia University Press, 1939), pp. 37-49; Gilbert Chinard, "Polybius and the American Constitution," *Journal of the History of Ideas*, I (Jan. 1940), 38-58.

2. Richard McKeon, "The Development of the Concept of Property in Political Philosophy: A Study of the Background of the Constitution," *Ethics*, XLVIII (April 1938), 298.

3. Richard Hofstadter, *The American Political Tradition* (New York: Vintage Books, 1956). Cf. Eugene V. Rostow, "The Supreme Court in the American Constitutional System," in Willmoore Kendall and George Carey (eds.), *Liberalism Verses Conservatism* (D. Van Nostrand & Co., Inc., 1966), pp. 285-300; Clinton Rossiter, *1787 The Grand Convention* (New York: The Macmillan Co., 1965). I regard Rossiter as at least an incipient historicist in view of the following considerations. After his having just completed a lengthy study of the men who drafted the Constitution, Rossiter concludes by saying that "most talk about the intentions of the Framers—whether in . . . the opinions of judges, or in the monographs of professors—is as irrelevant as it is unpersuasive, as stale as it is strained, as rhetorically absurd as it is historically unsound. No one, surely, can read the records of the Grand Convention . . . and not come to this harsh yet honest conclusion" (p. 333). That Rossiter should say *no one* can avoid this "harsh yet honest conclusion," when countless judges *and* professors have done precisely that, is a cause for wonder. And how he would evaluate his own work in view of this "harsh yet honest conclusion" is another cause for wonder—for he attempts to elucidate the intentions of the Framers for the better part of three hundred pages! Apparently, the only "clear intent of the Framers," according to Rossiter, "was that each generation of Americans should pursue its destiny as a community of free

men" (p. 334). If *this* is their only "clear" intent, why study their writings? Indeed, if their writings are as obscure as Rossiter here suggests, they are not worthy of being studied at all!

4. Hofstadter, *op. cit.*, p. 10.

5. *Ibid.*, pp. 16-17.

6. *Ibid.*, p. 3.

7. *Ibid.*, p. 16.

8. Is it not strange that Hamilton, who supposedly held a suspicious view of human nature, nevertheless wished to invest the new government with great powers; whereas Jefferson, who supposedly held a trusting view of human nature, wished to minimize these powers. ("Free government," Jefferson was to write in the Kentucky Resolutions, "is founded in jealousy, and not in confidence.")

9. Hofstadter, *op. cit.*, p. 16.

10. *Supra*, p. 151.

11. In the Introduction to his work (pp. viii-ix), Hofstadter refers to a "central faith" which has persisted throughout our post-revolutionary history, but which was not *politically* dominant during the eighteenth and nineteenth centuries. The ideas involved in this central faith were "confined to small groups of dissenters and alienated intellectuals" as opposed to "practical politicians." Except during revolutionary times, the ideas of practical politicians are "limited by the *climate of opinion* that sustains their culture" (italics added). (I might note in passing that this distinction between "alienated intellectuals" and "practical politicians" has little if any relevance to the American Revolution or to the Framers of the American Constitution. Many of the leaders of the Revolution were politicians as well as intellectuals; and many of the Framers of the Constitution were intellectuals as well as politicians. Furthermore, some of the opponents of the Constitution— whom Hofstadter would classify as alienated intellectuals—might also be classified as alienated politicians!)

12. *Ibid.*, p. 17.

13. *Ibid.*, p. 16.

14. *Ibid.*, p. 7 (italics added).

15. *Ibid.*, p. 5.

16. *Ibid.*, p. 10.

17. *Ibid.*, p. 11.

18. *Ibid.*, p. 15.

19. *Supra*, Chapter 4. Strangely enough, Hofstadter quotes John Adams as saying that there could be "no free government without a democratical branch in the constitution" (p. 14).

20. Hofstadter contends that "It was the opponents of the Constitution who were most active in demanding [these] vital liberties ..." (p. 11). Here he seems to have forgotten Madison's preeminent role on behalf of the first ten amendments, and perhaps the fact that

many members of the Convention were members of the First Congress. Of course, everything seems to hinge on what he means by the "most active" proponents of these amendments; but he brings forth not a scintilla of evidence bearing on the problem. On the other hand, Elbridge Gerry, who *opposed* the Constitution, tried, on at least two occasions, to postpone consideration of the amendments in question, though not necessarily because he opposed their *ultimate* adoption. Cf. *Annals of the Congress of the United States,* I, 461-462, 732; Max Farrand, *The Records of the Federal Convention of 1787* (4 vols.; New Haven: Yale University Press, 1937), II, 341, IV, 215, under "Slavery" (hereafter cited as *Farrand* unless otherwise indicated); *Federalist 84.* What is remarkable, however, is that Hofstadter admits that the Founders had "a statesmanlike sense of moderation and unscrupulously republican philosophy" (p. 15). But what is an "unscrupulously republican philosophy"? Is it the philosophy of balanced government —a philosophy which supposedly links liberty to property and not to democracy?

21. Charles A. Beard, *An Economic Interpretation of the Constitution of the United States* (New York: The Macmillan Co., 1954), first published in 1913.

22. Cf. McKeon, *op. cit.,* 297 *et seq.*

23. Cf. Robert Brown, *Charles Beard and the Constitution* (Princeton: Princeton University Press, 1956); Forest McDonald, *We the People: The Economic Origins of the Constitution* (Chicago: University of Chicago Press, 1958).

24. Beard, *op. cit.,* p. xii.

25. *Ibid.,* p. 15.

26. Max Weber, *Politics as a Vocation* (Philadelphia: Forcett Press Facet Books, 1965; H. H. Gerth and C. Wright Mills, trans.), p. 9.

27. Cf. Austin Ranney and Willmoore Kendall, *Democracy and the American Party System* (New York: Harcourt Brace & World, Inc., 1956), pp. 477-481, 29-38; James Allen Smith, *The Spirit of American Government* (New York: The Macmillan Co., 1907).

28. Cf. "Democracy and *The Federalist:* A Reconsideration of the Framers' Intent," *American Political Science Review,* LIII (March 1959), 52-68; Martin Diamond, Winston Fisk, and Herbert Garfinkel, *The Democratic Republic* (Chicago: Rand McNally & Co., 1966), Part One; Brown, *op. cit.* All further references to Diamond appear in his *APSR* article.

29. Diamond argues that: "An inflamed Marxian proletariat would not be indefinitely deterred by [such] institutional checks . . ." (p. 66). This is certainly true. But even had the Founders established an unmitigated monarchy, even such a government could not long survive an "inflamed Marxian proletariat"—especially at the time of Louis XVI! Diamond also argues that the amending provisions of the Constitution do not really constitute a check against the majority, that they only

insure "that passage of an amendment would require a nationally distributed majority" (p. 57). But what would be the political and economic composition of such a majority—and not today, but what is germane to Diamond's understanding of the Framers' *intent*—at the end of the eighteenth century? What Diamond does here is to use contemporary conditions as a gauge for measuring the Framers' intentions—hardly sound exegesis. But even today, the Senate, with its two-thirds rule for shutting off debate (Rule 22), slows down the passage of democratic legislation; and this Senate is but the shadow of the original one.

30. *Ibid.*, p. 54 (italics in the original).

31. Strangely enough, this is confirmed by the very title of the book which Diamond co-authored, namely, *The Democratic Republic!*

32. Ranney and Kendall, *op. cit.*, p. 38.

33. Diamond, p. 60.

34. *Farrand*, I, 423. According to *Federalist 57:* "The aim of every political constitution is, or ought to be, first to obtain for rulers men who possess most wisdom to discern, and most virtue to pursue, the common good . . ." And in *Federalist 64:* "[Because] the State legislatures who appoint the senators, will in general be composed of the most enlightened and respectable citizens, there is reason to presume [they will appoint] those men only who have become the most distinguished by their abilities and virtue . . ." In this connection, consider the caliber and political views of such Senators as Gouverneur Morris, Rufus King, George Cabot, Uriah Tracy, Theodore Sedgwick—but let us also add Albert Gallatin and John Quincy Adams.

35. Cf. *The Politics of Aristotle* (Oxford: Clarendon Press, 1952; Ernest Barker trans.), Book IV, esp. pp. 180-182 (hereafter cited as *Politics*).

36. Diamond, p. 61.

37. *Ibid.*, pp. 61-62.

38. *Ibid.*, p. 61.

39. *Ibid.*, p. 64.

40. *Politics*, p. 173. In *Federalist 63*, Madison notes that the Senate of Carthage was elected by the people.

41. *Farrand*, II, 616.

42. Cf. Appendix II.

43. This is especially evident in Chapter 8, where *Federalist* 62 and 63 are analyzed.

Chapter 2

1. *Farrand*, I, 2-6.

2. Cf. Article I, Section 5, of the Constitution, and the debates of August 10 (*Farrand*, II, 255).

3. *Ibid.*, I, 10.

4. *Ibid.*

5. *Ibid.*, I, 9-10.

6. *Ibid.*, I, 16.

7. *Ibid.*, I, 8.

8. *Ibid.*, I, 15.

9. *Documentary History of the Constitution of the United States of America 1787-1870* (5 vols.; Washington, D.C.: Dept. of State), IV, 183 (italics added). For commentary of the contemporary historian Jared Sparks on Madison's opinion regarding the importance of the rule of secrecy, see *Farrand*, III, 478-479.

10. *Ibid.*, III, 49-50 (italics added). Cf. *Documentary History of the Constitution*, IV, 401, Johnson to Washington.

11. *The Oxford Universal Dictionary* (Oxford: Clarendon Press, 1955). Cf. Washington's letters in *Documentary History of the Constitution*, IV, 331, 333, 371-373, 464, 500, 828, where he repeatedly uses the term "candor" in connection with the debates of the Convention and with those on ratification. Finally, in Edmund Randolph's criticism of the Constitution before the Virginia House of Delegates, note his admission that the debates of the Convention were conducted with *candor* (*Farrand*, III, 126).

12. *Ibid.*, III, 28. Similar thoughts are expressed by Alexander Martin of North Carolina to the governor of his state (*ibid.*, III, 64).

13. In a letter to his son dated May 20 (*ibid.*, III, 23), Mason expressed the belief that the success of the Convention would depend very much upon the "candor" and "liberality" of the delegates. Interestingly enough, the term "liberality," like the term "candor," also signified freedom from bias, although here it is to be understood as that quality which enables men to be friends despite their political differences. In this connection, cf. *Documentary History of the Constitution*, IV, 530-531, Washington to Madison, March 2, 1780.

14. *Farrand*, III, 368 (italics added). Cf. *Documentary History of the Constitution*, V, 18-20, Washington to Charles Pettit, Aug. 16, 1788.

15. Cf. Bertram M. Gross, *The Legislative Struggle: A Study in Social Combat* (New York: McGraw-Hill Book Co., 1953); David B. Truman, *The Governmental Process: Political Interests and Public Opinion* (New York: Alfred A. Knopf, 1953).

16. *Farrand*, III, 455 (italics added, with punctuation slightly altered). Franklin expressed the same sentiments at the close of the Convention (*ibid.*, II, 641-643; III, 104-105). Cf. debates of July 20 where "Gouverneur Morris' opinion had been changed by the arguments used in the discussion" on "the necessity of impeachments, if the Executive was to continue for any time in office" (*ibid.*, II, 68). As to whether Supreme Court justices change their opinions during the judicial conference, cf. Martin Shapiro, *Law and Politics in the Supreme Court* (New York: The Free Press, 1964), p. 22.

Chapter 3

1. *Farrand,* I, 18. Randolph does not use the term "cause" but "danger." It will be seen later that the substitution more clearly reveals Randolph's guiding intention.

2. *Ibid.*

3. *Ibid.,* I, 25-26.

4. *Ibid.,* I, 26.

5. *Ibid.,* I, 20-21 (italics added).

6. Rhode Island vacillated between annual and semi-annual elections.

7. Cf. *The Federal and State Constitutions, Colonial Charters, and Other Organic Laws of the United States* (2 vols.; Washington, D.C.: Government Printing Office, 1877-78). Cf. Appendix 1, *supra.*

8. In further confirmation of this, the sixth resolution invests the national legislature with the power to veto state laws, a power, to be sure, which is to be shared by the two legislative branches.

9. Cf. Appendix 1, *supra.*

Chapter 4

1. It is to be noted, however, that Franklin apparently preferred a unicameral legislature.

2. King's notes.

3. On June 26, by the way, Mason favored a property qualification for Senators.

4. Italics added. It should be pointed out in this connection that Mason's notion of the *people* is broader than Sherman's. Sherman seems to identify the people with the unenlightened many. For Mason, the people constitute all the classes of society. This distinction must be borne in mind when evaluating such notions as popular government and popular sovereignty.

5. Cf. Edward Dumbauld (ed.), *The Political Writings of Thomas Jefferson* (New York: Liberal Arts Press, 1955), p. 103, on the Virginia Constitution.

6. Pierce's notes.

7. Though Wilson would later favor popular election of the Senate and the Executive, he would also propose (1) a nine-year term for the Senate; (2) an absolute veto for the executive; (3) executive appointments of the judiciary; and (4) life tenure for members of the judiciary.

8. Cf. Aristotle, *Politics,* pp. 198-199. It may be noted that Aristotle regarded elections, in contradistinction to appointment by lot, as oligarchic (pp. 170, 177). Cf. Montesquieu, *The Spirit of the*

Laws (New York: Hafner Publishing Co., 1949; Thomas Nugent, trans.), p. 11 (hereafter cited as *Laws*); Rousseau, *The Social Contract*, III, 5, IV, 3; Charles W. Hendel (ed.), *David Hume's Political Essays*, (New York: Liberal Arts Press, 1949), p. 15 (hereafter cited as *Political Essays*).

9. This may be said of election per se. Cf. the debates of August 14, where John Mercer, a delegate from Maryland, declared: "Elective Governments . . . necessarily become aristocratic, because the rulers being few can and will draw emoluments for themselves from the many."

10. Cf. Aristotle, *Politics*, p. 267; Cicero *De re publica* i 60

11. Debates of June 7. As already noted, most of these upper branches had rather high property qualifications as is seen in Appendix 1.

12. Indeed, it was partly with this in mind that Wilson, almost alone among the delegates, favored an *absolute* executive veto over the legislature.

13. For example, the police powers may be left to the states, while there may be concurrent jurisdiction over taxation.

14. But cf. Martin Diamond, "What the Framers Meant by Federalism," in Robert Goldman (ed.), *A Nation of States* (Chicago: Rand McNally & Co., 1961), pp. 24-41. Diamond contends that the Framers identified the terms "federal" and "confederal" in opposition to the term "national," regarding the former as signifying a "league." But it is apparent from Randolph's enumeration of the properties of a federal government (*supra*, pp. 41-42) that he at least attributed *national* features to a federal government. The fact is that the Framers were far from being consistent in the use of these terms. (Cf., for example, the debates of May 30 and June 19.)

15. *Supra*, p. 41.

16. They may partly be inferred from what Randolph regarded as the defects of the Confederation, and from the first resolution of the Virginia Plan. *Supra*, p. 42.

17. Recall *Federalist 51:* "Justice is the end of government. It is the end of civil society. It ever has been and ever will be pursued until it be obtained, or until liberty be lost in the pursuit." In *Federalist 10*, Madison speaks of men being guided by a "love of justice." This suggests that justice involves more than respect for private rights.

18. Cf. *Federalist 51;* also, Hume, *Political Essays*, p. 13; Rousseau, *Social Contract*, I, Introduction.

19. Cf. Aristotle, *Politics*, p. 182; Machiavelli, *Discourses*, I, 4; Hume, *Political Essays*, pp. 157-158; Rousseau, *Social Contract*, II, Introduction; Montesquieu, *Laws*, p. 127; Montesquieu, *Grandeur and Decadence of the Romans*, (New York, 1882; Jehu Baker, trans.), pp. 184-185.

20. Monopolies would tend to make the working-class more "class-conscious."

21. Cf. Aristotle, *Politics*, pp. 181-183, 185-186.

22. *Federalist 10*.

23. *Ibid.*, where Madison concludes: "In the extent and proper structure of the Union, therefore, we behold a republican remedy for the diseases most incident to republican government."

24. The fact that Madison speaks of an "unmixed" republic is itself a warning that his distinction between a republic and a democracy is not sufficient. But of this, more in a moment.

25. A similar view of free government is expressed by Hamilton in J. C. Hamilton (ed.), *Works*, (7 vols.; Congressional Ed., 1850), II, 56. It may also be noted that John Adams regarded the British Constitution as a republic. Cf. George A. Peek Jr. (ed.), *The Political Writings of John Adams*, (New York: Liberal Arts Press, 1954), p. 44; and cf. p. 49 (hereafter cited as *Adams*).

26. From this it is apparent that Madison's defense of the representative principle is not simply motivated by democratic sentiment. The principle is essential to *any* plan of free government. But in addition to this, its adoption by the Convention was dictated by expediency. It makes possible the establishment of a government extending over a large territory. It augments the authority of this government and secures democratic support. At the same time, however, by enlarging the sphere of government, enlarged too is the scope of its purposes, which purposes are partly "democratic" and partly "oligarchic."

27. The issue was again raised on June 21, six days after the introduction of the New Jersey Plan. On this date New Jersey again voted against popular election of the first branch, nine states voted for, while the Maryland delegation was divided. Since the debates in question add little to those just examined, it will not be improper to pass them by.

Chapter 5

1. Pierce's notes, contrary to Madison's and Yates's, indicate that the vote occurred after discussion of the first clause of the fifth resolution.

2. The same point was made by Rufus King on May 31, and it was this that caused Spaight to withdraw his motion.

3. King's notes. (Compare Madison's of the same date.)

4. See Pinckney's suggestions in the debates now being discussed.

5. Cf. *Federalist 63*.

6. After all, Madison would have the state legislatures *nominate* the members of the Senate.

7. King's notes.

8. The reader will understand that it is the smallness of a *powerful* Senate which is here in question. This is presupposed in the following discussion.

9. To paraphrase a remark of Madison's quoted earlier: Respect for others, as well as self-respect, is always greater the fewer the number among whom blame and praise are to be divided. Here it is relevant to point out that a small Senate exercising important authority will be under closer public scrutiny, so that individual responsibility can more readily be determined.

10. Cf. *Federalist 51;* Hume, *Political Essays,* pp. 68-69; Spinoza, *Tractatus Politicus,* I, Secs. 5-6.

11. Cf. Hume, *Political Essays,* p. 13.

12. *Considerations sur les Causes de la Grandeur des Romains et de leur Decadence* (Paris, 1899), p. 4 (my translation). The original reads: "Dans la naissance des sociétés, ce sont les chefs des républiques qui font l'institution; et c'est ensuite l'institution qui forme les chefs des républiques." Baker, cited earlier, translates *républiques* as "states." This is unfortunate inasmuch as the term "state" is more abstract and lacks the specific qualities which Montesquieu attributes to a "republic" in *The Spirit of the Laws.*

13. Yates's notes.

14. King's notes.

15. Madison developed this idea in *Federalist 10.*

16. Oddly enough, these debates are most notable for the light they shed on the size of the Senate than on the mode of its appointment.

17. Consider, in this connection, the Tenth Amendment of the Constitution.

Chapter 6

1. Debates of June 21, Yates's notes.

2. *Ibid.,* Madison's notes.

3. This does not contradict Madison's position with respect to the size of the Senate as being more important than the personal character of its members.

4. It may be noted in this connection that *Federalist 53* also makes mention of the fact that "fit men" might be unwilling to serve in too brief an office.

5. The quoted phrase is from *Federalist 10.*

6. I am not unaware of the difficulty which this reference to "the unreflecting multitude" presents to my conjoining of Madison's and Jenifer's views. For the question arises: How can such a multitude be expected to elect men of caliber to the House of Representatives? It must be borne in mind, however that, whereas Jenifer is referring

to *popular election of the House,* Madison is referring to *ratification of the Constitution.*

7. Yates records Gerry as saying that he "could not be governed by the prejudices of the people [but that] their good sense will ever have its weight."

8. Again I quote from *Federalist 10.*

9. This decision was rendered without debate and will receive no further comment save to say that it should be considered in the light of Chapter 3.

10. The reader should bear in mind that the interval saw the introduction of the New Jersey Plan.

11. Cf. Yates's notes where Sherman is said to have feared the possibility of Representatives adopting "the interest of the state wherein they reside," that is, wherein happens to be the seat of the national government.

12. It should be noted that, according to *Federalist 62,* every election affecting the state legislatures (presumably their lower branches), resulted in a change of one half the number of representatives.

13. The words appear half-erased in Madison's original notes. Cf. *Documentary History of the Constitution,* III, 185.

Chapter 7

1. I shall return to this problem toward the end of the chapter.

2. It is to be noted, however, that discussion over the nature of the American union continued for another day.

3. It is unfortunate that we do not have a verbatim report of this remarkable speech. Hamilton's own notes are extensive but sketchy. Madison and Yates, however, do provide coherent accounts, and the notes of Rufus King are also helpful. While I shall always refer, whenever possible, to Hamilton's own notes, I remind the reader that all references are taken from Madison's unless otherwise indicated.

4. It should be noted that the plan itself was not *formally* submitted to the Convention.

5. Cf. Henry C. Lodge (ed.), *The Works of Alexander Hamilton* (12 vols.; New York: G. P. Putnam's Sons, 1904), II, 41, 60-61 (hereafter cited as *Works*).

6. Significantly enough, Hamilton was to elaborate the same principle on the very first page of *Federalist 1.*

7. Hamilton, *Works,* II, 92, *et seq.* Cf. *Adams,* p. 86.

8. The present writer is aware that there are important philosophical differences particularly between Montesquieu on the one hand, and Aristotle and Cicero on the other. Nevertheless, I feel justified in ignoring these differences for the purpose of elucidating

Hamilton's thought. It may be noted, however, that Montesquieu speaks of the British constitution as a "moderate" republic. For his description and evaluation of this republic, cf. Montesquieu, *Laws*, I, 150-162, 321.

9. This will no doubt remind the reader of Madison's reflections on civilized societies, namely, that they inevitably give rise to majority and minority faction. Cf. Plato *Republic* iii, where the transition is made from the "city of pigs" to the civilized city.

10. Though this inequality is to be found in all forms of society, the division it engenders between the few and the many is typical of civil societies, that is, of those societies where industry is encouraged. Cf. the correspondence between Adams and Jefferson on the *natural aristoi*, especially, Jefferson to Adams, October 28, 1813, and Adams to Jefferson, November 15, 1813. (A passage of the former is cited *infra*, n. 11.) It will be seen that Hamilton is closer to Adams than to Jefferson.

11. Cf. Jefferson to Adams, cited a moment ago, where he writes: "The natural aristocracy [as opposed to an aristocracy based on wealth or family] I consider the most precious gift of nature, for the instruction, the trusts, and government of society. And, indeed, it would have been inconsistent in Creation to have formed man for the social state and not to have provided virtue and wisdom enough to manage the concerns of society. May we not even say that that form of government is the best which provides the most effectually for the pure selection of these natural *aristoi* into the offices of government."

12. Indeed, this would be to establish an *artificial* division between the "few" and the "many."

13. Cf. Hamilton, *Works*, VIII, 4-5.

14. The appointment of the Senate by the state legislatures favors the actual representation of the wealthier classes of citizens. (Consider too, in this connection, the significance of the *contract clause*.) As for the judiciary, obviously this branch favors the actual representation of the legal profession to the virtual exclusion of all other classes.

15. Jonathan Elliot (ed.,) *The Debates in the Several State Conventions on the Adoption of the Federal Constitution* (5 vols.; Philadelphia: J. B. Lippincott Co., 1836), II, 257 (italics added); hereafter cited as *Elliot's Debates*. The omitted words are "The learned and the ignorant." Inasmuch as Hamilton contrasts only the rich and the poor, these words are left out so as not to encumber the exposition.

16. The political significance of envy will be considered in Chapter 8 in connection with Madison's speech of June 26.

17. Rather than burden the text, notice that in his speech of June 18, Hamilton said, in effect, that a well founded government would attract to its support the passions which "govern most indi-

viduals," namely, ambition, avarice, and interest. By "interest," he presumably meant self-interest, something which could hardly be said to distinguish one class from another. But since he was especially concerned to attract the rich to the support of the new government, it is reasonable to suppose he would attribute ambition and avarice to the rich more than to the poor—this, even though these passions are said to "govern most individuals."

18. Marshall's decision in *Marbury* v. *Madison* is instructive on this point.

19. *Documentary History of the Constitution,* III, 773.

20. Cited in Richard B. Morris (ed.), *Alexander Hamilton and the Founding of the Nation* (New York: The Dial Press, 1957), p. 144 (hereafter cited as *Morris*).

21. It should be borne in mind that no less than 26 of the 55 delegates at the Convention were lawyers or jurists, and that the Senate, then as now, was of a similar complexion.

22. Hamilton, *Works,* III, 13-14, and cf. II, 230-231, 331, 332, 335.

23 Cf. Alexis de Tocqueville, *Democracy in America* (2 vols.; New York: Vintage Books, 1954; Phillips Bradley, ed.), II, 129-132.

24. Cf. *Morris,* p. 155.

25. Hamilton's notes.

26. *Loc. cit.*

27. Although the Senate may also be said to embody the representative principle, it is the several states which are thus being represented. If it is true that an elective process is oligarchic or aristocratic, appointment by an elected body is the more so. But the weight of my argument does not depend on this aspect of the problem, since I am primarily concerned with Randolph's *intentions.*

28. *Supra,* p. 127.

29. Madison's notes of June 26 record Hamilton as saying he did "not think favorably of Republican Government." In Yates's notes of this date, Hamilton is reported to have said: "As long as offices are open to all men, and no constitutional rank is established, it is pure republicanism." In Hamilton's *Brief of Argument on the Constitution of the United States* (*Works,* II, 91-95), an outline of a speech addressed to the New York ratifying convention, he designates the proposed government as a "representative democracy." But consider the following: In the same brief he defines a democracy as one "where the whole power of the government [is] in the hands of the people" whether exercised by themselves, or by representatives "chosen by them either mediately or immediately." He then defines aristocracy as a government "where the whole sovereignty is permanently in the hands of a few for life or hereditary." Finally, he defines monarchy as a government "where the whole sovereignty is in the hands of one for life or hereditary." Where these three principles are

united, he says, the result is a "mixed government." Now, even assuming that Hamilton really did regard the proposed government as a representative democracy, two things are to be noted. First, his definitions of the democratic and non-democratic forms are not mutually exclusive! This is so because the definition of democracy is based, say, on some criterion of election; whereas his definitions of aristocracy and monarchy are based on the criterion of *tenure*. Obviously the Supreme Court is consistent with both criteria, so that the proposed government would exemplify some form of mixed regime. Second, whatever *name* we give to the form of the proposed government, we are to understand the *character* of this government primarily in terms of the *ends or values which it was intended to serve*. These ends or values are democratic, oligarchic and aristocratic: equality, wealth, and excellence, all of which are included in the republican idea of justice.

30. *Farrand*, III, 266.

31. *Politics*, pp. 177-178.

32. Yates's notes.

33. Cited in *Morris*, p. 134.

34. As we have seen, however, the large turnover of state *representatives* did not have too great an effect on the composition of the *annually* elected Congress under the Articles. Cf. *Federalist 62* and Madison's notes of June 7.

35. Hamilton, *Works*, II, 42-55. Hamilton's portrayal of the proposed Senate in these pages clearly indicates that his critique of June 18 was rhetorical, meaning only, that he thereby hoped to persuade the Convention to elevate the tone of the Senate even further.

36. Cf. *Adams*, pp. 115-116, 138-139; *Farrand*, I, 511-514 (speech by Gouverneur Morris).

37. Cited in *Morris*, p. 359 (italics added).

38. *Ibid.*, pp. 334-335, 343-353, 361-373, 375-376.

39. The executive, of course, would provide the "energy" for that will.

40. Cited in *Morris*, pp. 134-135. Cf. Hamilton, *Works*, II, 42-43, 53.

Chapter 8

1. I shall refer only to Pinckney's own version of his speech of June 25 which is to be found in *Farrand*, IV, 28-37.

2. Cf. *Adams*, pp. 144-145, for an "aristocrat's" vision of a similar America.

3. Not to be confused with the Pinckney mentioned earlier, and who was also from South Carolina.

4. Later in the day, Wilson supported Read's motion. It might

also be noted that Read had proposed, on the previous day, a senatorial tenure during good behavior.

5. The other number is *Federalist 62* which, when contrasted
with his speech of June 6, may also be regarded primarily as the
work of Madison. It should not need saying, however, that there is
utterly no way of showing that Hamilton did not *contribute* to the
formulation of the numbers in question. Indeed, there is reason to
believe he did. (Consider, for example, Hamilton's speeches of June
18 and June 29 so far as concerns the need for "permanency" and
"respectability" in the senatorial institution.) Language analysis with
computers may be helpful if we do not take them too seriously, that
is, if we do not sacrifice our common sense.

6. A similar statement in Madison's speech of June 26 will be
cited shortly.

7. Cf. Yates's notes of June 12 and Randolph's speech of the
same date.

8. Italics added.

9. These are the same qualities which Madison later associated
with the Senate in his speech of June 26. Cf. *supra*, p. 296, n. 34.

10. Italics added.

11. That Madison, toward the end of *Federalist 63*, should deem
it necessary to anticipate and refute the objection that the Senate,
as described earlier, might become transformed into a "tyrannical
aristocracy," or into an "independent aristocratic body," only confirms
my interpretation! Again we must not be deceived by Madison's
rhetoric, which is intended to say, simultaneously, different things to
different persons. His purpose here was to anticipate those adversaries of the Constitution who, for various reasons, might foster the
belief that the proposed Senate would become a *hereditary* aristocracy. But that the proposed Senate might be regarded as an aristocratic body (as indeed it was by some opponents of the Constitution) is evidence—to be sure, only collateral evidence—supporting my
position. Finally, the reader should know that in *Federalist 62*, when
the character of the Senate is compared with that of the House, it is
said that the "genius" of the two bodies must be distinguished from
each other "by every circumstance which will consist . . . with the
genuine principles of republican government." The only question is,
what are the "genuine principles of republican government" according to Madison? But we have already seen, and shall yet see more
clearly, a republican government, for Madison, admits of a non-
hereditary aristocratic principle.

12. I shall show, in the chapter on the Supreme Court, that the
formal cause or *generic* character of the Constitution is not reducible
to its *efficient* cause or the principle of popular sovereignty. Cf.
supra, p. 216 n.

13. I say this despite the following statement of *Federalist 63:* "The people can never wilfully betray their own interests; but they may possibly be betrayed by the representatives of the people . . ." This can only mean that men *intend* what they *believe* to be good for them. It cannot mean that *what* they intend or will *is* good for them. But here again is an example of Madison's rhetoric.

14. *Federalist 63.*

15. Both meanings, it should be noted, conform to eighteenth-century usage; Cf. *Oxford Dictionary,* previously cited.

16. The leveling spirit is also connected with majority faction in Madison's speech of June 26.

17. It may be assumed that, for Madison, this diversity gives rise to invention and discovery, advances the various kinds of manufacturing, fosters agriculture and commerce, promotes wealth and leisure, the arts and sciences.

18. This conclusion is drawn in the light of Madison's speeches of June 6 and June 26.

19. Cited in Saul K. Padover, *The Complete Madison* (New York: Harper & Row, 1953), pp. 267-268. "Government," Madison continues, "is instituted to protect property of every sort;" and "Conscience is the most sacred of all property." Cf. *Letters and Other Writings of James Madison* (4 vols.; Philadelphia: J. B. Lippincott & Co., 1865), IV, 478-480.

20. Cf. Leo Strauss, *Natural Right and History* (Chicago: University of Chicago Press, 1953), p. 245, where the author interprets Madison as having said: "The protection of [different and unequal faculties of *acquiring* property] is the first object of government." (Professor Strauss's brackets and italics.) What Madison actually said is this: "The diversity in the faculties of men, from which the rights of property originate, is not less an insuperable obstacle to a uniformity of interests. The protection of these faculties is the first object of government." Notice that the first object of government is not to protect the rights of property, nor the faculties *of* acquiring property, but rather the faculties *from* which the rights of property originate. (Note the comma between "men" and "from" in the first sentence.) Now even apart from the fact that Madison's conception of property extends beyond material possessions (and this is not clearly evident in *Federalist 10*), the protection of the different and unequal faculties "of" acquiring property may well be the *first* object of government—*but only for practical purposes.* In other words, this protection need not be the *ultimate* object of government. Assuming that Madison is the author of *Federalist 51,* recall the statement that "justice is the end of government." As there implied, this justice involves more than the protection of property—unless property be understood to include one's rights and privileges, the rights and privileges achieved by the use of one's faculties.

21. The reader should bear in mind that the institutional limits of any of the constitutive principles of a republic cannot be finely drawn. This is because each of the diverse principles of a republic has diverse exemplifications (quantitative as well as qualitative), and these may be variously combined in each branch of the regime.

22. It should be obvious that political equality stands on another footing, for it entails no more than the right of all citizens to have some voice in political affairs.

23. For example: rich and poor, learned and unlearned, are equally punishable by law for the same offense. Or, regardless of wealth or talent, "one man one vote."

24. The manner of constituting the Senate has this notion of justice in view. But the mere protection of private property insures the political influence of wealth, and hence, of the respectable members of the community. Another example of aristocratic justice may be found in the standards of excellence required for entry into the civil service.

25. The equalitarian aspects would consist, for example, in the liberty to pursue a lawful calling or to participate in political affairs. Above and beyond this, however, would be the liberty to enjoy the superior advantages of wealth and talent.

26. *Farrand,* I, 605. Recall that Wilson supported Madison's and Pinckney's proposal to invest Congress with the power to establish a national university.

27. In this connection, consider the following passage from *Federalist 50:* "When men exercise their reason coolly and freely on a variety of distinct questions, they inevitably fall into different opinions on some of them. When they are governed by a common passion, their opinions, if they are so to be called, will be the same." Now it should be noted that, although Madison first speaks of "pluralism" in connection with the representative principle, hence, with the House, nevertheless it is this branch which poses the danger of egalitarian tyranny. It may therefore be said that while the House is to make a greater degree of pluralism *possible,* the preservation of that pluralism will depend largely upon the Senate.

28. *Federalist 63.* In his second annual message to Congress, December 5, 1810, President Madison proposed the establishment of a national university. "Such an institution," he urged, ". . . [by] enlightening the opinions, by expanding the patriotism, and by assimilating the principles, the sentiments, and the manners of those who might resort to this temple of science, to be redistributed in due time through every part of the community, sources of jealousy and prejudice would be diminished. The features of national character would be multiplied, and greater extent given to social harmony." Cited in Padover, *The Complete Madison,* p. 316. Cf. *Elliot's Debates,* II, 320, 301-307, where Hamilton speaks of the Senate's func-

tion as one of fostering national character on the one hand, and of overcoming faction on the other.

29. *Federalist 62.* Cf. Rousseau, *Origin of Inequality,* Dedicatory Letter.

30. Cf. Aristotle, *Politics,* pp. 72-73.

31. *Federalist 62.*

32. Hamilton, *Works,* IV, 70-198.

33. See Hamilton's notes of June 6 commenting on Madison's speech of that date; also his speech of June 26 as reported by Madison. The difference in motive between Madison and Hamilton may be highly significant for their later opposition, hence for the depth of their aristocratic and nationalist principles. The present writer does not wish to suggest, however, that he has any explanation, satisfactory to himself, for Madison's later conversion to Jeffersonianism.

34. Cf. *Morris,* p. 173, and Hamilton's notes of June 6 *in re* the objects of the state governments.

35. *Farrand,* I, 168 (Madison's own notes). This is the "same" Madison who authored the Virginia Resolutions!

Chapter 9

1. *Farrand,* III, 410.

2. It will not be necessary, for the purpose of my mixed regime thesis, to examine the specific powers of the two houses of Congress. Nor is there required any additional discussion of the issue concerning the representation of the states in the Senate, the significance of which was developed in Chapter 5.

3. To explain this in terms of a struggle for power masquerading behind different "ideologies" is a gross, but by now a common, oversimplification. If we would descend from abstractions and be truly realistic, we would see that men cannot struggle for power save in the name of something other than power—unless power itself involves greatness or heightened existence. So-called ideologies may be facades, may be conscious or unconscious deceptions. But look beneath them. At the very least we shall find the idea that the strong *ought* to rule the weak. (Cf., in Thucydides, the speech of the Athenian envoy at the first Spartan congress as well as Pericles' funeral oration.) Or consider. If it is generally true that men conceal their desire for power behind the facade of some ideology, may it not be that man is so constituted by *nature* that he is compelled to do this, meaning, that he is compelled by his very nature to *justify* his actions? If so, the desire for "justification" would be as elemental as the desire for power. If it be argued, however, that the desire for "justification" is subordinated to the desire for power, against this it can be said that the desire for "justification" is itself a power, or that power, in the ordinary sense of the term, is but one of the means by which men seek

"justification." Of course, the decisive question is whether the different ways in which men seek "justification" are equally just. But there is no overpowering reason to reduce the problem to the struggle for mere power.

4. I say "opposing" principles to facilitate the discussion. Actually, the two legislative bodies are not opposed in all respects, nor could they be if the system is to be viable. After all, since they must legislate, they must have some common ground of agreement, for example: that men should settle their differences through peaceful persuasion, and, having done so, should abide by their agreements. A third body will have an interest in seeing that they do.

5. Here the term "oligarchic" is taken in its indefinite sense, meaning, that it may signify either the rule of wealth or of merit or both.

6. Cf. Charles C. Thach, *The Creation of the Presidency, 1775-1789* (Baltimore: Johns Hopkins Press, 1922). Although Thach analyzes the debates on the Presidency in a masterly way, his inquiry suffers from two defects. First, it makes no use of Hamilton's commentary in *The Federalist;* and second, its historical exegesis does not afford *philosophical* insight into the intended role of the Presidency in American political life.

7. From the debates of June 2 and June 9.

8. Actually, the motion was divided into two parts. Thus, the first part, *that the President be appointed by Electors,* was carried six states to three, with the delegation of one state divided. The second part, *that the Electors be chosen by the state legislatures,* was carried eight states to two.

9. This was actually anticipated by Morris on July 24.

10. Actually, this issue was anticipated on August 7.

11. This point has been well established by David A. McKnight, *The Electoral System of the United States* (Philadelphia: J. B. Lippincott & Co., 1878), pp. 44-48, 249; and is affirmed by J. Hampden Dougherty, *The Electoral System of the United States* (New York: G. P. Putnam's Sons 1906), p. 21. McKnight (p. 61), believes that the Convention probably expected or preferred the state legislatures to choose Electors themselves. Compare, however, Lucius Wilmerding, Jr., *The Electoral College* (New Jersey: Rutgers University Press, 1958), pref., ix, xi, and pp. 19-22, 170-175. It is Wilmerding's position that the general sentiment of the Convention was to have the Electors chosen by the people. But even he admits that "too many members of the Federal Convention expressed a contrary view" (p. 21). Furthermore, the thesis of Wilmerding's otherwise excellent work suffers from a fundamental error. His thesis is that the purpose of the Constitution "is, and has always been, to elevate to the executive chair the man who is the choice of the majority of the people in the nation as a whole" (pref., ix). Wilmerding cites in support of

his thesis such men as Hamilton, Gouverneur Morris, Rufus King, and Timothy Pickering—all Federalists! Whatever their views on the manner of choosing Electors, these men would have deplored the democratic conception of the Presidency which underlies Wilmerding's thesis. (I do not wish to suggest, however, that the evidence is conclusive as to how the majority of the Convention intended to have Electors chosen.) But as for Hamilton, I refer the reader to *Farrand,* III, 617-618, 622-624, where three different modes of electing the President are indicated: (1) by Electors chosen by Electors chosen by the people—that is, by what Farrand calls a "tertiary" election; (2) by Electors immediately chosen by the people; and (3) by Electors chosen by the state legislatures. The *first* method is elaborated in Hamilton's copy of his plan of government.

12. "The roster of Electors in our first elections reads like a 'Who's Who' in the State Goverments!" Wilmerding, *op. cit.*, p. 175, where he also cites Lanman's *Dictionary of Congress:* "As late as 1855 it was noticed that in Alabama and Mississippi the ablest men of the state were Electors and went among the people to instruct, excite, and arouse them upon the issues between the parties." But cf. *Farrand,* II, 58.

13. The Electors are to "ballot," meaning, they are to vote in *secrecy,* and "transmit *sealed* to the Seat of Government" the list of persons for whom they have voted. Cf. *Oxford Dictionary.* That the voting was intended to be conducted in secret is confirmed by Charles Pinckney and Jonathan Dayton, *Farrand,* III, 390, 364.

14. The latter contingency arises from the fact that each Elector is to ballot for two persons but may not designate which of the two he prefers as President. Since the number of ballots cast is *twice* the number of appointed Electors, it is mathematically possible for three persons to receive equal majorities of the total electoral vote. For a technical and historical treatment of the general problem (apart from its implications for the intended character of the Presidency), I refer the reader to Wilmerding's work cited above.

15. But cf. *supra, n. 12.*

16. I have in mind the Lincoln-Douglas debates.

17. Madison's notes of July 17.

18. In his notes of June 1, Hamilton uses the term "vigor" rather than the term "energy." But both terms are used synonymously in *Federalist 70.*

19. Hamilton continues: "If they should unfortunately assail the executive magistracy of a country, consisting of a plurality of persons . . . they might split the community into the most violent and irreconcilable factions, adhering differently to the different individuals who composed the magistracy." (This is precisely the same argument advanced by Wilson during the debates of June 4.)

20. *Federalist 71.*

21. *Ibid.* (italics added).

22. I have in mind both religious and political precepts. For the latter, the Constitution and the Declaration are of fundamental importance. But consider also my commentary on *Federalist 49, supra,* pp. 226-234.

23. The question as to whether a nation can achieve unity by pursuing a multiplicity of *equal* ends is taken up in the concluding chapter.

24. Cf. Jacob E. Cooke (ed.), *The Reports of Alexander Hamilton* (New York: Harper Torchbooks, 1964).

25. Compassion, be it noted, is the predominant emotion of democratic eras.

26. Cf. *Federalist 71.*

Chapter 10

1. *Debates of the Senate of the United States on the Judiciary during the First Session of the Seventh Congress* (Philadelphia: 1802), p. 30.

2. For confirmation of judicial review, cf. Charles A. Beard, "The Supreme Court—Usurper or Grantee?" in Robert G. McCloskey (ed.) *Essays in Constitutional Law* (New York: Vintage Books, 1957), pp. 24-58. A more recent work is Alexander M. Bickel, *The Least Dangerous Branch* (New York: The Bobbs-Merril Co., 1962), chap. 1. Here is one of the most brilliant studies of the Supreme Court. Bickel's primary concern is to reconcile judicial review, which he confirms, with democratic principles. I believe he fails. Two other failures are to be noted. Bickel well recognizes the Court's pedagogic function, its role as a teacher of America's enduring values. Unfortunately, he fails to elucidate or elaborate upon these values. Finally, Bickel's rejection of Marshall's argument in *Marbury* v. *Madison* is surprisingly superficial in view of the profundity of the work as a whole. In denial of judicial review, cf. Horace A. Davis, *The Judicial Veto* (Boston: Houghton Mifflin Co., 1914), chap. 3, which includes a critique of Beard's analysis; Louis B. Boudin, *Government by Judiciary* (New York: William Godwin Inc., 1932), chap. 6, which proceeds from a democratic interpretation of the Constitution.

3. Cf. Robert G. McCloskey, *The American Supreme Court* (Chicago: University of Chicago Press, 1960), chap. 1. McCloskey admits that most of the framers *expected* the Court to exercise judicial review, but: "The most that can be said is that the language [of the Constitution] and intent did not preclude the Court from becoming the puissant tribunal of later history" (p. 9).

4. Cf. James B. Thayer, *The Origin and Scope of the American Doctrine of Constitutional Law* (Boston: Little, Brown & Co., 1893).

I shall refer to this work later. Here I only note that Thayer's doctrine of "the clear mistake" (only when the legislature has made such a mistake can its acts be nullified by the Court) would render the Court the mere creature of the legislature. A less extreme view is to be found in Edward S. Corwin, *Court Over Constitution* (New York: Peter Smith, 1950), chap. 1. Corwin's notion of "departmental" review will be taken to task later. The following works are cited for their bearing on judicial review generally: Andrew C. McLaughlin, *The Court, The Constitution, and Parties* (Chicago: University of Chicago Press, 1912), chaps. 1, 4 and 5; Charles G. Haines, *The American Doctrine of Judicial Supremacy* (New York: The Macmillan Co., 1914), Pt. I.

5. Cf. *Federalist 78*. It will be shown—although by now it should be obvious—that whenever the Founders speak of checking the "legislature," they mean, primarily, the House of Representatives or a legislature no longer restrained by the Senate. This fact has been overlooked even by those who affirm the doctrine of judicial review.

6. The omitted provisions concern review of acts of the state legislatures which, under the sixth resolution, may be vetoed by the national legislature.

7. Pierce's notes (italics added).

8. For example, Ghorum and Strong on July 21, and Charles Pinckney on August 15.

9. See Charles Pinckney's remark of August 15.

10. It should be pointed out that King also opposed the council on grounds that it conflicted with the idea of a unitary executive (debates of June 6). Critics of judicial review have failed to appreciate the significance of this fact.

11. However, during his defense of the proposed council of revision on July 21, Mason declared: "Notwithstanding the precautions taken in the Constitution of the Legislature, it would so much resemble that of the individual States, that it must be expected frequently to pass unjust and pernicious laws." The sequel of this statement will be examined later, at which time it will be seen to be an exercise in rhetoric on behalf of the proposed council of revision.

12. Recall Madison's proposal to invest the Senate, rather than the legislature as a whole, with a veto over all acts passed by the several states.

13. Is it not remarkable that, with one exception, every link in the Virginia Plan which would have made the composition of these three branches partially dependent upon the House of Representatives was severed during the proceedings of the Constitutional Convention—this plan which was itself proposed as a check against the democracy! The one exception is the election of the President by the House in the event of an indecisive choice by the electoral college. But even here, notice, the House does not *nominate* the President.

14. While defending the council of revision on July 21, Madison declared: "Experience in all the States had evinced a powerful tendency in the Legislature to absorb all powers into its vortex." Earlier, on June 4, when the council was first proposed, Madison warned of the "danger of oppression from an unjust and interested majority"— this, after referring to the difference of interests between rich and poor, creditors and debtors (King's notes). The following day, when Madison first objected to an appointment of judges by the entire legislature, he seems to have identified the legislature with the House of Representatives. The inference is clear: When Madison referred to the revisionary council as a check against the legislature, he had principally in view the democratic branch of that legislature. And so it was with Gouverneur Morris who, on August 15, unambiguously referred to the revisionary council as a check against "the popular branch."

15. Debates of July 21 (italics added). I underscore the word "additional" because it suggests that, absent the council of revision, the Supreme Court could still nullify laws which were unconstitutional.

16. See also Madison's notes of June 6.

17. Debates of July 21 (italics added).

18. I say "plainly" unjust in view of Mason's "however" unjust. Besides, if the law is not plainly unjust to the Supreme Court, there is no problem: for in that event we would no longer be dealing with Mason's principle.

19. Negative sanction, should the Court disclaim jurisdiction. Admittedly, and as Hamilton says in *Federalist 78*, the Court might mitigate the severity of an unjust law without declaring it unconstitutional.

20. Yet this is precisely the implication of Thayer's position referred to earlier (*supra* p. 312, *n.* 4). Thayer quotes this statement of Wilson's in support of his own thesis regarding the scope of judicial review (pp. 14-15). In so doing he failed to grasp the rhetoric of the debates (a failure common among students of the Constitution). But this failure of Thayer's springs from the very heart of his thinking. Consider Thayer's standard (p. 18) as to what acts of the legislature may be set aside as unconstitutional. The Court, says Thayer, "can only disregard the Act when those who have the right to make laws have not merely made a mistake, but have made a very clear one—so clear that it is not open to rational question." One can hardly treat such absurdities without sarcasm. For virtually no cases coming before the Court conform to Thayer's standard! This standard would reduce the scope of judicial review to a nullity. But the secret of Thayer's position is contained in these words which he italicizes (p. 24): *"The ultimate question is not what is the true meaning of the constitution, but whether legislation is sustainable or not."* Here,

as elsewhere, Thayer gives voice to the *pragmatic* movement in American politics: Not *lawfulness*, so much as *expediency*, not long-range considerations, so much as "ever-enfolding exigencies"—this is the dominant principle of Thayer's work and, indeed, of the contemporary scene.

21. Notice, however, that on July 18, Madison proposed that the jurisdiction of the Court "shall extend to all cases arising under the National laws, and to such other questions as may involve the National peace and harmony." This proposal was adopted without dissent.

22. The fate of the council was sealed on July 21, and then, only by a plurality of the states voting (four nays, three yeas, and two divided). Evidently, the proponents of the council made some conversions. For when the council was first proposed on June 4, and motion was made to have the executive alone exercise the revisionary veto, the motion was carried eight to two. (But compare the voting of each state on the two dates in question.) On August 15, by the way, Madison made one last attempt to introduce the judiciary into the legislative process. He proposed "that all acts before they become laws should be submitted to the Executive and Supreme Judiciary Departments, that if either of these should object two-thirds of each House, if both object, three-fourths of each House, should be necessary to overrule the objections and give to the acts the force of law." This motion was defeated eight to three. What is remarkable, however, is that Mercer (who, together with Dickenson, denied the principle of judicial review) approved of Madison's proposal. This fact has been overlooked by critics of judicial review.

23. Cf. *Federalist 78*, where Hamilton wrote: "There is no position which depends on clearer principles, than that every act of a delegated authority, contrary to the tenor of the commission under which it is exercised, is void. No legislative act, therefore, contrary to the Constitution, can be valid. To deny this, would be to affirm, that the deputy is greater than his principal . . . that the representatives of the people are superior to the people themselves . . ."

24. Cf. Gouverneur Morris' speech (February 3, 1802) before the Senate on the repeal of the Judiciary Act of 1801, *Annals of Congress,* 7th Cong., 1st Sess., pp. 180-181, where he associates certain constitutional principles (to be mentioned shortly) with the very nature of man.

25. Notice that in *Federalist 78*, Hamilton refers to the "intentions," rather than to the will, of the people. In contrast, the judiciary is to exercise not "will," but "judgment."

26. It should not be thought that the contract clause may never be impared by the national government. No absolute property rights are posited in the Constitution, and as Hamilton well knew (*supra,*

p. 126), the public interest may sometimes necessitate their lawful suspension. (That Marshall should have spoken of property rights as absolute should be understood as having been dictated by considerations of prudence.)

27. Had the Constitution contemplated such a change, it would probably have enabled simple majorities to effectuate amendments, or it would have referred constitutional changes to a decision of the people acting through conventions as proposed in Jefferson's draft of a constitution for the state of Virginia. (Of this, more later.) Nevertheless, should the principles of the Constitution be amended to the extent of altering its generic form, the act of amendment would in truth be an act of revolution: the Constitution would not have been amended but annulled. In this connection it may be noted that, taken together, Articles XIII, XIV, XV, XVI (but not per se), XVII, and XIX (I ignore XXIV), may well have changed the form of the Constitution. But the reader should bear in mind that mine is an inquiry into the political philosophy of the *original* Constitution.

28. I have in mind the development of organized political parties and the national political conventions. The latter, we have seen, have circumvented Article II of the Constitution. Now it may be noted that whereas the nineteenth century augmented, as it were, the power of the oligarchic principle, the twentieth century has augmented the power of the democratic principle.

29. The Court's interpretation of the "equal protection clause" of the Fourteenth Amendment, especially in connection with the reapportionment cases (of which, more later), has obviously increased the power of the democratic principle. That interpretation, it will be understood, is reflexively related to the egalitarianism of contemporary society.

30. Cf. Thomas R. Powell, "The Logic and Rhetoric of Constitutional Law," in McCloskey, *Essays on Constitutional Law*, pp. 85-107. Powell's essay involves a democratic (sociological) reduction of judicial judgment to the level of common sense. We are given to understand, in effect, that judges are merely human. This is a sad commentary on humanity, inasmuch as the judges, according to Powell's interpretation of what determines their opinions, are little more than knaves, that they knowingly violate what they have sworn to support! Of course, Powell (along with the many who take this position) does not mean to insinuate such a thing, having never fully reflected upon the moral implications of what he sees in the "rhetoric" of the Court. But the real issue, which Powell's pragmatism prevents him from facing is this: Are judges really concerned with justice or with the long-range implications of their decisions? Powell's *implicit* answer to both aspects of this question appears to be no. Cf. John P. Roche, "Judicial Self-Restraint," *American Political Science Review*, XLIX

(Sept. 1955), 762-772, for an unrestrained sequel to Powell. For a collection of essays on legal realism and neo-realism or the mathematically oriented school of judicial behavioralism, cf. Glendon Schubert (ed.), *Judicial Behavior* (Chicago: Rand McNally & Co., 1964). For a critique of the behavioralist school, cf. Theodore L. Becker, *Political Behavioralism and Modern Jurisprudence* (Chicago: Rand McNally & Co., 1964); and cf., also, Martin Shapiro, *op. cit.*

31. I say this in the belief that the errors of the present Court, as concerns the First and Fourteenth Amendments, are destructive of the fabric of the Constitution and of the very order of society.

32. Cf. Albert J. Beveridge, *The Life of John Marshall* (4 vols.; Boston: Houghton Mifflin Co., 1919), III, 50-156; IV, 282-339, for background on Marshall's decision in *Marbury* v. *Madison* and in *McCulloch* v. *Maryland*. (When Marshall says in the latter case that "it is a *constitution* we are expounding," he certainly has in mind considerations of public policy.)

33. Powell, *op. cit.*, p. 97.

34. I must apologize to the reader for taking his time to refute a puerile argument. He should understand, however, that beneath that argument is a pragmatist conception of law and of judicial review which is repugnant to the Constitution.

35. I fully appreciate the fact that the judges may preserve the "form" of the Constitution while destroying its substance; or that they may base their decisions on a tendentious selection of the evidence, more precisely, may appeal exclusively to "one side" of the Founders' intentions. But here I am addressing myself to the philosophy of the Constitution as understood by its authors, a philosophy, we have seen, which admits of democratic and aristocratic principles.

36. Implicit in the notion of covenants is the notion of "divested sovereignty," although this may be qualified by the terms of the covenant, as, for example, in a limited constitution. That the people did divest themselves of some of their sovereignty is borne out by the Tenth Amendment which reads, in part: "The powers not delegated to the United States by the Constitution . . . are reserved . . . to the people"—meaning, conversely, that the powers delegated to the United States by the Constitution may not be reclaimed by the people. Cf. *Federalist 33* and *59;* Hobbes, *Leviathan*, chaps. xvii (beginning) and xiii *passim;* Locke, *Second Treatise*, chap. xix, sec. 243; chap. viii *passim;* and compare Rousseau, *Social Contract*, III, 16.

37. Earlier in the paragraph from which this is taken, Hamilton acknowledged "the right of the people to alter or abolish the established Constitution whenever they find it inconsistent with their happiness." Cf. *Federalist 28.*

38. H. A. Washington (ed.), *The Works of Thomas Jefferson* (9 vols.; New York: H. W. Derby, 1861); letters to Madison, Sep-

tember 6, 1789, III, 102-108; to John W. Eppes, June 24, 1813, VI, 136-137; to Samuel Kirchival, July 12, 1816, VII, 15-16.

39. The fact that this number does not make mention of judicial review in its critique of Jefferson favors Madison as the main author. But the boldness of the argument suggests Hamilton's influence, as do certain phrases, for example, "legitimate fountain of power" in 49 and "fountain of all legitimate authority" in 22. Cf., also, *Federalist 17*.

40. Cf. Corwin, *op. cit.* pp. 5-7, where he sets forth the "departmental" conception of judicial review. This conception conforms to Jefferson's post-Marbury views. See Jefferson's letter to Judge Roane, September 6, 1819 where he writes: ". . . each department is truly independent of the others, and has an equal right to decide for itself what is the meaning of the constitution in the cases submitted to its action; . . . [and] without any regard to what the others may have decided for themselves under a similar question." *Works* (H. A. Washington ed.), VII, 135-136. Before Jefferson assumed the Presidency he expressed opinions favorable to judicial review: Paul L. Ford (ed.), *The Works of Thomas Jefferson* (12 vols.; New York: G. P. Putnam's Sons, 1904); letters to Meusnier, January 4, 1786, V, 31-32; and to Rowan, September 26, 1798, VIII, 448. Nevertheless, it must be said that Jefferson was generally opposed to the notion of a constitution as a fundamental and permanent law; *Works* (H. A. Washington ed.), letters to Noah Webster, December 4, 1790, III, 202; to Priestley, June 19, 1802, IV, 404; and those letters cited above where Jefferson limits the binding force of constitutions to nineteen years.

41. Clearly Madison and Hamilton have primarily in view the House of Representatives.

42. Again I cite from *Federalist 63* on the Senate. But see also *Federalist 62* which discusses the evils stemming from mutability in the laws, mutability which the Senate was to prevent.

43. This is one of the conclusions implicit in Marshall's argument in *Marbury* v. *Madison*, 1 *Cranch* 137. I have in mind his statement: "The exercise of this original right [of the people to establish the fundamental principles of government], is a very great exertion; nor can it, nor ought it, to be frequently repeated" (*ibid.*, p. 176).

44. Jefferson was consistent enough to recognize this in his letter to Judge Roane cited above, *n.* 40.

45. What is truly remarkable, however, is that the judiciary could not only save the essential element of that "system," but it could do so while ultimately enlarging the legislative powers—not beyond that which this "system" would ironically justify—but beyond the strict-construction theory of the Constitution fostered by Jefferson (whose inconsistencies, by the way, are both legion and enormous). Indeed, this is precisely what Marshall's genius accomplished in *McCulloch*

v. *Maryland* on the one hand, and in *Marbury* v. *Madison* on the other. Here is the kernel of the argument. Under the Constitution, it is the function of the legislature "to make all Laws which shall be necessary and proper for carrying into Execution" its own powers and all other powers vested in the government of the United States. Now whether a particular law is *necessary*—and what is necessary includes what is *expedient*—here the legislature is the final authority. But whether that particular law is *proper*, which is to say, constitutional, here the Supreme Court is the final authority.

46. As Hamilton said in *Federalist 81:* "There is an absurdity in referring the determination of causes, in the first instance, to judges of permanent standing; in the last, to those of a temporary and mutable constitution. And there is still a greater absurdity in subjecting the decisions of men, selected for their knowledge of the laws, acquired by long and laborious study, to the revision and control of men who, for want of the same advantage, cannot but be deficient in that knowledge."

47. "The members of the legislature will rarely be chosen with a view to those qualifications which fit men for the stations of judges; and as, on this account, there will be great reason to apprehend all the ill consequences of defective information, so, on account of the natural propensity of such bodies to party divisions, there will be no less reason to fear that the pestilential breath of faction may poison the fountains of justice" (*ibid.*).

48. *Federalist 78.*

49. 1 *Cranch* 176 (italics in the original).

50. *Ibid.* (The word *justice* is not italicized in the original.)

51. Why, indeed, secure the independence of judges if not, in part, to enable them to pass impartial judgment between the government and the citizen who might be prosecuted by that government—prosecuted, perhaps, under a law whose enactment exceeded the legislature's constitutional authority? (Cf. *Federalist 78.*)

52. The reader will understand that I have not considered in any detail the *scope* of judicial review—a most important problem, but one which is not fundamental to this inquiry.

53. Cf. Tocqueville, *op. cit.*, I, 157.

54. Cf. Rostow, *op. cit.*, p. 298, where Rostow's historicism is most evident. Also, cf. Chief Justice Warren's opinion in *Reynolds* v. *Sims*, 377 U.S. 533 (1964), and compare with Justice Frankfurter's opinion in *Colegrove* v. *Green*, 328 U.S. 549 (1946), and with Justice Holmes's dissent in *Lochner* v. *New York*, 198 U.S. 45 (1905). In the line of reapportionment cases commencing with *Baker* v. *Carr*, 369 U.S. 186 (1961), and culminating in *Reynolds* v. *Sims*, I find the clearest erosion of long-established principles, but this, under the steady impact of the democracy. Still the Court seeks to justify its decisions by the intentions of the Founders—of course, by a tenden-

tious selection of the evidence.

55. This was one of Jefferson's fondest wishes: *Works* (Ford ed.) VII, 256; *Works* (H. A. Washington ed.), I, 81; VI, 96; and VII, 9-13. Jefferson felt that ordinary law was of the same rank as the "fundamental" law.

Chapter 11

1. Cf. John Dewey, *The Public and Its Problems* (Chicago: Gateway Books, 1946). Dewey's insistence on the public's need for organized or "embodied" intelligence is but the insistence that government use scientific methods to serve and adjust the multifarious and changing wants of society. It is not a question of considering whether the wants of individuals and groups are good or bad, moderate or excessive, but rather of weighing their *consequences* for "conjoint behavior" (chap. 1, *passim*). According to Dewey (p. 191), "the genuine problem is that of adjusting groups and individuals to one another," which means adjusting their various and conflicting wants or interests. Government is thus conceived as the mere instrument of society, solving its problems not by the methods of compromise, but by the methods of the experimental sciences. Because the public and its problems change from time to time, what constitutes a good or the best form of government cannot be known "a priori" (p. 33). Political philosophies or ideologies or "isms" which profess such knowledge are but antiquated myths. (But cf. pp. 148, 167, 181, 182, 184, 206-209, where Dewey opts for democracy as the ideal form of government, it being in his view, the most conducive to *freedom* and science.) An example of Dewey's pragmatic approach to the function of government may be seen in Robert A. Dahl and Charles E. Lindblom, *Politics, Economics, and Welfare* (New York: Harper Torchbooks, 1963), pp. 3, 4, 19, 21, 25-54. The last term of the title is the ultimate function of the first; for qualifications to the contrary notwithstanding, the authors accept Bertrand Russell's definition of freedom, which they quote on page 29, viz., "the absence of obstacles to the realization of desires."

2. Granted that particular laws may serve the purpose of education. But education has no higher status, *de jure*, than any other purpose served by the laws. In other words, it is not the *paramount* purpose of the laws to elevate men's moral and intellectual character. Indeed, so far as concerns the laws *qua* laws, education is but one of a multiplicity of wants which, in a democratic society, enjoy a more or less equal status. Perhaps this is why public education today is little more than a means of making men comfortable.

3. Conflict, in its many forms, is fast becoming the rule of American life "despite" the vast number of laws aimed at making men comfortable. And far from resolving conflicts, the laws merely

sustain a "cold war" at home more demoralizing than the "cold war" abroad. (It may even be said that the vast number of laws enacted today is itself a sign of lawlessness.) Furthermore, "despite" the modern comforts, nothing is more discomforting than life in contemporary urban society. It is precisely in urban society that men's wants are constantly being stimulated. More wants are being *manufactured* every day. The entire economic system, by means of advertising and planned obsolescence, is directed to making men dissatisfied with what they have (but not dissatisfied with *what they are*). The laws encourage that system while seeking to make men comfortable.

4. Cf. Dewey, *op. cit.*, p. 12: "We must in any case start from acts which are performed, not from hypothetical causes for these acts, and consider their consequences." (But whereas Dewey never gets back to these causes, the Founders constantly take them into account while seeking to control their effects.)

5. The following critique is written in full cognizance of my chapter on Madison (Chapter 8), wherein I discussed his conception of faction (especially the leveling spirit of majority faction), its causes and ramifications. There I was concerned to elucidate the heights of Madison's intentions; here I am concerned to elucidate why the Constitution cannot achieve those heights.

6. But notice that *tranquility*, which presupposes friendship, is one of the ends for which the Constitution was established.

7. The criterion is no longer whether a would-be statesman possesses the moral and intellectual virtues but whether he is *pragmatic*, a term which has supplanted wisdom in political discourse.

8. See Chapter 7 on Hamilton.

9. Addressing the Federal Convention on August 14, Mercer declared: "It is a first principle in political science, that whenever the rights of property are secured, an aristocracy will grow out of it." (Cf. Gouverneur Morris' speech of July 2.)

10. This is one of the secrets of true statesmanship. Thus, suppose a particular opinion should emerge in society at large, an opinion having intrinsic moral value. At some stage of its progress, the opinion should be fostered by law. Suppose statesmen, anticipating that Negroes would soon hold the balance of power in the cities, had been attentive to the growing liberal opinion that segregation is unjust. Laws might have been passed reflecting this opinion, but controlling its consequences to the ultimate advantage of the Negro and to the community as a whole. Instead, the laws are largely determined by the *de facto* and changing distribution of power within society. This is pragmatic statesmanship.

11. It is to be borne in mind that several of the state constitutions attempted to do precisely this. Cf. Appendix 2.

12. I leave aside age, citizenship, and residence qualifications. But the reader should bear in mind that a vast number of men would

be precluded from public office by such *de facto* qualifications as race, religion, property, and education. Indeed, election to public office would depend very much upon whether one was a member of the legal profession. Cf. Appendix 1 which outlines the qualifications for state legislators and their electors, this being relevant to the character of those appointed to the Senate, but also to those appointed as Electors of the President.

13. To improve the probabilities such that the *de jure* is superior to the *de facto*, qualifications would be required for the offices in question or for their electors. This would give the indirect modes of election a qualitative status which is explicit rather than implicit.

14. Cf. his "Report on Manufactures."

Bibliography

Public Documents

Annals of Congress. Vols. I-XIII.

Documentary History of the Constitution of the United States 1787-1870. 5 vols. Washington, D.C., 1900. Department of State.

Federal and State Constitutions, Colonial Charter, and Other Organic Laws of the United States. 2 vols. Washington, D.C., Government Printing Office, 1877-1888.

U.S. Reports.

Books and Collected Works

Adams, Henry. *History of the United States of America.* 9 vols. New York: Charles Scribner's Sons, 1921.

Aristotle. *Politics.* Ernest Barker, trans. London: Oxford University Press, 1952.

———. *Nicomachean Ethics.*

Beard, Charles A. *An Economic Interpretation of the Constitution of the United States.* New York: The Macmillan Co., 1954.

Becker, Theodore L. *Political Behavioralism and Modern Jurisprudence.* Chicago: Rand McNally & Co., 1964.

Beveridge, Albert J. *The Life of John Marshall.* 4 vols. Boston: Houghton Mifflin Co., 1919.

Bickel, Alexander M. *The Least Dangerous Branch.* Indianapolis: Bobbs-Merrill Co., Inc., 1962.

Blackstone, William. *Commentaries on the Laws of England*. 2 vols. Chicago: Callaghan & Co., 1876.

Boudin, Louis B. *Government by Judiciary*. New York: William Godwin, Inc., 1932.

Brown, Robert. *Charles Beard and the Constitution*. Princeton: Princeton University Press, 1956.

Burke, Edmund. *Reflections on the Revolution in France*. Chicago: Gateway Editions, Inc., 1955.

Calhoun, John C. *A Disquisition on Government*. Indianapolis: Bobbs-Merrill Co., Inc., 1953.

Cicero. *De re publica*.

Corwin, Edward S. *Court Over Constitution*. New York: Peter Smith, 1950.

Crèvecoeur, J. Hector St. John de. *Letters from an American Farmer*. New York: E. P. Dutton & Co., Inc., 1957.

Davis, Horace A. *The Judicial Veto*. Boston: Houghton Mifflin Co., 1914.

Dewey, John. *The Public and Its Problems*. Chicago: Gateway Books, 1946.

Diamond, Martin, Winston Mills Fisk, and Herbert Garfinkel. *The Democratic Republic*. Chicago: Rand McNally & Co., 1966.

Dougherty, Hampden J. *The Electoral System of the United States*. New York: G. P. Putnam's Sons, 1906.

Dumbauld, Edward (ed.). *The Political Writings of Thomas Jefferson*. New York: Liberal Arts Press, 1956.

Elliot, Jonathan (ed.). *The Debates in the Several State Conventions on the Adoption of the Federal Constitution*. 5 vols. Philadelphia: J. B. Lippincott Co., 1836.

Farrand, Max (ed.). *The Records of the Federal Convention of 1787*. 4 vols. New Haven: Yale University Press, 1937.

Ford, Paul L. *Essays on the Constitution of the United States 1787-1788*. Brooklyn: Historical Printing Club, 1892.

Goldwin, Robert A. (ed.). *A Nation of States*. Chicago: Rand McNally & Co., 1966.

Gross, Bertram M. *The Legislative Struggle: A Study in Social Combat*. New York: McGraw-Hill Book Co., Inc., 1953.

Haines, Charles G. *The American Doctrine of Judicial Supremacy*. New York: The Macmillan Co., 1914.

Hamilton, Alexander. *Works.* John C. Hamilton (ed.). 7 vols. Congress ed., 1850-1851.

——. *Works.* Henry C. Lodge (ed.). 12 vols. New York: G. P. Putnam's Sons, 1904.

Hamilton, Madison, Jay. *The Federalist.*

Hendel, Charles W. (ed.). *David Hume's Political Essays.* New York: Liberal Arts Press, 1953.

Hobbes, Thomas. *Leviathan.*

Hofstadter, Richard. *The American Political Tradition.* New York: Vintage Books, 1956.

Jefferson, Thomas. *Works.* H. A. Washington (ed.). 9 vols. New York: H. W. Derby, 1861.

——. *Works.* Paul L. Ford (ed.). 12 vols. New York: G. P. Putnam's Sons, 1904.

Kendall, Willmoore and George Carey (eds.). *Liberalism Verses Conservatism.* Princeton: D. Van Nostrand & Co., Inc., 1966.

Locke, John. *Second Treatise of Civil Government.*

Machiavelli, Niccolo. *Discourses.*

Madison, James. *Letters and Other Writings.* 4 vols. Philadelphia: J. B. Lippincott & Co., 1865.

McCloskey, Robert G. *The American Supreme Court.* Chicago: University of Chicago Press, 1960.

——. (ed.). *Essays on Constitutional Law.* New York: Vintage Books, 1957.

McDonald, Forest. *We the People: The Economic Origins of the Constitution.* Chicago: University of Chicago Press, 1958.

McKinley, Albert E. *Suffrage Franchise in the Thirteen English Colonies in America.* Philadelphia: University of Pennsylvania, 1905.

McKnight, David A. *The Electoral System of the United States.* Philadelphia: J. B. Lippincott & Co., 1878.

McLaughlin, Andrew C. *The Court, the Constitution, and Parties.* Chicago: University of Chicago Press, 1912.

Montesquieu, Baron de, *The Spirit of the Laws.* Thomas Nugent, trans. New York: Hafner Publishing Co., 1949.

——. *Considerations sur les causes de la Grandeur des Romains et de leur Decadence.* Paris: 1898.

Morgenthau, Hans J. *The Purpose of American Politics.* New York: Alfred A. Knopf, 1960.

Morris, Richard B. (ed.). *Alexander Hamilton and the Founding of the Nation.* New York: The Dial Press, 1957.

Neustadt, Richard E. *Presidential Power.* New York: John Wiley & Sons, Inc., 1962.

Padover, Saul K. (ed.). *The Complete Madison.* New York: Harper & Row, 1953.

Peek, George A., Jr. (ed.). *The Political Writings of John Adams.* New York: Liberal Arts Press, 1954.

Plato. *Republic.*

———. *Laws.*

———. *Statesman.*

Polybius. *Histories.*

Potter, Elisha R. *Considerations on the Rhode Island Question.* Boston: Thomas H. Webb & Co., 1842.

Pritchett, Herman C. *The American Constitution.* New York: McGraw-Hill Book Co., Inc., 1959.

Ranney, Austin and Willmoore Kendall. *Democracy and the American Party System.* New York: Harcourt Brace & World, Inc., 1956.

Read, Conyers (ed.). *The Constitution Reconsidered.* New York: Columbia University Press, 1938.

Rossiter, Clinton. *1787 the Grand Convention.* New York: Macmillan Co., 1965.

Rousseau, Jean-Jacques. *Social Contract.*

———. *Origin of Inequality.*

Schubert, Glendon. (ed.). *Judicial Behavior.* Chicago: Rand McNally & Co., 1964.

Shapiro, Martin. *Law and Politics in the Supreme Court.* New York: The Free Press, 1964.

Smith, James Allen. *The Spirit of American Government.* New York: The Macmillan Co., 1907.

Spinoza. *Tractatus Politicus.*

Stern, Phillip (ed.). *The Life and Writings of Abraham Lincoln.* New York: Modern Library, 1940.

Strauss, Leo. *Natural Right and History.* Chicago: University of Chicago Press, 1953.

Thach, Charles C. *The Creation of the Presidency 1775-1789.* Baltimore: Johns Hopkins Press, 1922.

Thayer, James B. *The Origin and Scope of the American Doctrine of Constitutional Law.* Boston: Little, Brown & Co., 1893.

Thucydides. *History of the Peloponnesian War.*

Tocqueville, Alexis de. *Democracy in America.* 2 vols. New York: Vintage Books, 1954.

Truman, David B. *The Governmental Process.* New York: Alfred A. Knopf, 1953.

Weber, Max. *Politics as a Vocation.* H. H. Gerth and C. Wright Mills, trans. Philadelphia: Fortress Press Facet Books, 1965.

Wilmerding, Lucius Jr. *The Electoral College.* New Jersey: Rutgers University Press, 1958.

Williamson, Chilton. *American Suffrage from Property to Democracy 1760-1860.* Princeton: Princeton University Press, 1960.

Periodicals

Chinard, Gilbert. "Polybius and the American Constitution," *Journal of the History of Ideas,* I (Jan. 1940), 38-58.

Diamond, Martin. "Democracy and *The Federalist:* A Reconsideration of the Framers' Intent," *American Political Science Review,* LIII (March 1959), 52-68.

McKeon, Richard. "The Development of the Concept of Property in Political Philosophy: A Study of the Background of the Constitution," *Ethics,* XLVIII (April 1938), 297-366.

Roche, John P. "Judicial Self-Restraint," *American Political Science Review,* XLIX (Sept. 1955), 762-772.

———. "The Founding Fathers: A Reform Caucus in Action," *American Political Science Review,* LV (Dec. 1961), 799-816.

Acknowledgments

THIS inquiry into the Constitution had its origin in a course I took with Professors Martin Diamond and Herbert Storing at the University of Chicago. The course was on *The Federalist,* and the treatment of this work was not only scintillating in its originality, but classical in its seriousness and candor. Never, to my knowledge, had the thoughts of Hamilton and Madison received such politically pertinent and penetrating analysis. The fundamental problems of these statesmen were shown to be *our* problems, their wisdom and courage a challenge to our own times. And yet, presented here were men whose political sagacity was not only to be admired, but critically assimilated and surpassed. The high seriousness which was thus brought to the study of *The Federalist* evoked in me the desire to bring to the study of the Constitution the discipline of political philosophy; and here I was most fortunate in having a teacher whose contribution to political philosophy is profound and permanent: Professor Leo Strauss. It was, however, under the guidance of Professor Storing that the original version of the present work—my doctoral dissertation—was written. His provocative questions and challenging comments were invaluable; I could hardly have had a more incisive and constructive critic. Meanwhile, and throughout this inquiry, there were the many illuminating talks with my friend Harry Clor. Whether we conversed on politics, on philosophy, or on the meaning of the Constitution, never did I depart from these talks without new or deeper insight. Thus, when I look back on all this good fortune and contemplate the present work, I can truly say that whatever merit it may possess it owes mainly to these my friends and teachers; its errors and shortcomings are solely my own.

To my wife I owe a special debt of gratitude. With womanly wisdom she made it possible to overcome many of the perplexities besetting this inquiry.

Finally, I should like to express my gratitude to friends unnamed here, but whose share in this venture is not forgotten.

Index

Index

[333]